RURAL INDUSTRIALIZATION IN CHINA

by Jon Sigurdson

Published by
Council on East Asian Studies
Harvard University

Distributed by
Harvard University Press
Cambridge, Massachusetts
and
London, England
1977

This book is produced by the John K. Fairbank Center for East
Asian Research at Harvard University, which administers research
projects designed to further scholarly understanding of China,
Japan, Korea, Vietnam, Inner Asia, and adjacent areas. These
studies have been assisted by grants from the Ford Foundation.

Library of Congress Cataloging in Publication Data

Sigurdson, Jon.
    Rural industrialization in China.

    (Harvard East Asian monographs; 73)
    Bibliography: p. 259
    Includes index.
    1. Rural development—China. 2. China—
Industries. I. Title. II. Series.
HC427.9.S542   338'.0951   77-7233

ISBN 0-674-78072-8

To Whom It May Concern

FOREWORD

In 1958, China embarked on a massive campaign for rural industrialization. The First Five Year Plan, 1953–1957, had centered on large-scale projects, with help from Soviet technology and planning. Because these projects had benefited only certain parts of the country, the Chinese leaders decided in 1958 to concentrate on spreading the fruits of modernization to workers and peasants throughout the country. With collectivization essentially completed in late 1956, and with the new commune organization of 1958, the leaders had an administrative structure for introducing a national program for rural development.

In the first years after 1958 many local areas tried to expand industry too quickly, without adequate planning, technology, and analysis of available resources. By the early 1960s, the Chinese leaders were more sober-minded, and the regime set about planning a better coordinated program for developing the countryside.

China's program had many features different from rural developments elsewhere and, beginning in the 1970s, other developing countries began to show great interest in the Chinese approach. The United States, for example, had given massive infusions of outside aid to the most modern sectors of other developing countries, but that brought few benefits to the rural areas. The U.S. Agency for International Development, viewing their efforts since World War II, recognized that many developing countries were suffering from the same problems that afflicted China in the First Five Year Plan. It was clear that overall growth rate was not enough to ensure benefits going to peasants in backward areas. China, having done perhaps more than any other country to develop a program of rural industrialization, naturally attracted the interest of planners in developing countries.

The problem has been that there has been insufficient information through which to examine the utility and benefits of the Chinese rural industrialization program. Jon Sigurdson, who has collected more data on this topic than perhaps any other scholar, here makes an effort to evaluate this program.

Sigurdson focuses his analysis on the county level, the key administrative unit for Chinese rural industrialization. (The 2,100 counties in the country average over 300,000 in population.) Certain aspects of very light industry have been decentralized below the county, to the commune (which averages over 8,000 population in size), and sometimes even to the brigades under the direction of the commune. Sigurdson here analyzes rural industrialization within counties, giving the rationale for the various programs, an analysis of two model counties, and some estimate of how well the programs have worked.

Sigurdson brings to this task a variety of unique advantages. A trained engineer, he has been interested in technology in relation to development, and has taken field trips to India and other developing countries, which provides a useful perspective for viewing China. He was a scientific attaché at the Swedish Embassy in Peking for three years, and later, in December 1971 and July 1973, was given perhaps the most detailed opportunity to visit and examine local industry of any visitor to China. Before and after these visits, Sigurdson read broadly in the Chinese press and in secondary studies of China to provide a larger context for his observations, so that data from his visits could serve as examples, shedding light on the broader range of policies.

The picture that emerges from Sigurdson's work is that China's rural industrial program has proved itself effective in many areas and will undoubtedly remain a part of the Chinese industrial development strategy until advances in the modern sectors replace those parts which are no longer justified.

The five basic plants, aside from consumer goods industries, that China attempted to introduce are fertilizer, cement, farm machinery, iron and steel, and electricity and energy. In the case of fertilizer, it became clear that local plants were far more expensive than the very large-scale plants when some of the economic constraints were relieved; therefore, since 1973, China has made an effort to move to a new stage with the importation of very large foreign plants. With cement, because the costs of small plants are relatively modest with shaft technology, the cost of transporting larger amounts of cement long distances from the more efficient large-scale rotary kilns is not justifiable economically. It is therefore at this stage of development more fruitful to make cement locally. As for farm machinery, much of the more complicated machine tools, tractors, electric machinery, and other farm tools cannot always be produced locally. However, various forms of subcontracting are available so that larger implements can be completed and assembled, and later serviced at the county level by subcontractors who can also repair the machinery. The cost of operating very small iron and steel plants has proved very high, and, except in some areas where appropriate raw materials are readily available, small plants have not proved to be realistic alternatives for the manufacture of iron and steel. In the case of electrical energy, where the resources are available, hydroelectric stations have been built locally, and coal has also been mined in a large number of counties.

The program has lessons for developing countries, although precise data and blueprints are not readily enough available to serve as the basis for specific plans. In conception, the Chinese program may not be so different from what many developing countries advocate. What is different is that China has had the rural organizational structure, leadership, and appropriate technology, which other countries need if they are to embark on a comparable program of rural industrialization.

Ezra F. Vogel
Cambridge, Massachusetts

PREFACE

This monograph on rural industrialization in China has been made possible through generous grants from a number of different sources. The Bank of Sweden Tercentenary Fund has provided the means of support during the main period of research—through a two-year grant to study the internal transfer of technology in China. The research project was initiated through an offer from Dr. Geoffrey Oldham at the Science Policy Research Unit (SPRU) at the University of Sussex in England to join his group for the study of technology and development in China. The idea then received strong support from Professor S. Brohult and Mr. H. Forsberg of the Swedish Academy of Engineering Sciences, which continued to serve as formal employer during the main period of research. As a preparation for the research project, a travel and study award was provided by the Ford Foundation, which made it possible to visit the major China study centers in the United States and Japan and also to pay short visits to Hong Kong, New Delhi, and Moscow before joining SPRU.

The emphasis of the research project at an early stage became centered on rural industrialization where a large number of small-scale enterprises are at the receiving end of an internal technology transfer from cities to rural areas. So the system approach of rural industrialization and the manifold, mutual supporting objectives became the main focus of attention at an early stage of the project.

The description and analysis in this monograph is, aside from the traditional sources available to China scholars, to a considerable extent based upon information and insight gained during two individually undertaken study visits to China—in December 1971 and in July 1973. China International Travel Service was host during the first stay in China, made possible through Ford Foundation funding. The Academy of Sciences in Peking was host during the second visit, part of an informal exchange program sponsored by the Swedish Academy of Engineering Sciences and the Chinese

Academy of Sciences. The hospitality and services rendered by the Chinese hosts are greatly appreciated, and large parts of this monograph would not have been possible without their full cooperation.

The Swedish Board of Technical Development provided travel funds for the second visit and an additional study grant in order to extend the research project so that information from the latest visit could be incorporated in this monograph.

The author had a further opportunity during spring 1974 to elaborate the system characteristics of rural industrialization in China in a report made possible through financial support from the Swedish International Development Authority (SIDA).[1] This was part of a larger attempt by a research team at the Economic Research Institute of the Stockholm School of Economics to describe and analyze China's development strategy—sponsored by SIDA.

My research project has benefited from encouragement and valuable suggestions from a large number of colleagues at the Science Policy Research Unit and other centers and from discussions with colleagues at seminars and international conferences. Among others, I want to thank Professors Roy Hofheinz and Ezra Vogel for valuable ideas and assistance during my stay at the East Asian Research Center at Harvard University in April–June 1973, a stay made possible thanks to a grant from the Center. In particular I am grateful to Professor Shigeru Ishikawa, Hitotsubashi University, who made valuable suggestions during my early work on the subject and also provided detailed and illuminating comments shortly before the manuscript was completed. Finally, I want to thank Ms. Leena Höskuldsson, who not only did much of the final typing but also systematically tried to improve my English, and Ms. Cynthia Morehouse, who with great care worked out the index.

During the extended period of getting the manuscript finally ready for publication, I had additional opportunities to make field visits to study regional development and local/rural industrialization programs in Pakistan, India, and Mexico. This brought out more clearly the relevance of Chinese rural industrialization as a critical element of integrated programs for rural modernization—in particular in countries where the size of the rural population exerts itself as an overriding issue in manpower planning. On the other hand, it also brought out the limitations to duplicating a Chinese approach that are embedded in the country's political structure, tradition, and earlier experience.

For this and other reasons familiar to all who attempt to evaluate aspects of modernization in a continent-sized country like China, the information and analysis in this monograph can be nothing but tentative. However, they may provide some added insight into an aspect of economic planning that is important in China and is receiving increasing attention in other developing countries. It is my hope that this monograph may serve as a stepping stone for further analysis of industrialization and modernization in achieving growth with equity.

Copenhagen, May 1977   Jon Sigurdson

CONTENTS

INTRODUCTION

The existence of a rapidly growing rural industrial sector which consists of a large number of small- and medium-sized enterprises is one important characteristic of the present development strategy in China. The encouragement of small-scale industries in rural areas in China is an essential element of China's regional development programs which today focus on agricultural development and diversification, local raw material utilization, resource mobilization, and long-term employment impact. The systematic and integrated development of rural industry has hardly any parallel in other developing countries—even if similarities of detail can be found in other places.

The small-scale industrial sector in China consists of two different parts—urban small-scale industries (not discussed here) and rural small-scale industries.[1] The sophistication and scope of industrial activities are dependent on the level of education, economic development, natural resource endowment, and nearness to ideas and new information. Consequently, it is realistic to differentiate between *rural industry in city-near locations* and *rural industry in rural areas proper.* The former seems to have much more in common with urban-based small-scale industry than is the case for the rest of rural industry.

Rural industry is, in this monograph, not defined on the basis of size but as any local industrial unit run by county, commune, or brigade. The enterprises may be collectively owned, jointly financed by the state and collective units, or wholly owned by the state but under local management. Rural industry also includes units attached to middle schools, hospitals, and health clinics. Rural industry within a county (hsien) is usually discussed because of the importance attached to this administrative level in industrial news reports from China. Production technology in rural industry ranges from the very primitive to modern, up-to-date process technology, depending on product, size, and stage of development.

1

Rural industry is distributed within a county at brigade, commune, and county level, with most of the heavy industry and larger enterprises located in the county capitals. The county capitals would usually have a population not exceeding 20,000. Most of the rural industrial enterprises are relatively small, rarely exceeding a few hundred employees. In any discussion of rural industry in China it is essential to realize that many enterprises are not small by international classification and that many of them are located in small urban centers.[2]

The rural industrial sector appears to be rather complex both in organization and in objectives. First, it should provide agriculture with many of the needed industrial inputs and industrial services with provision for local adaptations and changing requirements. Second, it should tap local mineral and energy resources as far as possible. Third, it should establish new industrial structures where the future potential market is. Fourth, it should establish industrial systems which can be used for the manufacture of complex products needed locally as well as for subcontracting to urban enterprises, and, lately, also manufacture export items. Overriding objectives are to provide rural areas with more opportunities for economic and social development and to reduce the differential between cities and countryside in order, among other things, to control migration.

Obviously, rural industry in China is not a homogenous concept and should rather be seen as the outflow of two different strategies. First, it is the logical outcome of a *sector strategy* involving technology choices in a number of industrial sectors—most of them initiated during the Great Leap Forward or earlier. This has required the *scaling down* of modern large-scale technology through a product and/or quality choice combined with design changes in the manufacturing process. Second, rural industry is part of an *integrated rural development strategy*—also initiated during the Great Leap Forward—where a number of activities are integrated within or closely related to the commune system. It is then often rooted in the traditional sector of the economy and has often been preceded by a long tradition of village crafts. Such industries are often based on the *scaling up* of village crafts. The scaling up of cottage industries in China is not based on improvement of technology alone, but the cottage industries have been converted into modern small-scale industries through cooperativization, electrification, and access to low-cost simple machinery. The assumption for both categories is that they, in the main, should be using local resources and be meeting a local demand for goods and industrial services.

The total number of rural industrial units is very high. The largest category consists of the very small brigade-level repair and manufacture shops, of which there may be several hundred thousand. The second largest category is likely to be the small mines—or mining spots—of which there are likely to be considerably more than 100,000. There are also 50,000 small hydroelectric stations. A large number of the 50,000 communes are likely to have their own workshops for grain milling, oil pressing, and other food-processing plants, wood-working shops, and so forth, which are usually run by the brigades or in multi-purpose units at the commune level. Rural heavy industry—small iron and steel plants, cement plants, chemical fertilizer plants, and other chemical plants—may amount to between 5,000 and 10,000 units. The number of county-run machinery plants may amount to more than 3,000 units. Then there is also a large number of light (consumer) industry enterprises in counties, communes, and brigades, and these may amount to more than 100,000 units. So the total number of industrial units—within the rural industrial sector—is likely to be in the region of 500,000 or more.

China has not released any national figures for employment in county-, commune-, and brigade-level enterprises. There can be no doubt that employment in various parts of the country varies widely. Rural areas which are under the administration of big industrial cities have 20 percent or more of the labor force in industry. Remote places in the interior of the country may hardly have any rural industrial activity at all. Information from a number of relatively (in terms of rural industrialization) well-developed regions in Hopei province indicates that less than 5 percent of China's total labor force in those areas is engaged in rural industries.[3]

Consequently the national average is likely to be considerably lower. A realistic assessment may be that rural industrial employment would be in the region of 7.5—15 million, and the higher estimate could correspond to approximately 50 percent of total employment in manufacturing and mining.

What, then, is the economic impact of roughly 500,000 rural industrial units employing between 7.5 and 15.0 million people? Assume—using the higher estimate—that in 1973 a rural industrial labor force was distributed with the ratio 3:6:6 in county-, commune-, and brigade-level enterprises. Further, assume that the production value is 5,000 yuan, 1,000 yuan, and 500 yuan per worker respectively in enterprises at the three levels. The total production value would then amount to 24 billion yuan, which is almost one-third of an estimated agricultural production value in 1973 of 80 billion (approximately 70 billion yuan in 1970 according to information given to Edgar Snow). The lower employment figure would yield a production value of 12 billion.

These estimates indicate—assuming that they are realistic—that rural industries have had a considerable impact on the pattern of industrial employment. They further indicate that the economic impact of rural industries is quite considerable in rural areas but contributes relatively less to the overall industrialization efforts of the country.

Before a discussion of the Chinese experience in rural industrialization, it might be useful to mention some characteristic features that are important in understanding Chinese development strategy. China is a big, developing, socialist, and independent country and has a partly decentralized economy.

The total area is only a little less than 10 million square kilometers with a population of about 850 million. Arable land per capita is only about 0.15 hectares. China has a modern industrial sector, which among other things produces as much steel as Great Britain, but rural areas in China account for over 80 percent of the population; the Chinese leaders have often pointed to their relatively little mechanized agriculture as a mark of backwardness.

China is a socialist country in a transitional phase, aiming at the establishment of a communist state, which means a commitment to plan economic, political, and social development in order to achieve certain goals defined in terms of communist ideology. These include, among other things, that the means of production should be owned by the whole people—the state—not yet the case in agriculture and small- and medium-sized industry which still are largely owned by collectives.

China has come to stress self-reliance, and the country is today economically independent with no foreign debts. China engages in foreign trade—which makes up approximately 5 percent of GNP, both ways—in order to achieve rapid development of certain economic sectors, in order to be able to give foreign aid, and so forth. China cooperated with the Soviet Union during the 1950s but has since then chosen not to use long-term credits to finance her industrial imports.

China is a planned economy. But local industries—in contrast to enterprises directly under the national ministries—operate at all administrative levels: in the 29 provinces, nearly 200 regions, about 2,000 counties, about 50,000 communes, and also in the roughly 750,000 brigades which are not administrative units.

Because of the scarcity of data it has not been possible comprehensively to describe and analyze rural industry in China. Consequently, the author has selected certain aspects to be dealt with in separate chapters.

A considerable amount of information used in this monograph is based on data given by Chinese officials during two visits to China. On both occasions Zunhua county in Hopei province and Lin county in Honan province were visited. Considerably more data could be collected for Zunhua than for Lin, which may indicate that the former area is industrially more advanced than the latter. However, the reader should be aware that Zunhua is a model county in China; data from Zunhua should be viewed in the light of this fact. Information from one particular place is better than no information at all, and information from a model county can certainly be used to exemplify what the Chinese planners intend to do—when certain conditions are fulfilled. To make the models come alive and exemplify the different components, information available to the author from Zunhua and Tangshan region in Hopei province has been summarized in a separate chapter.

An attempt is also made to summarize in economic and political terms the rationality of the Chinese attempt to use rural industrialization as an essential and integral component of her development strategy and the applicability of the Chinese approach in other developing countries.

Finally, this monograph deals, unfortunately, much more with policy than implementation and the problems associated with realization of actual policies. This must constantly be borne in mind by the reader.[4] There is still no clear-cut evidence that rural industrial policies are universally implemented in China. However, sufficient quantitative data are available to indicate that local industrialization programs are today widely implemented, even if they are facing more problems and undergoing more changes than appear in those national news media immediately available to a foreign observer.

Chapter 1

MODELS OF RURAL INDUSTRIALIZATION

Industrial Policies[1]

The new government in 1949 almost immediately launched its program of economic development, with a central economic strategy more or less based on the Soviet model. All efforts were to be directed towards building a core of heavy industry in a limited number of sectors with savings generated largely by the remainder of the economy. Following the Soviet model, the new government chose the organizational instrument of central economic planning. The planned sector was not only granted investment preference but was actively directed by the state. The non-planned sector was subject to a number of controls largely for the purpose of maximizing savings in the interest of the preferred sector. All major economic enterprises came under direct central control, by-passing local authorities. The handicraft industry was gradually transformed into cooperatives.

Only in 1954, however, had the organizational prerequisites for centralized planning been achieved. Even then, the entire economy of the country—still backward and economically disunited— could not be integrated into a single planning system. Thus the economy was divided into a planned and a non-planned sector. The former consisted of the country's major goods and service industries and the latter of the remainder of the economy.

The adoption of a Soviet-type economic strategy had its parallels in political and social policies. A new bureaucracy had to be created and staffed with able administrators. The revolution brought about the loss of a sizable group of technical and administrative talent which had to be replaced. During this period the party became top-heavy with cadres, and the party organization was unevenly distributed throughout the country, with its greatest strength in the major cities. Too much attention was paid to central state-owned industries and not enough to local industries, agriculture,

7

commerce, educational and cultural work, and other sectors. It was further realized that the planning should be made less detailed with more flexibility at lower levels of the economic system, in particular allowing lower echelons greater flexibility in setting their own targets. But the leadership did not react until late in 1957 with a series of far-reaching decentralization measures. The changes decided on at this time occurred in the context of a general political and social situation. The most significant element was the steady growth of a regional and local party apparatus that was becoming increasingly important at the lower levels of the system.

Decentralization aimed not only at improving economic coordination by reducing central control, but mainly at creating conditions which would activate and speed up economic development at the most basic levels of the economy: agriculture, and medium- and small-scale industry. Rapid development of agriculture and regional industry would not only create an imbalance that could not be rectified because of the distant and cumbersome machinery of the state, but would generate constantly changing supply and demand conditions necessitating great flexibility at the lowest possible levels. Furthermore, rapid economic development would create demand for new products that could not be supplied on a national scale. It was then necessary to find substitute materials within the local economic region. But this meant a shift in relative emphasis from large- to medium- and small-scale industry, in relative emphasis from industry in general to agriculture, in relative emphasis from city to village.

The emphasis on small-scale and rural industry in China cannot be fully understood without discussing the concept of "walking on two legs." The concept stands for balance of five relationships— industry and agriculture, heavy industry and light industry, large enterprises and medium-to-small enterprises, modern production methods and indigenous methods, enterprises run by the central government and those run by local authorities.

The first relationship is usually explained in the following way.[2] China is still a large agricultural country and a majority of her population lives in the countryside. Agriculture must be rapidly developed in order to meet requirements for food, clothing, and industrial raw materials. Agriculture is also a large potential market for industrial products. However, agricultural development depends on the support of industry to provide agricultural inputs which are needed in large quantities. Thus, industry and agriculture must be developed simultaneously since they complement each other.

The second relationship states that heavy industry and light industry must develop simultaneously. Modernization of industry and agriculture and building a strong defense require advanced equipment and materials which mainly come from heavy industry. Heavy industry expansion requires funds for which the main source is the profits of light-industry enterprises. Light industry needs comparatively fewer funds and goes into production faster, and the period of capital turnover is short. So the outcome of a balanced development is that more consumer goods are produced to satisfy the increasing needs of the people and growing amounts of funds for heavy industry. This is, of course, one way of saying that the development strategy should be such that the share of the national product invested is high while at the same time people's requirements for consumer goods are met.

The remaining three relationships essential for the development of rural industry indicate an industrial dualism which should manifest itself as a spectrum of sizes, technologies, and initiatives (control). These three relations are restated in Table 1.

Table 1. Industrial Spectrum of the "Two-Leg" Policy.[3]

Enterprise size	Technology	Initiative (control) level
Big	Advanced	Nation
Medium	Intermediate	Province
Small	Intermediate/Primitive	County/Commune

China stresses today that it is necessary to build large leading-core enterprises with a high level of technology and productivity. However, the lower end of the industrial spectrum should also be pursued, since the enterprises there train technicians and accumulate experience and funds for the larger enterprises to be built while providing people with urgently needed industrial products. In the main, the newest technology should be adopted but, where various constraints hinder this development, simple, practical methods should be used. These methods are then continually improved upon and this enables speedier development than would otherwise be the case.

China still considers herself to be an economically underdeveloped country where it is not possible for the central government to run everything in economic construction. By developing national and local enterprises at the same time, local initiative can be given fuller play, and the natural resources, funds, equipment, and technology in the localities can be better utilized.

These comments have mainly touched upon the economics of the two-leg policy. However, another consequence is that increasing numbers of relatively modern industries in the countryside are training many peasants into workers and technicians and engineers. This, then, leads to reducing the differences between workers and peasants, city and countryside, mental and manual labor, which are important political goals in China today.

The industrial dualism of the two-leg policy is evident in both rural and urban areas and involves constant choices and changes in most industrial sectors. Simultaneously, the lower end of the industrial spectrum is, in rural areas, also part of an attempt to achieve integrated rural development based in communes and counties. A choice has then been made here to concentrate the description and analysis on industries—mainly small ones—located in rural areas.

The principles for a new development strategy had evolved gradually from 1956 onwards and were slowly tried out in the period up to May 1958, when a full-scale Great Leap Forward was launched. In contrast to the First Five-Year Plan (1953–1957), the Leap policy emphasized:

1. Improvement in the farming techniques through extended, more systematic use of manpower available within the agricultural sector.
2. Expansion of small local industries—manned with rural manpower—using indigenous, labor-intensive technologies.

During the early, fairly unplanned proliferation of small industries, transportation costs and/or the technical feasibility were not always properly considered. At the same time, the small industries may have been too much geared to the needs of the urban industrial sector. The rural industrialization approach of this period was still a set of sector strategies. The integrated approach of rural development appears to have been introduced considerably later than the setting up of the communes.

The new development approach meant that the rural population had to provide the manpower for agricultural tasks as well as the manpower needed in the new labor-intensive industrial undertakings. The early Great Leap Forward emphasized certain discrete technologies, particularly within the metallurgical sector, but the development of the transportation and energy sectors was promoted less. However, a new view on the role of rural small-scale industries evolved. They should primarily be serving agriculture, but only at a later stage, joining forces with the modern urban-based sector. This approach is clearly evident from the following comment in 1960:

> Owing to the complicated character of agricultural production, agriculture imposes diversified demands on industry. Meanwhile, industrial raw materials are spread over the countryside ... By the developing of medium and small enterprises, the demands of agricultural production can be extensively met on the one hand and local materials can be obtained and local activity developed on the other ... Experience in the three years' Leap Forward has clearly shown that without a gradual equipping of agriculture with modern technology it is impossible to shift more labor power gradually from the rural areas to the industrial front ... Transfer of labor power from the agricultural front to the industrial front has virtually to be effected at the price of equivalent agricultural machinery and motive power.[4]

For a number of reasons affecting the Chinese economy—consecutive years of bad weather for agriculture, Soviet withdrawal of assistance to develop the modern sector of the economy—it became impossible to continue the modified Great Leap Forward, and most of the small-scale industries were closed down in 1961. Some of them continued to operate, but not until the late 1960s did a new proliferation begin. The new development is based on the application of the two-leg policies. The process is now more gradual and cautious and has little resemblance to the early part of the Great Leap Forward in 1958.

The Chinese labor policies have seldom been clearly spelled out, but it appears evident that the modern industrial sector will not in the foreseeable future provide many new employment opportunities. The following quotation discussing Shanghai may still be considered typical as a comment on how industrial bases like Peking, Tientsin, Wuhan, and the cities in the northeast should be developed.

To increase the number of workers is one of the ways of developing industrial production. That rural population accounts for over 80 percent of the people of our country is a hallmark of the backwardness of our country. Therefore our country must continue to develop large, medium, and small industrial enterprises and continue to swell the ranks of the working class. This is fully correct insofar as the whole country is concerned. However, insofar as this old industrial base of Shanghai is concerned, it is inadvisable to build and expand industrial enterprises excessively because it is too far away from raw materials and fuel-producing centers and from the inland markets and because it is necessary to place geographical distribution of industry on a rational basis and to change the uneven growth of the economy between coastal areas and the hinterland. For this reason, increase in the number of workers should not be taken as the main way of developing Shanghai's industry from now on . . . To raise labor productivity, too, is one of the ways of developing industrial production . . . in the case of Shanghai, it is particularly essential to take the constant rising of labor productivity as the main way.[5]

This leaves labor absorption to take place mainly in the rural industrial sector and within agriculture. The rural industrial sector

plays an important role in a number of industrial sectors, which
will be evident from the discussion in Chapter 4. Production is
generally more labor-intensive and production technology more
primitive than in the modern industrial sector and also contains a
strong element of local indigenous technology. After the proliferation of small-scale rural industries in 1969–1971, the emphasis
appears now to be shifting towards increasing labor productivity.
Technical innovations and use of more machinery are suggested
measures for increasing production in these enterprises instead of
increasing employment. This may be taken as an indication that
the local industrial systems have basically been established and
that the task is now shifting towards a more efficient use of rural
industrial structures. With simultaneous expansion of national and
local enterprises in rural areas, the national enterprises can increasingly draw on the manufacturing potential of a large number of
small enterprises. However, before the discussion continues, it is
necessary to make a clear distinction between rural industrialization
and decentralization of industry.

Rural Industrialization versus Industrial Decentralization[6]
    To explain the difference between these concepts, it is neces-
sary to classify population centers according to size. Communities
may usefully be categorized in four size ranges:
1. Rural communities with up to 10,000–20,000 inhabitants
   (market towns)
2. Small urban centers with up to about 200,000 inhabitants
3. Secondary urban centers with up to about 1,000,000
   inhabitants
4. Metropolitan centers with over 1,000,000 inhabitants.
The population figures are only approximate. The basic distinguish-
ing feature is the economic base of the community. Small urban
centers are defined as those whose existence is based mainly on the
services they furnish to the surrounding rural areas. In secondary
urban centers other activities take precedence over agro-related
activities, and agriculture in the surrounding countryside is based
mainly on the demand for food created by the urban center. Metropolitan areas are the one or few largest population centers in almost

any country, in which most industry, government, and commerce are concentrated.[7]

Industrial decentralization is a generic name for moving industry out of the metropolis to any other communities. The chief aim of an industrial decentralization policy is usually to achieve a shift of future industrial growth from a metropolitan area to secondary urban centers. In most countries only a minority of the new industries—mostly those which process natural resources—are decentralized down to smaller urban centers and, to a much smaller extent, to rural communities. It is suggested that such industries be termed *regional industries*. This pattern of industrial decentralization and the place of rural industry are shown in Figure 1.

Industrial concentration in one or a few centers is commonly found in countries in the early stages of industrialization. The spreading of industrialization to secondary urban centers is found in industrially more advanced developing countries like Pakistan and India. The further spreading of industry to rural communities is found in mature industrial countries. The hypothesis has been advanced that the above order of industrial development is the optimal one. However, the experience in Japan and more recently in China indicates that an entirely different pattern involving rural communities at an early stage of development is feasible—even if the circumstances and necessary conditions are not yet fully known.

Industrial decentralization to secondary urban centers is, it is generally agreed, an entirely feasible goal involving minimal short-term economic disadvantages for the enterprises concerned and contributing substantially to overall economic efficiency. However, it has in the past been argued that it is an entirely different matter to locate industry in rural locations, which is said to involve great costs because of reduced economic efficiency.

There are two divergent views on how to use industry to bring employment and income opportunities to the majority of the population (which in many developing countries is still to be found in the villages) at present and in the foreseeable future. One extreme viewpoint advocates that industrialization should continue where it started—in the large urban centers. The other extreme advocates the

Figure 1. The Relation Between Rural Industrialization and Industrial Decentralization

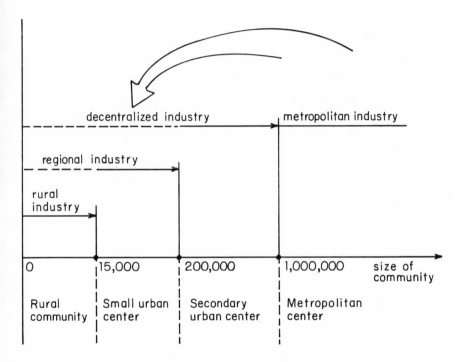

decentralization of industry into the villages. Neither is very realistic, and a middle way advocates the promotion of industry in urban centers of intermediate size with considerably more emphasis than in the past on promoting productive linkages between the smaller urban centers and the villages. In this way agriculture and industry would become more integrated. Rural industrialization in China can basically be seen as an integral component of this second approach.

It is certainly desirable to bring industrial employment and income, and the indirect employment and income generated by industry, closer to the majority of the population living in the villages. But it does not follow that the best way to do this is to seek to locate a considerable proportion of manufacturing industry directly in the villages or even in the small urban centers (market towns). In order to achieve the objectives mentioned, it is likely to be more effective to focus on the industrial development of selected towns and cities which are intermediaries between villages on the one hand and secondary urban and metropolitan centers on the other hand, with a considerable emphasis on upgrading traditional village crafts serving agriculture. Industrial development would then take place in urban places, which are intermediaries between villages and the metropolitan areas. This would then take advantages of reasonably low costs for industrial facilities like power and transportation and provide important external economies associated with urban locations. Yet it would bring industry and related services substantially closer to the majority of the population, who still live in villages.

In this context it is necessary to formulate programs to foster small industry and a full range of economic and cultural activities for intermediate cities and towns, to link such programs to the surrounding areas, and at the same time to promote trade and other connections between industry and agriculture.

The industrial development in intermediate urban centers would focus mainly on the following products:

1. Agricultural inputs—fertilizers and farm implements such as hand tools and ploughs, small tractors at a later stage
2. Transportation equipment—bicycles, carts, wheelbarrows
3. Construction materials—bricks, tiles, and lumber
4. Construction tools
5. Consumer goods—textiles, canned food, furniture, utensils
6. Glass products, chemicals

The social and political benefits of decentralization are worth some economic cost. If decentralization were taken to mean pushing industry directly into the villages, which was partly the case in China during the initial stage of the Great Leap Forward in 1958, the cost would be very great, both in terms of material and human resources required and in terms of lost efficiency. The cost would certainly be much less under a decentralization policy focused on intermediate cities and towns. There are good reasons for believing that there might be no economic cost at all in the long run, but even a net economic gain. There are two main reasons for this. First, the social overheads are lower in the intermediate towns. Second, creating dispersed centers of innovation and economic change in the intermediate places is likely to speed up the development of the country as a whole more effectively than a highly centralized industrial pattern would do. Most industrial economists would agree with this argument so far and would generally not favor any industrial promotion program which goes into the villages or the very small urban centers.

It is often argued that the hand production of folklorish artistic articles is the only activity that has a great development potential in rural communities. However, there are other exceptions to the principle that manufacturing needs an urban location. Certain agro-industries, like sugar, grain, and timber mills, may find a village location best. But as transportation improves, even these are likely to gravitate to towns, or towns will develop around them.

In many areas, however, traditional village industries meeting a traditional type of local demand will continue to have a function for some years to come. Most of the traditional village industries will have to undergo transformation, and many of their activities will gravitate to urban locations as modernization proceeds, bringing more purchasing power, new tastes, and increased communications. But an integrated program for upgrading village service and producing a rural industrial extension service may make it possible to retain a considerable amount of industrial activity in the villages, a situation evident in many areas of China.

Linkages Between Agriculture, Rural Industry, and Modern Industry
China has in her rural industrialization programs always stressed the complementarity of agriculture and industry, which includes two different aspects. On the one hand, rural industry should serve as a complement to the modern industrial sector, but on the

other hand—and at present more important—rural industry should also serve as a complement to agriculture. However, no explicit models of how rural industrialization should be carried out, or how rural industry should function in a wider context, have been published. As it is often useful to have a model as a basis for analysis and discussion, an attempt has been made here to describe the Chinese approach in a few models. It must be remembered, however, that few localities have identical conditions for rural industrialization, and the Chinese reality, therefore, may only partially conform to the models presented here.

Integrated rural development, of which rural industrialization programs form an essential part, should in China, as in other countries, fulfill multiple objectives. Provision of industrial inputs for agriculture, processing of primary products, employment and income generation are among these. Consequently, a successful program for rural industrialization requires close links between rural industry and agriculture, since the agricultural sector provides manpower, raw materials, and capital. But the links with the modern industrial sector are equally important, since modern industry initially supplies rural industry with much of the needed technologies and also provides markets for ancilliary industries at a later stage of development. So, as a basis for further discussion, it may be helpful to look briefly at the linkages between agriculture, rural industry, and modern industry, as they are illustrated in Figure 2, where the development of the linkages is indicated in three stages.

Modern industry, which in terms of employment is relatively small, is characterized by a relatively high degree of mechanization, and further expansion of this sector cannot create sufficient employment to absorb the manpower coming of working age. Agriculture, on the other hand, provides much of China's exports which are exchanged mainly for industrial commodities needed by the modern industrial sector. Agriculture requires industrial inputs to raise yields, but the low degree of mechanization and relatively low productivity initially prevent the substantial accumulation of capital which is required for the mechanization of agriculture.

Stage 1. In the first stage of changing the relations between the

modern industrial sector and agriculture, rural industry is introduced as an intermediary. Rural industry is developed more or less
from scratch, initially providing many of the repair and maintenance

Figure 2. Development Stages of Rural Industry's
Interaction With Agriculture and Modern
Industry

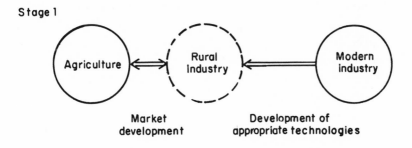

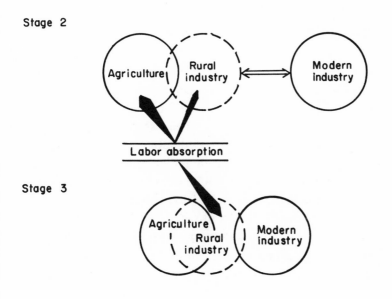

facilities needed for tools and machinery used in agriculture, but also producing industrial inputs for agriculture as well as processing agricultural produce. Consequently, the linkage between rural industry and agriculture is a mutual relationship where rural industry provides much of the technical skill formation which takes place in the rural sector of the economy. Industrial manpower for the rural industrial sector is recruited from agriculture, although on a modest scale. As agriculture develops, more raw materials and more local capital can be provided for the further development of rural industry. At this stage of development, the linkage between the modern industrial sector and rural industry is mainly a one-way relationship whereby rural industry is given much of the required technology. This comes both in the form of machinery and in the form of on-the-spot instructions or training in the modern industrial enterprises. Important factors in the further development of linkages are the level of market demand (purchasing power of the locality) and the availability of technologies appropriate for relatively small rural industries. The price mechanism is initially of little importance, and the initiative of the local leadership at different administrative levels explains much of the new activity.

Stage 2. Rural industry and agriculture now become partly integrated. Agriculture supplies rural industry with increasing amounts of raw materials for light industrial products, and rural industry also processes increasing amounts of farm produce. The increase in purchasing power arising from the increased productivity in agriculture makes it possible to finance more farm machinery out of which only the larger units are manufactured within the modern industrial sector. Labor absorption, at this stage, will still mainly take place within agriculture or related activities, but will also to a limited extent take place in the rural industrial sector. Consequently, urbanization in rural areas will still be rather slow. But rural industry reaches a certain degree of sophistication and differentiation and ancilliary rural industries can supply modern industry with certain components and products. Technology will continue to flow from the modern industrial sector. Thus, in the second stage, the linkage between the two sectors develops into a mutual relationship.

Stage 3. In this stage of the sequence, rural industry and modern industry become more or less integrated. Some lines of production can be shifted from the modern sector to the rural industrial sector. Quality standards and standardization within the rural industrial sector improve considerably, thus permitting a considerable expansion of the subcontracting system. A growing amount of export products can be manufactured within the rural industrial sector, and the difference in enterprise size and quality standards between rural industry and modern industry is beginning to disappear. Rural industry and related services are becoming increasingly important for labor absorption. A fairly substantial transfer of employment from agriculture to rural industry can take place as agriculture is mechanized. This is then accompanied by a relatively rapid urbanization of the centers which have served as nuclei in the rural industrialization process.

Thus, it can be seen that rural industrialization in this model, based on local resources of manpower and capital, is going to provide the basis for the mechanization of agriculture, which in turn will make it possible for peasants to engage in new tasks (such as multiple cropping) and raise agricultural yields. With higher yields more industrial crops can be grown, and this, in turn, will give local light industry more raw materials. In the process, labor is absorbed into rural industry, and purchasing power is also increased, thus creating a local market for light and other industrial products.

Basically, rural industry should use locally available raw materials, produce locally, and distribute locally. This implies that arranging plans, allocating raw materials, and organizing factory production should ideally be based on local decisions. But as soon as secondary objectives—such as the manufacture of components or products for the modern industrial sector—are emphasized, local planning must increasingly be coordinated with central plans, which often means those of the next higher administrative level. In meeting the primary objective of serving agriculture, in the first stage, a symbiotic interaction develops between the rural industrial sector and the surrounding agricultural sector. In the third stage of development, when secondary objectives begin to come into the picture, a similar symbiotic interaction develops between the rural industrial sector and that of the modern industry. These interactions appear to be very important not only for economic but also for social development in gradually transforming the relatively backward areas of China.

Rural industry should ideally be developed gradually, and closely coordinated with agricultural development so as not to cause any disruption of the local economy, and there is evidence to support the conclusion that this is done in many places in China today. In many localities all over the country a problem-finding and problem-solving capacity will gradually be built up. This will make it possible to specify local resource availability and request outside resources more accurately. The countryside would then be in the position to put forward demands on the basis of increasing purchasing power and increasing knowledge. The difference between the countryside and the cities may then diminish, and this is an important social goal.

Rural Industrial Systems

Although rural industry is an integral part of the Chinese development strategy, there is no general pattern of rural industrialization that applies to the whole country. China's widely differing natural conditions and uneven level of economic development are obvious explanations of why this must be so. However, it appears to be a basic requirement all over the country that rural industry—or the rural industrial system within a locality—should be geared towards serving agriculture. In doing so, rural industry should fulfill three general conditions. First, it should use raw materials that are locally available. Second, it should manufacture locally. Third, the products should mainly be distributed locally. There are, of course, exceptions to these requirements—particularly near the big cities. The resource base and the size of the locality are also likely to influence the emphasis given to the above-mentioned three requirements.

However, there can be no doubt that in most places the interaction between rural industry and agriculture is considered to be of overriding importance, particularly in the initial stages of developing rural industry in a locality. It is thought that the interaction can be best understood in the context of a county industrial system, and Figure 3 shows a model of the kind of economic and industrial system evident today in a number of counties. The commodity flow in the diagram clearly shows that the rural industrial system primarily serves agriculture. The agricultural sector is provided with agricultural technology (including improved seed strains), improved irrigation and drainage facilities, chemical fertilizer and agro-chemicals, and farm machinery. This creates the basis for increased agricultural productivity which, if above a certain level, means that production of industrial crops can be expanded. Industry can then be supplied with more raw materials, and more light industrial products can be manufactured for local consumption. With increasing mechanization more manpower can be released for industrial employment.

Figure 3 illustrates the flow chart for a county or a locality that is well endowed with natural resources including coal, iron ore, and limestone. In such a locality the industrial activities can be divided into five different components. The first is the heavy small-scale industry which includes what the Chinese often term "five small industries." These supply energy, cement, chemical fertilizer, iron and steel, and machinery, which directly or indirectly provide agriculture with the inputs necessary for raising productivity. These plants are usually run by the county.

The second component is various resource-specific industries which may provide raw materials such as coal, iron ore, limestone, and other minerals to the "five small industries" or to larger national enterprises. It is evident that the resource base—location, size, and quality—decides to what extent small-scale heavy industries can be set up. Economies of scale and the development of the transportation system are other important factors, all of which will be discussed later.

The third and fourth components of industrial activity in a county both belong to light industry. The main responsibility of this sector is to process agricultural and side-line produce and to

Figure 3. Model of a Rural Industrial System in China Showing Commodity Flow

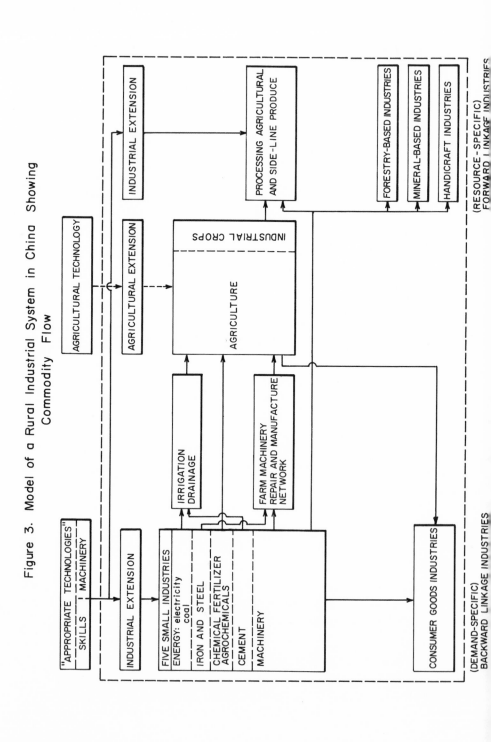

provide the locality with some of the needed consumer goods. This may include flour milling, oil pressing, cotton ginning, and so forth, as well as manufacture of textiles and shoes, household goods of porcelain and metal, canned fruit, and other goods. The expansion of the local light industrial sector is closely dependent on increased productivity in the agricultural sector, which provides most of the raw materials. Light industrial enterprises are at county, commune, and brigade levels.

The fifth component, the farm machinery repair and manufacture network, produces simple farm implements, tools, and also heavier equipment. Of primary importance is the repair and maintenance of farm implements and machinery in order to sustain a high rate of machinery utilization. Therefore the repair and manufacture network has a three-tier structure where in principle each brigade and commune within a county should have its own unit. Naturally, the smallest units are run by the brigades, medium-sized ones by the communes, and the relatively large units by the county. The goal is to develop a clear division of labor among units at different levels. The brigade units should engage in simple repairs and manufacturing. The commune units should be able to carry out more complex repairs and also manufacture heavier equipment. The county stations should be able to carry out the repairs of any complex farm machinery being used within the county and also manufacture heavy equipment to be used in agriculture or in the units of the repair and manufacture network.

Obviously, not all of China's 2,110 counties have the resources to create a complete industrial system of the kind described above. The size and diversity of a county industrial system depend on the natural resource base and the level of economic development. Some counties are well advanced, the value of their total industrial production exceeding that of agriculture. But most of the counties are likely to be still in the initial stage of developing their industrial systems. This would usually correspond to the first stage of the previously described three-step model.

Figure 4. Different Modes of Rural Modernization in China

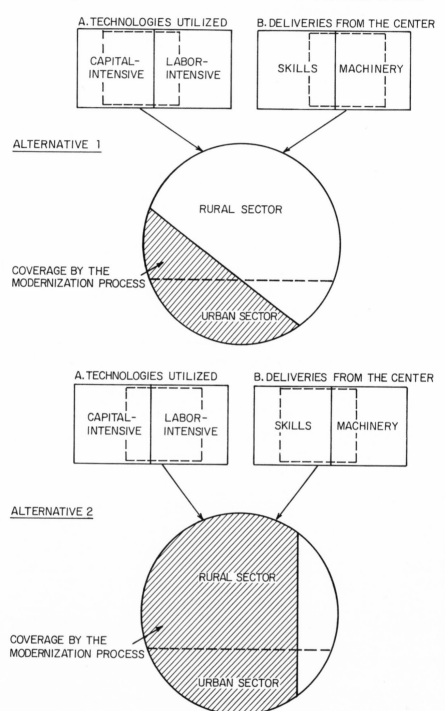

Urban-Rural Relationships

There exist—in theory—two basically different development alternatives for the rural areas. The first is to concentrate almost all the resources on the development of the modern, city-based industrial sector, and meet the needs of the rural sector only when a sufficiently large city-based industrial sector has been created. The rural areas would then be left for a considerable period of time more or less to themselves and only selectively be drawn into the modernization process on the basis of modern technology and deliveries of machinery from the center. This would correspond to alternative 1 in Figure 4. In this alternative, scarcity of resources available to the center sets a limit to the coverage of the modernization process in rural areas.

The second alternative involves a fundamental change in the relationship between rural areas and the center and in providing rural areas with technologies. If the balance between deliveries of skills and machinery is shifted towards the skill side, the result will be that a considerably larger proportion of the rural areas can be drawn into the modernization. The explanation is that skill transfer will only temporarily reduce the center's capacity for further development. This alternative, however, requires a considerable local resource mobilization in order to sustain the modernization process. If, at the same time, more labor-intensive technologies are used and further developed than is traditionally the case in the modern industrial sector, considerably more people can be drawn into the industrial phase of modernization. This corresponds to alternative 2 in Figure 4.

The development and application of labor-intensive technologies in cities—mainly collectively owned enterprises—has in China had the further effect that a larger share of the cities' population, such as students, housewives, and retired people, have been drawn into productive occupations.

If a majority of rural areas can be drawn into the modernization process as indicated in alternative 2 in Figure 4, this is likely to have some important consequences. First, it will considerably influence or even reverse the traditional migration pattern from rural areas to cities. Second, it will also greatly influence the urbanization pattern so that small urban places will expand much more quickly than the large urban places. Some foreign observers have even thought that China is going to avoid urbanization altogether. However, there is hardly any evidence to support that conclusion.

Administrative reforms have considerably changed the relations between urban places and the surrounding agricultural areas. The administrative units of cities and towns all include in their responsibilities considerable rural areas which on the average constitute 40 percent of the population in the administrative area. On the one hand, the coordinated supply of vegetables and other farm products is part of the justification for including large rural areas. On the other hand, there is no doubt that expanding urban centers draw on the labor pool in their rural areas and that employment and occupational patterns in urban rural areas generally are different from rural areas proper. However, the migration from the rural areas—and the internal brain drain—which was very much in evidence during the 1950s, has basically been reversed. The largely uncontrolled migration to the cities was, through a number of administrative measures, stopped in the early 1960s, when temporary difficulties forced leadership to consolidate the economy and to allocate more resources to the development of agriculture. A large number of newly arrived city dwellers were then sent back to their native villages to strengthen the agricultural front. The migration regulations, which are now combined with local rationing cards for certain essential commodities like cereals, edible oil, and cotton, have been well observed. Since the Cultural Revolution, the countryside has been affected by two flows of reverse migration.

First, in the process of changing the school system to conform better with the needs of a developing country, a substantial number of urban middle-school students were asked to resettle more or less permanently in rural areas.[8] Zunhua county in Hopei province, for example, received at least 4,600 middle school and university students who had come to the county to receive "re-education among peasants and workers." Of this number, 40 had in 1971 been selected for university studies and another 70 joined commercial enterprises.

And no less than 820 had been recruited for industrial work. Their different training and outlook are likely to have been beneficial to Zunhua not only in the activities mentioned but also in agriculture and side-line occupations.

Second, in the process of setting up various infrastructure services, a very large number of professionals—teachers, administrators, doctors and other medical personnel—have gone to the countryside. There they have provided valuable services, trained paratechnical personnel, and assisted in setting up the framework for rural services. The Chinese have on occasion indicated that about 30 percent of the total urban medical personnel have during the past years been allocated to rural areas.

The central administration has at the same time been cut down. The central ministries and agencies in Peking have been reduced to less than half of the earlier number. The number of people employed in the central administration is reported to have been reduced by about 80 percent. Simultaneously, the administrative structure at provincial, regional, and county levels appears to have been considerably strengthened both in number and power.

Simultaneously with the reversed migration, a substantial number of employment opportunities have been created in rural areas. Employment in rural areas has increased, but still more new employment has been generated through expansion of commerce, transportation, public health and other services, animal husbandry, and agricultural side-line production. All these are likely to play an important role in providing employment and "career" opportunities for the young and mobile people who, under different circumstances, would have moved into the cities. A substantial number of the educated youth who have resettled in the rural areas have been recruited into new rural activities.

The rural modernization and rural industrialization programs have not only influenced the migration pattern between rural and urban areas. They also appear to have important consequences for the distribution of urban population in cities of different sizes. When rural industrialization programs were actively promoted during the Great Leap Forward in the late 1950s, the then considerably larger communes were centers for almost all rural industrial activities, and only gradually did a more differentiated approach develop. The heavy industry component of rural industrialization appeared at the time to have been the responsibility of the communes. This is no longer so. Almost all heavy-industry-type rural industries—chemical fertilizer, iron and steel, cement plants, and so forth—are now located in or near the county seats and run by the county administration.

The apices of service networks are also located in the county seats. It consequently appears that the county capitals have been constituted as growth centers for rural areas. That this should be so appears natural when one sees the size and distribution of cities in China, given in Table 2 below.

The statistical information relates to 1953; the "urban population" today has almost doubled and is around 170 million, which includes approximately 40 percent peasants. But the relative importance of the size categories is not likely to have undergone considerable changes. A striking feature of the distribution is that more than 4,000 towns with between 2,000 and 19,999 people in 1953 accounted for 32 percent of the urban population. Almost all the county capitals are to be found in this category, and it appears that the rural industrialization in China to a considerable extent will be based on the further development of these towns.

China has on the whole been much more successful in controlling the migration into the big cities and has established better industrial-economic relations between cities and rural areas than most other countries. But this does not mean that problems do not exist. The present consolidation phase of rural industrialization and the limited employment impact of the programs so far may create considerable frustration among two categories of people. First, a proportion of the resettled educated youth cannot quickly be drawn into activities where their background and outlook would make them suited to support the modernization. Second, large rural groups would most probably like to move into activities that are more exciting, less hard, and economically more rewarding than agricultural work. There does not seem to be much of a prospect

Table 2. Size and Distribution of Cities in China in 1953

Size	Number of Cities	Population in Millions	Percentage of Urban Population
> 1,000,000	9	17.5	22.6
500,000-999,999	16	9.4	12.1
200,000-499,999	28	7.1	9.1
100,000-199,999	49	6.0	7.8
50,000-99,999	71	4.6	5.9
20,000-49,999	247	6.8	8.9
2,000-19,999	4,228	24.7	32.0
1,000-1,999	727	1.1	1.4
< 1,000	193	1.4	0.2
TOTAL:	5,568	77.3	100.0%

Source: Morris Benjamin Ullman, *Cities of Mainland China, 1953 and 1958,* Washington, D.C., U.S. Department of Commerce, Bureau of the Census, Foreign Manpower Research Office, 1961.

for meeting such hopes in the near future. Therefore it is essential to reduce the cultural differential between cities and countryside and not let the economic differential develop. Cultural conditions in rural areas have been considerably improved since the Cultural Revolution started in 1966; and it could be argued that people in the cities are culturally less privileged than they were in the mid-1960s. Income for certain groups in the cities increased in 1971 but there is no indication that the overall economic differential between cities and countryside has increased.

Chapter 2

RURAL INDUSTRY CHARACTERISTICS

Rural industrialization is a function of both demand and
availability of local resources; it is easier to influence the former
than the latter. Rural industry can—with reference to the model
for the rural industry system in Figure 3—be categorized into *backward linkage industries* meeting a demand for agricultural inputs
and consumer goods, and *forward linkage industries* mainly based
on locally available physical and human resources. The various
categories are listed in Table 3 below. The backward linkage industries, of course, require local human resources but are initially very
dependent on external technological and financial resources.

The Chinese planners have attempted to use the demand
arising from a modernizing agriculture to create backward linkages
—in a rural context—for almost all the important inputs required
by agriculture. Some of the backward linkage industries—like
cement and chemical fertilizer—are justified because of the existence of local raw material resources. However, their development
has not been triggered because of existing local resources but from
a demand caused mainly by changes in agricultural technology,
and lacks justification without this local demand.

Mechanical inputs are manufactured in county-, commune-,
and brigade-level units, the activity at brigade level usually consisting only of a couple of blacksmiths using a few pieces of relatively simple machinery. Chemical inputs are usually produced in
county-level enterprises, even though mixing and simple phosphate
fertilizer production may be found in commune-level enterprises.
The manufacture of consumer goods is carried out at all three
levels but more complex products—such as plastic sandals—only in
county-level units. Processing of agricultural and side-line produce
is mainly carried out by brigades and communes. Forestry-based
and mineral-based industry is generally carried out by brigades and
communes, depending on the resource base, the manpower situa-

33

Table 3. Rural, Agro-Related Industrial Categories

A. *Backward linkage industries—meeting a demand for:*
1. Agricultural inputs
    a. Mechanical inputs
        – direct demand for farm equipment and tools
        – derived demand for productive equipment to manufacture farm equipment and tools
    b. Chemical inputs (chemical fertilizers, pesticides, etc.)
    c. Construction materials (cement, stone, bricks, etc.)
2. Consumer goods
    a. Direct demand for products
    b. Derived demand for productive equipment to manufacture consumer goods

B. *Forward linkage industries*
3. Agro-based industries
    a. Direct demand for processing of agricultural produce
    b. Derived demand for equipment for processing agricultural produce
4. Services
    a. Direct demand for transport, storage, and distribution
    b. Derived demand for equipment for transport, etc.
5. Forestry-based industries
6. Mineral-based industries
7. Handicraft industries
    a. Rural consumer goods
    b. Artistic handicrafts

tion, and the technology utilized. Handicraft industry is found at commune, brigade, and household levels. All this relates to industry in rural areas proper; the situation may be quite different in city-near locations.

Rural industries generally serve a small market, the size of which varies with the level—brigade, commune, county, or region—where the enterprise is found. Some economists have tended to interpret this as a tendency to develop a cellular economy.[1] The evidence in the rest of this paper does not support this viewpoint. Through choice of enterprise size and manufacturing technology it has been possible in many industrial sectors to transfer industry into rural areas and manufacture economically to meet a local demand—if all externalities are considered. Further, size of enterprise and technology are closely related to the control-initiative level, and many localities—communes and counties—are already being drawn into subcontracting and manufacturing export items, thus also meeting an external demand. This is particularly true for rural industry in city-near locations.

Planning Levels

It appears that the Chinese planners are now guided by a conviction that most of the facilities for economic and social activities in rural areas can be provided most effectively and economically when they are clustered in space so as to take advantage of interdependence in their functions and use. For many social and economic activities, hierarchical structures are desirable and in some cases necessary. The particular levels of the hierarchies of a number of different activities cluster naturally on the basis of similarities in the areas or populations which they serve most efficiently. These levels appear to relate naturally to villages and towns, that is, brigades and counties, on the basis of the accessibility of these places to appropriate areas or number of uses. Activities or institutions can be grouped well when their ideal service or trade areas are similar. So grouping of activities in centers is usually advantageous when they can all be served by the same transport system.

Many of the projects decided at the provincial level require an intimate knowledge of local conditions. The higher the degree of the geographic disaggregation of economic planning, the greater must be the specificity of the plan. At the local level, planning consists of detailed project design, and plan implementation consists of the actual completion of particular projects and the provision of the planned productive and social services. So local planning must be based on local expertise comprising detailed knowledge of the geographic, climatic, hydrological, and the diverse economic and social conditions in each particular locality.

Consequently, rural industrialization in China is based on a multi-tier industrial structure involving enterprises in brigades (villages), communes, counties, and also a limited number of enterprises at regional level. The size and ownership is closely related to capital/labor-intensity, capital requirements, and what production to engage in. To understand the place of rural industry in the economy, it might be useful first to look at the administrative structure. China has five administrative levels—nation, province, region, county, and commune. The number of units at each administrative level is given in Table 4.

Table 4. Administrative Levels in China

1. Nation	
2. Province	29 provinces, autonomous regions, and municipalities
3. Region	192 regions
4. County	2,100 counties + 167 cities
5. Commune	74,000 communes*
– brigade	the commune/brigade ratio is approximately 1:10
– team	the brigade/team ratio is approximately 1:10

Source: *Handbook for the administrative structure of the People's Republic of China,* Cartography Publishing House, Peking, 1965.

*It has for a number of years been assumed—based on earlier information—that the number of people's communes was around 74,000. However, a NCNA report dated June 25, 1973 referred to "China's 50,000 people's communes" (BBC Summary of World Broadcasts, Part 3, The Far East, *Weekly Economic Report,* FE/W731, 4 July 1973).

China's being a planned economy means, among other things, that the targets of the enterprises must be included in yearly state plans. With a total number of at least half a million industrial units in rural areas, this cannot be done at the national level. Decentralization measures were already taken in 1957, and province, region, and county agencies are today involved in drawing up and implementing plans, as illustrated in Figure 5.

The production targets of the rural industries are only partly included in state planning, which is evident from Table 5 below. All state-owned county-level enterprises usually have their planning

Figure 5. Hierarchy of Lower-Level Planning (areas)

Province

Region

County

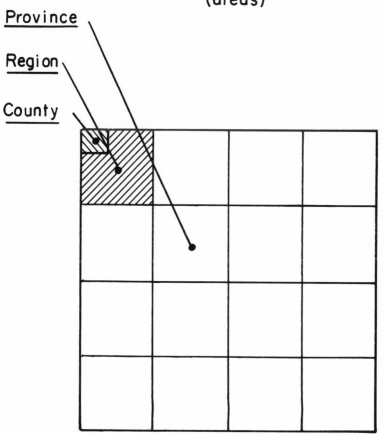

targets included in the state plan. The same is true only for the more important of the collectively owned units at county level, and all others are excluded. However, it must be noted that many of the commune-level and brigade-level enterprises are indirectly drawn into the state plan if they are providing minerals or other raw materials to state-owned, county-level enterprises.

It is becoming increasingly common that items for export are produced within rural industrial systems—items such as nails, machinery parts, or handicraft products. In the case of such products' being manufactured in a collectively owned county-level enterprise, the planning targets will be included in the state plan.

Table 5. Categories of Industrial Enterprises in Rural Areas

Administrative level	Ownership	Planning targets
1. County	State	Included in the state plan
2a. County	Collective	Included in the state plan
2b. County	Collective	Not included in the state plan
3. Commune	Collective	Not included in the state plan
4. Brigade	Collective	Not included in the state plan

The same is likely to be true for an essential product like paper coming from a collectively owned county-level enterprise.

People's communes and the counties require some explanation. The communes are the outcome of a gradual collectivization process of Chinese agriculture, which started in 1950, even earlier in some areas. Small, relatively informal, mutual-aid teams were further developed into larger co-op farms, which then became collective farms, which in turn were rapidly developed into a relatively small number of people's communes in 1958. Changes and consolidation led to a considerable decrease in the size of communes after 1958, and the ownership is now generally divided among three levels—commune, brigade, and team—except for a few cases where teams have been merged into brigades, or the very rare cases where the brigades further have been merged into communes. The brigades are often the old natural villages.

The number of counties is at present more than 2,110 and is rising only slowly. However, the number of counties has undergone great changes since the liberation in 1949. The counties are very important units for rural industrialization programs. The counties in the densely populated areas of China cover an area of about 2,000 sq. km., and each has on an average 300,000 residents. The average population of a commune is almost 10,000 but varies considerably from one area to another.

Rural areas in China consist of both rural communes and towns. The latter are county capitals as well as townships within the county. The cities and towns are divided into urban districts, neighborhoods, and street committees. The political structure of rural and urban areas is displayed in Figure 6. The numbers given

Figure 6. China's Administrative-Political Structure

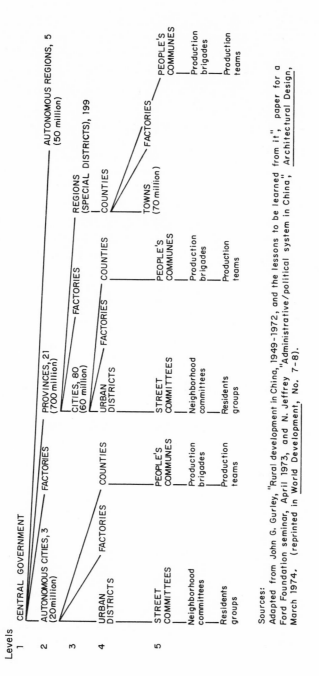

Sources:
Adapted from John G. Gurley, "Rural development in China, 1949-1972, and the lessons to be learned from it", paper for a Ford Foundation seminar, April 1973, and N. Jeffrey "Administrative/political system in China", Architectural Design, March 1974. (reprinted in World Development, No. 7-8).

differ slightly from those elsewhere in this monograph, but the function of the figure is to show the political structure in China. The urban districts, neighborhoods, and street committees are responsible for a large number of industrial activities—mainly manufacturing light (consumer) products or products on a subcontracting basis for large plants.

Many of the industrial enterprises in rural areas are not small by international classification. (See Table 6 below.) This is true for most of the county-level enterprises, which in terms of employment represent some 40 percent of rural industry and usually have 50–250 workers and employees. Some of the county-run enterprises may have up to 1,000 people employed, in which case the county is likely to have a long tradition of local industries, an ideal location on a main railway line, or a favorable situation in other ways.

Table 6. Size Characteristics of Industries
in Rural Areas in China*

Level	Ownership	Size
County	State-owned	50–250 workers
Commune	Collectively-owned	10–100 workers
Brigade	Collectively-owned	2–20 workers

*A number of the counties have enterprises with employment substantially higher than 250. For example, some of the local coal-mining enterprises may have more than 1,000 employees.

A majority of the commune-level enterprises in rural areas proper are small by international classification, having 10–100 workers. The commune-level enterprises in rural areas around the big industrial cities are quite different. They are usually considerably larger and should be compared with county-level enterprises in rural areas proper. They usually engage in a considerable degree of subcontracting for big city-based enterprises. To exemplify this point, information on industrial activity in a commune in the Peking suburbs is displayed in Table 15 in the section on employment considerations (p. 54).

Brigade-level enterprises are always small, and many of the activities they undertake are modernized village crafts like oil pressing, cotton ginning, grain milling, timber sawing, and so forth.

The wage characteristics for rural industries are summarized in Table 7 below. Rural industries have different forms of wage systems. The state-owned county-level enterprises pay fixed wages set in accordance with precise state regulations. Collectively owned units at commune and brigade level pay agricultural work points plus a percentage. The work points vary from place to place, depending on productivity in agriculture. Workers in agriculturally well-developed areas may earn as much in commune-level enterprises as their colleagues do in state-owned enterprises. But industrial workers in commune-level enterprises usually have wages far below state wages.

Table 7. Wage System in Enterprises at
Various Administrative Levels

Level	Ownership	Remuneration
County	State	Stage wage scale
County	Collective	Modified wage scale
Commune	Collective	Work points + 10–20%
Brigade	Collective	Work points + 10–20%

Differences in departments and trades further contribute to different wage levels, and the historical development in enterprises is also a decisive factor in explaining the wage level.[2] It is usually explained that collectively owned enterprises have a lower productivity. Consequently, the wages should be lower—in the present stage of economic development—since they create less wealth. County-level collectively owned enterprises should be seen as an intermediate form of ownership. They are the outcome of the handicraft cooperatives established in the 1950s, some of which have grown into substantial undertakings. The county local government has much wider control of profits from such enterprises and also greater responsibility for financing further expansion. These as well as other county-level enterprises may have a large number of contract workers, who receive "pocket money" from the factory and remuneration based on work points from the agricultural units to which they belong. So this wage system conforms closely to the one used for commune- and brigade-level enterprises. The difference between the state wages and what the contract workers get is handed over to the units where the workers belong.

Similarly, the adjustment in seasonal employment varies considerably for different types of enterprises, and is summarized in Table 8 below. The state-owned county-level enterprises are hardly affected at all, while the brigade-run enterprises adjust almost completely, which means that most brigade-level industrial undertakings are almost completely closed down in busy farming seasons. The other types of enterprises fall somewhere in between.

Table 8. Employment System in Enterprises at
Various Administrative Levels

Level	Ownership	Employment system	Seasonal adjustment in employment
County	State	Fixed + some contract	Negligible
County	Collective	Fixed + contract	Usually negligible
Commune	Collective	Some fixed + contract	Considerable
Brigade	Collective	Contract	Complete

Employment Considerations

A February 1958 article in the *People's Daily*[3] discussed ways to solve the country's population problem. It pointed out that medium and small enterprises provide additional employment even though these local industries have shortcomings such as higher production costs. The article noted that socialism has no preference for only medium and small enterprises to the exclusion of large modern enterprises, but under certain conditions the policy of a combination of large, medium, and small enterprises will help to overcome difficulties and accelerate industrialization. The exclusive pursuit of large enterprises employing advanced techniques would result in the engagement of a part of the labor force in actual production, which requires the allocation of a large part of the available means of production. As a consequence, another part of the labor force would not be engaged in actual production through lack of sufficient means of production. The result would be that part of the labor force engaged in actual production would have to support the other part temporarily not engaged in actual production, thus wasting much available labor power. Furthermore, as far as the acceleration of the rate of accumulation of capital is concerned, the exclusive pursuit of large enterprises employing advanced techniques is not wholly reasonable under certain conditions.

Such were some of the views expressed in the light of the two-leg industrialization policy formulated in the late 1950s and preceding the Great Leap Forward approach in spring 1958. What is the situation today? Does China have an employment problem? The answer to the latter question must be "yes and no." The communes and various social control mechanisms have made it possible to control urbanization and provide every able-bodied person with employment. However, the Chinese planners are today facing a serious challenge in manpower planning as the following facts suggest.

China's working age population (15–64 years) is estimated to be roughly 500 million with a yearly increase of 11 million. The expansion of the school system, a number of women staying at home as housewives, and various other factors make it realistic to assume that the actual labor force and net increase is one-third less, that is, 335 million and 7 million respectively.

The yearly economic expansion has in the 1970s been in the region of 8–10 percent—most of it within the modern sector of the economy. Assuming that this sector employs 70 million—which is most likely too high—the expansion of the modern part of the economy could in principle almost have accommodated the yearly increase of the labor force. However, there are important reservations. First, the modern sector employs less than 70 million people. Second, a considerable amount of economic expansion results from increased productivity as the result of improved technology and organization. Third, agriculture is undergoing fairly rapid—even if selective—mechanization, which reduces the demand for labor to perform certain traditional tasks.[4]

The population of China will, according to estimates made by U.N. demographers, be in the region of 1,200 million in the year 2000, which is an increase of 69 percent over 1965, or 43 percent over the 1974 population. The estimates are made on the assumption that the present net increase is 8 percent per five-year period. These and other figures are taken from a booklet published by the United Nations.[5] The U.N. demographers have not had access to aggregate national demographic figures, but their estimates and trends conform to fragmentary data given visiting foreigners and/or reported by Chinese news media.

The figures already presented and all other information in the following tables and diagrams refer to what the U.N. demographers have called "Asia: Mainland Region," which includes Taiwan and Hong Kong. No corrections have been made in the tables and the following discussion, since the relatively small populations of those two areas, even if of demographically somewhat different character, do not really influence the demographic facts for China proper.

Table 9 gives estimated population by age groups for five-year intervals from 1965 to 2000. Table 10 gives percentages for the same age groups in the same time interval. The age pyramid for two years—1965 and 2000—is presented in Figure 7. The 1965 pyramid has the broad base typical of all developing countries today, while the onion-shaped one for the year 2000 indicates that the population is still likely to continue to increase.

The U.N. figures show factors which—at least in the long run—must be favorable for modernization and industrialization. China is today a young nation with approximately 45 percent of the population in the age groups below 20. This share is expected to decrease gradually and reach 36 percent by the year 2000, which indicates that the main school-age groups are already becoming stable and not expected to increase very much during the period discussed. See also Figure 8.

The age groups above 65 are expected to increase rapidly, but their share will not yet exceed 6.5 percent at the turn of the century. What is really interesting and also disturbing is the fact that the share of population of working age (15–64 years) increases

Table 9. Population By Age Groups (in millions)

Year	0-14	5-14	0-19	15-64	65 +	Total
1965	270.7	175.7	343.6	414.5	27.2	712.5
1970	286.5	181.6	367.7	462.0	30.9	779.4
1975	295.6	189.0	385.8	516.8	35.6	848.0
1980	310.4	201.7	398.1	566.8	41.5	918.8
1985	319.2	207.1	417.3	624.7	48.5	992.4
1990	325.3	214.0	426.2	682.0	56.8	1,064.2
1995	328.4	218.0	432.4	738.6	66.7	1,133.8
2000	327.5	217.8	435.6	795.4	78.0	1,200.8

Table 10. Population By Age Groups (percentage)

Year	0-14	5-14	0-19	15-64	65 +	Total
1965	38.0	24.7	48.2	58.2	3.8	100.0
1970	36.8	23.3	47.2	59.3	4.0	100.0
1975	34.9	22.3	45.5	60.9	4.2	100.0
1980	33.8	22.0	43.3	61.7	4.5	100.0
1985	32.2	20.9	42.0	62.9	4.9	100.0
1990	30.6	20.1	40.0	64.1	5.3	100.0
1995	29.0	19.2	38.1	65.1	5.9	100.0
2000	27.3	18.1	36.3	66.2	6.5	100.0

Source for Tables 9 and 10: *World Population Prospects as Assessed in 1968 Population Studies,* No. 53, United Nations, New York, 1973.

much more rapidly than the population as a whole. The increase between 1965 and 2000 is 92 percent, between 1974 and 2000, 60 percent. A consequence of this is that the share of people of working age increases from 58 percent in 1965 to 66 percent at the turn of the century.

Table 11 shows the increases of total population and working-age population for five-year periods and calculated as yearly averages. Table 12 shows the population increases in percent per five-year period for total population as well as working-age population. In discussions of working age population, it should be noted that the retirement age is 60 for men and 55 for women. However, this

Table 11. Population Increase (in millions)

Period	Total population		Working-age population	
	5-year period	yearly average	5-year period	yearly average
1965–1970	66.9	13.4	47.5	9.5
1970–1975	68.6	13.7	54.8	11.0
1975–1980	70.7	14.1	50.0	10.0
1980–1985	73.6	14.7	57.9	11.6
1985–1990	71.7	14.3	57.3	11.5
1990–1995	69.6	13.9	56.6	11.3
1995–2000	67.1	13.4	56.8	11.4

Table 12. Population Increase
(percentage per five-year period)

Period	Total population	Working-age population
1965–1970	9.4	11.5
1970–1975	8.8	11.9
1975–1980	8.3	9.7
1980–1985	8.0	10.2
1985–1990	7.2	9.2
1990–1995	6.5	8.3
1995–2000	5.9	7.7

Source for Tables 11 and 12: *World Population Prospects as
Assessed in 1968 Population Studies,* No. 53, United
Nations, New York, 1973.

applies basically to state-owned enterprises and to similar employment in the modern sector of the economy, which employs only a
small fraction of the total labor force. Furthermore, it is very common to rehire industrial workers who have left state employment
in collectively owned enterprises.

The relatively rapid increase of total population, which is
small percentage-wise compared with other developing countries,
and the still more rapid increase of working-age population pose
two major problems the Chinese planners have to deal with. One

Figure 7. Population By Sex and Five-Year Age Groups (in million)

Year 1965

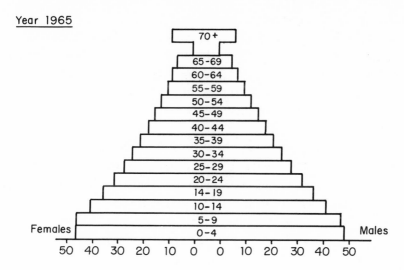

Year 2000

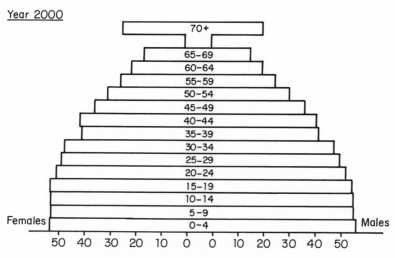

Source: World Population Prospects as Assessed in 1968
Population Studies, No. 53, United Nations, New York, 1973.

is the obvious food problem, and the other is where to employ meaningfully the increase of the labor force.

China has recently experienced a favorable development of increased productivity in agriculture. Officially it is often claimed that the population has increased by 50 percent since 1949 while grain production has increased by more than 100 percent. If the comparison is based on 1957, the picture turns out to be slightly different. The population increase is then 30 percent while the increase in production is 40 percent. To keep pace with population, grain production has to increase by another 40 percent before the year 2000. Furthermore, it is desirable to use more than the present 30 percent of the area under cultivation for purposes other than grain crops. Increased agricultural production can be achieved through increased acreage or increased yields. The first alternative includes expanding the area under cultivation as well as increasing the cropping index. This alternative as well as the second one requires more machinery and more industrial products. Consequently, agriculture and, subsequently, rural areas must undergo constant transformation in order to guarantee increased food production as well as meaningful employment for the increasing working-age groups.

Figure 8 shows the development over time of the three main age groups—the 65 and above, the below–15, and the major group of people between 15 and 64. Figure 9 shows the working-age group separately. The total figure is 500 million in 1974, with the previously mentioned reservations, which increases to almost 800 million in the year 2000. The modern sector holds at most 20 percent in 1974. A selective mechanization of agriculture is estimated to reduce labor requirements in agriculture proper by about 40 percent by the turn of the century—if present cropping practices are maintained.

Consequently, the natural increase in the labor force as well as the manpower released from agriculture—totally about 450 million —will have to be absorbed in the modern industrial sector and within a reorganized economic structure in rural areas. As noted already, the total labor force should be reduced by one-third because of the

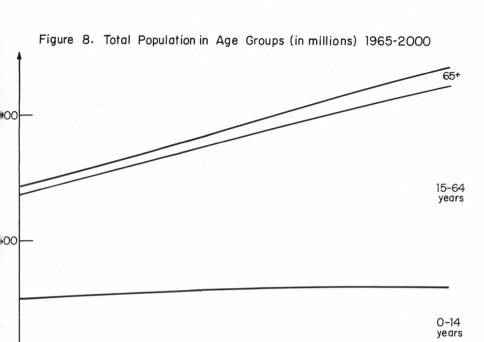

Figure 8. Total Population in Age Groups (in millions) 1965-2000

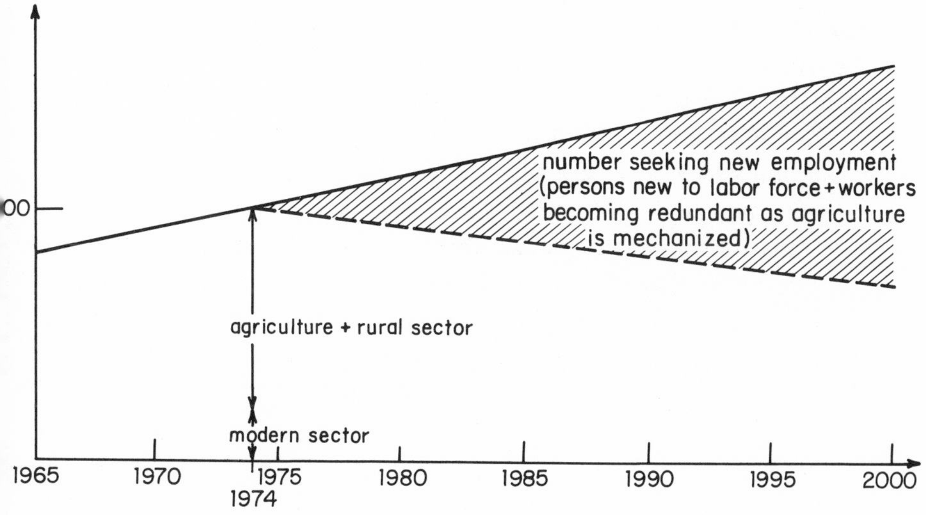

Figure 9. Working-age (15-64) Population (in millions) 1965-2000

number of women remaining in homes as housewives, the increase of young people attending school, and so forth. It is not yet evident how Chinese planners and politicians are going to cope with the employment problem. Two things should be made clear. First, China's population and manpower problem is small compared with that of India or other large developing countries where family planning programs have been much less successful than in China.[6] Second, the commune system provides social security and enables a social control which has no parallel in other developing countries, and furthermore provides a framework for economic planning which may still be in the formation stage.

What is the impact of rural industry in providing employment? Before starting to analyze some—only fragmentary—statistics, it is necessary, as noted earlier, to differentiate clearly between city-near localities and rural areas proper. In the second category the direct employment impact of county-level and commune-level industry appears to be limited. Table 13 gives the number of enterprises and total employment at various administrative levels in Hopei province, which appears from Chinese press reports to be one of the best developed provinces in terms of rural industrialization.

The table shows that industrial employment in county- and commune-level enterprises is not more than 2.6 percent of the estimated labor force in Hopei province. The figure may be somewhat higher in specific counties. At county level—in a model county (Zunhua)—employment in county- and commune-level enterprises amounts to 3.5 percent of the total labor force. The labor force is here calculated as 40 percent of the total population, which corresponds approximately to two-thirds of the working age population as defined earlier. However, in order to arrive at a more correct industrial development figure, it is necessary to add the industrial employment in units which are under control of the brigades and consider various indirect effects on the pattern of employment.

What can then be inferred from the information available on employment in Zunhua, which is a model county? Employment in the county-run enterprises was 3,000 in 1966 and had increased to

Table 13. Employment in Rural Industries—Hopei Province, 1972

| | | | | Employment | |
Level	Population	Estimated Labor Force	No. of Enterprises*	Total	% of Labor Force
Province (Hopei)	48 million	19.2 million	7,500	500,000	2.6%
Region (Tangshan)	6.84 million	2.74 million	1.200	70,000	2.6%
County (Zunhua)	0.58 million	0.23 million	110	8,000	3.5%

Source: Interviews with officials of the industrial bureaus at the various administrative levels, July 1973.

*Only county- and commune-level enterprises.

5,500 by 1971. See Figure 10. This expansion of employment is
certainly not very impressive in relation to the total population
figure of 550,000 for the whole county. But the total employment
figures reveal a somewhat different picture. The labor force of the
county is likely to be close to 200,000 people, excluding those who
are almost completely employed at home. Industrial employment
in the county-run enterprises would then be less than 3 percent of
this labor force. However, the communes have an additional employment of approximately 2,500 in 71 industrial units, and there are
another 5,000 employed in the brigades. Consequently, total industrial employment adds up to 13,000 people for the whole county.
See Figure 10. Another 10,000 people are engaged in agricultural
side-line occupations which to a considerable extent supply inputs
for local light industrial enterprises. The county has also more than
7,000 rubber-wheeled horsecarts which engage at least one person
per cart, and many of these are used to transport industrial raw
materials and finished products during part of the year. So, if all
the groups whose employment is related to industrial activities are
added together, between 10 and 15 percent of the labor force in
Zunhua appears to be in one way or another connected with the
industrial sector.

Figure 10. Employment Statistics for Rural Industry in
Zunhua County

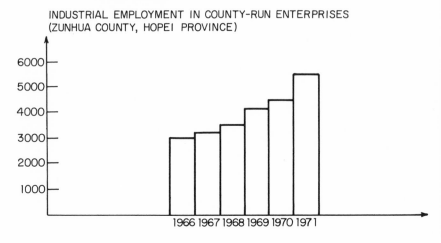

INDUSTRIAL EMPLOYMENT IN COUNTY-RUN ENTERPRISES
(ZUNHUA COUNTY, HOPEI PROVINCE)

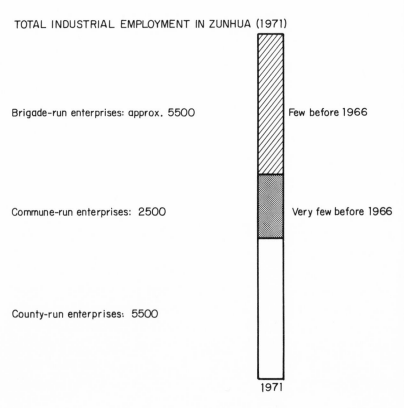

TOTAL INDUSTRIAL EMPLOYMENT IN ZUNHUA (1971)

Brigade-run enterprises: approx. 5500   Few before 1966

Commune-run enterprises: 2500   Very few before 1966

County-run enterprises: 5500

1971

Sulu, a county in another region in Hopei province located on a main railway line, shows a considerably higher-than-average employment figure. Total employment in county-level and commune-level enterprises was 11,000 in 1972, which, with a population of 475,000, gives a percentage figure of 5.8 of the labor force earlier calculated. Sulu county has had a substantial industrial structure during a number of years—which is evident from Table 14—with the biggest enterprise employing more than 1,000 people.

The commune-level industrial activities in a city-near location[7] near Peking are illustrated in Table 15. Total industrial employment in commune-run enterprises, which also includes farms for cows, horses, pigs, and ducks, was 2,300 in 1971. The labor force in the commune was approximately 35,000. Employment in manufacturing only in the commune-run enterprises—1,380—would then amount to 4 percent of the total labor force.

Production value in the commune-run enterprises amounted to 22 million yuan including production in the above-mentioned farms, which should be set against agricultural production value of 16 million, all figures referring to 1971. The production value of manufacturing only is likely to be in the region of 10 million yuan.

The influence of city-near location on the employment pattern can be further illustrated with figures from China's largest city. Shanghai rural areas—divided into 10 counties and 199 people's communes and 12 state farms—have a total population of 6 million. The labor force may then be estimated to be around 2.5 million. Out of these, 97,000 are employed in more than 1,000 collectively owned commune-level enterprises. Another 100,000 are found in county-level enterprises which are usually state-owned. The 2,800 brigades employ 150,000 people in industrial activities, but most of this employment is seasonal in character. Consequently, total employment in county-, commune-, and brigade-level enterprises is 350,000, which is 14 percent of the total labor force in rural areas of Shanghai. Counting employment in county- and commune-level enterprises only gives a share of 8 percent. Further, it should be noted that the higher level state-owned enterprises which are usually located in Shanghai proper recruit some of their workers

Table 14. Example of Industrial Development in Rural Areas
Sulu County, Shihchiachuang Region, Hopei Province

| | | | Production Value | |
Year	Number of Enterprises	Employment, Workers	Total, million	Per Worker, yuan
1949	n.a.	500	0.050	.100
1958	73	5,800	38.6	6.655
1963	43	3,000	21.5	7.167
1966			30.76	
1968	67	6,100	42.08	6.898
1972	94	11,000	67.62	6.147

Table 15. Industrial Activity in the Red Star
Chinese-Korean Friendship Commune, Tahsing County, Peking

Industrial Unit	Established	Employment	Production Value
1. Agricultural machinery	1957–58	150	
2. Paper mill	1958	110	0.24 million
3. Brick plant	1958	350	
4. Cereal processing plant	1964	108	
5. Oil pressing plant (3–5 months per year)	1964	45	
6. Cotton ginning plant (3–4 months per year)	1964	30	
7. Nuts and screws factory (state subcontractor)	1966	177	1.2 million
8. Electric switches factory (state subcontractor)	1960	300	
9. Sewing machine frame factory (state subcontractor)	1965	110	
		1,380	

from rural areas. So total industrial employment in rural areas is still higher than the figures indicate.

The discussion of the employment impact resulting from rural industrialization does not show very impressive figures in relation to

the earlier discussion of the global demographic situation in China
—except in favored city-near locations. The following question
should then be raised. Is employment essential or is it more important to keep a majority of the population in the countryside until
the modern sector can absorb more people, through reducing wage,
cultural, and other differentials between rural and urban areas? If
that is the case, the job opportunities offered to those young and
mobile groups which in other developing countries tend to migrate
into the cities may be quite impressive. This group would mainly
consist of males between 15 and 35, which constitute slightly less
than 30 percent of the working-age population in 1974. See Figure
11. The employment figures mentioned above are, of course, much
more impressive if they are related only to this much smaller target
group.

Finally, it should be mentioned that increased employment in
rural areas does not result from industrial employment only but
also comes from the following three areas. First, more labor time
is invested in infrastructure activities: roads, water control and
irrigation systems, land terracing, reforestation, and the construction of schools, hospitals and public buildings as well as housing.
Second, these infrastructure activities, especially improved water
control, have made possible a considerable shift of acreage from
single to double crops. They also make possible greater use of
fertilizer, which substantially increases crop yields. All this requires
more labor. Third, there has been a marked diversification of farm
activities into fruit and vegetable production and into animal husbandry, particularly in areas near city markets. These activities are
more labor-intensive than grain growing.

It has usually been argued that backward linkages vary with
agricultural technology in different ways. As regards links to manufacturing industry, a shift to improved seeds or HYV technology
will create a demand for such manufactured inputs as chemical
fertilizer, herbicides, and pesticides. Shifting from traditional to
intermediate or mechanized techniques requires a rising supply of
improved implements and machinery. In the case of provision of
inputs from the light engineering industry, there is a considerable

employment potential which, however, will vary greatly depending on whether an intermediate or a mechanized innovation path is followed in grain production.

Figure 11. Population Pyramid and Demographic Groups

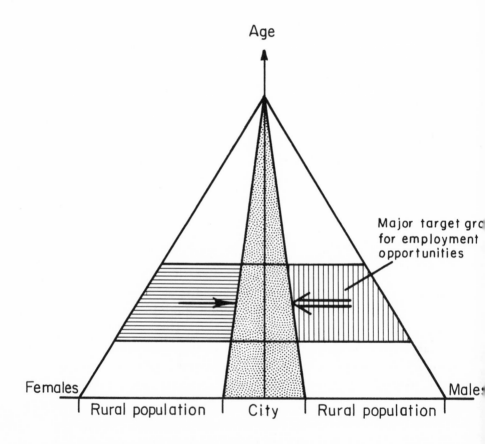

The arrows and the surrounding shaded areas indicate major migratory flows and the groups that support these flows, as they exist in many developing countries.

This is because the equipment required under each is quite different, and the manufacture of such equipment varies greatly in degree of labor intensity. Thus the items associated with intermediate techniques, such as hand hoes, pedal threshers, animal-drawn reapers, hand sprayers and dusters, and manually operated seeders, can all be produced by artisans or in small workshops in very labor-intensive operations and thus generate considerable employment. On the other hand, the more sophisticated machinery, including tractors, power tillers, and combines, must all be manufactured in plants where the capital intensity is much higher than in the workshops. This is certainly true, but the Chinese experience in no way shows that the first alternative will considerably influence the employment pattern.

The mechanization of agriculture requires tractor drivers, tube well operators, tractor engine mechanics, and people skilled in the servicing of tractors. Rural homes need better furniture, fixtures, fabrics, modern shoes, improved kitchen utensils, and so forth. These and a variety of other requirements are in most developing countries either not fulfilled or met from the cities. It would seem natural to upgrade the skills and organization of village blacksmiths, carpenters, shoemakers, weavers, potters, and so forth, so that they could assume new manufacturing and service roles in modernizing rural communities. The support of rural crafts to achieve their expansion and modernization certainly cannot be done in isolation. It should be part of an integrated plan to modernize rural communities, and development should preferably start in those villages that have a sizable population of craftsmen.

Modernization of village industry and partial transfer to market towns might have the consequence that close linkages between industry and agriculture are retained and developed. If so, such industry might rely on agricultural surplus for a considerable part of their financial requirements. Market town industrialization might also support other rural modernization programs. Furthermore, industrialization in market towns might not stem urbanization as such but might contribute to stemming the considerable flow of young mobile people leaving the villages for the large urban centers.

All available information indicates that villages in developing countries cannot be industrialized—in the traditional sense of the word. It appears equally true that employment generation in developing countries with a dominant majority of the labor force in agriculture cannot take place in urban-based modern industry at a rate that can cope with the increase in labor force. So modernized village crafts may still have an important role to play. To illustrate the potential for modernized village industrial activities, employment figures for such activities in a Chinese village located in a modernizing agricultural area are given in Table 16 below.

All these activities, which involve a total of 42 people, are seasonally adjusted to accommodate the peak labor requirements of the farming seasons. Except for the people engaged in leather tanning and fruit basket knitting—who work only for a short period every year—most are engaged more or less around the year.

In December 1971 the village population was reported to be 1,130; the present industrial employment consequently amounts to about 4 percent of the population or approximately 10 percent of the labor force. Aggregate information for the region where the village is located indicates that average industrial employment is approximately 10 workers per village—about 1 percent of the population or 2.5 percent of the labor force.

If the industrial workers engaged in mining and rock excavation are deducted from the figure given in Table 16, the remaining industrial employment may still be twice the village average. The fact that this village can sustain a considerably higher industrial activity than the average may largely be seen as a consequence of two contributing factors. First, agricultural development has created demand and purchasing power for new industrial products and services. Second, the mining activities can be undertaken as manpower can be saved from agriculture and at the same time contribute to local savings, which can be used for further investment in agricultural development.

It is evident that most of the village industrial activities—in terms of employment—are dependent on the availability of a local resource basis which mainly lies outside agriculture proper. The

Table 16. Industrial Activities in a Chinese Village.
Hsipu Brigade, Zunhua County, Tangshan Region,
Hopei Province, 1973

Activity	Number of People Engaged
1. Blacksmithy	2
2. Farm tools repair	2
3. Carpentry	5
4. Tanning (leather items for horse carts)	2
5. Agro-processing (flour milling)	2
6. Food processing (bean-curd and noodles manufacture)	2
7. Knitting (fruit baskets, etc.)	2
8. Capital construction (rock excavation)	10
9. Mining	15
Total	42

only exceptions in the village referred to are flour milling, black-smithy, repair of farm tools, and the manufacture of bean-curd and noodles. Employment in these activities amounts to 10 persons, which comes close to the average for the whole region.

Even if none of the activities listed are any longer traditional village crafts—except the knitting of fruit baskets—they have been developed on the basis of an earlier demand for village crafts, products, and services. Basic differences in the situation today as compared with that of 10–15 years ago are that all units today use power and machinery (usually makeshift equipment or machinery manufactured in local shops), even if production technology still is primitive and labor-intensive. Two requirements seem to appear essential from the Chinese experience, aside from the urgency for political commitment to develop rural areas and to establish the necessary institutional framework. First, it is essential for the villages to have *access to electricity,* which should primarily be used for productive purposes. Second, it is equally essential to *develop a capacity to design and manufacture simple producer goods locally,* that is, goods appropriate for the small scale of operation in the villages. So village industrial activities interact both with agriculture and with small-scale industries in urban places.

However, rural industries—even in model counties—are not likely to absorb in the near future the yearly increases in manpower. But the linkages of some industries are likely to have important employment-generating consequences. This seems to be particularly true for some of the agro-processing industries with their main employment impact in the farming sector through influence on the cropping pattern.

The labor requirements of different crops have varied widely, and the cropping pattern is possibly the single most important factor determining the level of rural employment. It appears from Chinese comments and from studies in other countries that changes in cropping pattern which make a favorable impact on employment are possible in both irrigated and unirrigated areas and may also be planned to absorb labor during the slack farming seasons.

The introduction of local industries often comes simultaneously with improved irrigation and increased cropping index. Grain crops are reduced in relative importance, and industrial crops like sugar cane and sugar beet, oil-bearing crops, and potatoes are gaining in importance. The nature of many of the new crops and some empirical evidence from other countries suggest that most of them have higher labor requirements than competing crops. Increased multiple cropping and other land-saving innovations also increase the demand for labor.

Many of the labor-intensive crops are also crops that produce commodities with high-income elasticities of demand. There are many crops such as sugar, potatoes, and fresh vegetables for which demand will continue to increase rapidly with rising incomes. The establishment of agro-processing industries offers prospects for raising incomes of members of teams and brigades supplying the crops, and the members are then likely to be induced to contribute to the initial capital costs for the new agro-processing industries. Thus investible surplus is mobilized for local development.

Relative prices, of course, affect the cropping pattern. This indicates that it is possible to increase areas under labor-intensive crops by evolving a positive price policy. But the return to the cultivator also depends on the yield. So the local research policy for developing technologies for labor-intensive crops must be consistent with local employment and other objectives. This appears to be part of the justification for the strong local control of the agricultural scientific networks which have been established in rural areas.

The points mentioned above clearly indicate that manpower and crop pattern policies must be carefully coordinated with irrigation plans and local research policy. If it is desired that employment should be generated through changes in the cropping pattern —which appears to be evident in China today—then the pace of mechanization and the extent to which machinery displaces human labor must be brought under local control. This is apparently also part of the explanation of why the mechanization of agriculture to a large extent has been made dependent on the capability of the locality to create and develop its own farm machinery enterprises.

Transport Considerations

The underdevelopment of the transport sector manifests itself in two ways. First, the means for physical transportation are scarce. Second, the capability of manufacturing transport equipment and road-building equipment in large quantities is also limited. The consequences are that transportation costs are high where cheap water and railway transportation are not available, and that truck transportation costs are inflated through shadow-pricing.

Rural industrialization includes—as mentioned earlier—both integrated rural development and sector policies. The communication system, which in most parts of the country is still relatively undeveloped, has consequences for both. First, those industries where service and adaptation are involved, which usually means specialized or diversified end products, have required a close interaction with the local market, which has consequently decided the location. The transportation costs per se have then played a subordinated role. This applies to repair and maintenance of farm machinery and to the manufacture of many types of small machinery and equipment. Consequently, the policy for the spatial distribution of machine-building enterprises stresses the widest possible coverage for certain types of machine manufacture. Second, in some industrial sectors which are included in rural industry, it has often been possible to achieve lower total costs through proper location of small plants—producing homogenous and standardized products—near the raw materials and near a local market.

The costs for different means of transportation are illustrated in Figure 12, based on information in an industrial handbook published in the early 1960s.[8] The figures refer to Hopei province in early 1958, but information given in various rural industrial plants in 1973 confirmed that the charges have not undergone any significant changes.

Figure 12 shows that transportation by horsecart is cheaper than truck transportation only up to distances less than 2 km. With increasing diversification and economic activity in rural areas, horsecart transportation will have to be emphasized if truck transportation is not available. However, the horses or other draught animals have to be fed. Such a development may then conflict with the commitment to develop grain and fibre production in order to relieve the country of critical bottlenecks in agriculture. It is of interest to note that in areas where horses are bred in large numbers, such as Inner Mongolia, horsecart transportation is cheaper than truck transportation for distances up to approximately 16 km. See Figure 12. Truck transportation charges vary somewhat from province to province but are almost uniform.

Railway transportation charges vary from 0.1162 yuan per ton km. for mercury down to 0.0140 per ton km. for coal for distances from 50 to 100 km. The charges are reduced with increased distances and are uniform all over the country. The charges for most industrial raw materials and intermediate goods are slightly above those for coal. However, the differences between railway charges and the 0.24 yuan per ton km. charged for truck transportation are quite considerable.

The majority of all trucks in China today are still relatively small vehicles using petrol engines and with a loading capacity in

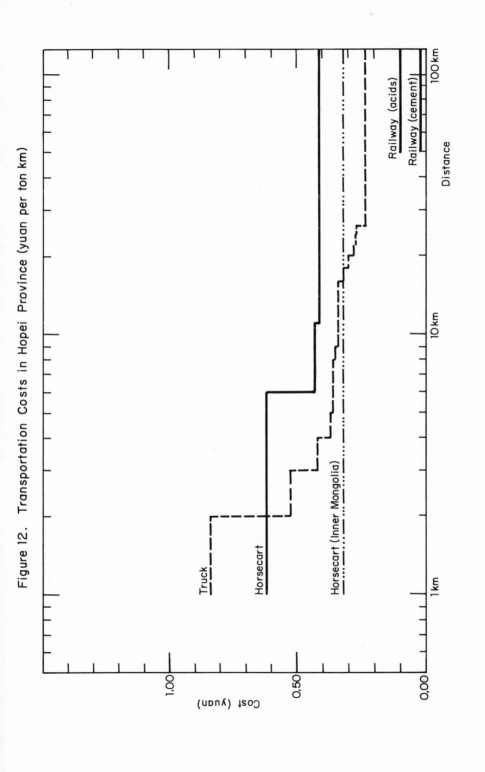

Figure 12. Transportation Costs in Hopei Province (yuan per ton km)

the region of 4–5 tons. Petrol consumption is about 0.3 liter per km. The price of petrol is assumed to be in the region of 1.5 yuan per liter. Petrol costs would then be approximately 0.11 yuan per ton km. for a fully loaded vehicle. Assume that the cost of a four-ton Liberation truck is 20,000 yuan and yearly depreciation, repair and maintenance costs (and capital charge) amount to 25 percent. Assume further that the truck is traveling with full load 100,000 kilometers per year. The above charges would then amount to less than 0.02 yuan per ton km.

The transportation charges levied would then clearly indicate that there is a considerable underutilization of vehicle capacity or that the cost is inflated through shadow-pricing. With access only to a limited number of rather small vehicles and a still underdeveloped road network (and in the past a poorly developed petroleum industry), the second explanation is the more likely one. It is also likely that the costs charged for truck transportation will be kept at their present high level for a considerable period of time.

The consequences are not negligible. Transportation costs for coal are slightly more than 0.01 yuan per ton km. when sent by railway against 0.24 yuan per ton km. if transported by truck. The wide disparity affects industrial location in two ways. First, it favors industrial development in localities on or near railway lines. Second, it also provides the potential for industrial development in places that have their own local resources of coal and other industrial raw materials and where a potential demand exists.

The question of transportation costs is closely related to pricing policy. Most products and services in China have uniform prices. A number of industrial products—including a large number of consumer goods—are supplied all over China at prices that are independent of transportation costs. However, many intermediate products and almost all industrial raw materials are supplied at ex-factory prices (or slightly higher transfer prices) plus transportation costs. Consequently, production costs and the costs to the consumer of industrial products are dependent on the location of a manufacturing unit. The still relatively undeveloped transport system in China has thus given added weight to the choice of local small-scale industries in a number of sectors. However, this is only part of the explanation, as will become evident in Chapter 4, in a discussion of small-scale plants in some important industrial sectors.

Naturally, transport considerations play a varying role in various industrial sectors. It is obvious that transportation costs play a much less important role for wrapping paper at a production cost of roughly 500 yuan than for cement which can be manufactured at 40 yuan per ton. It should be noted that cement is a commodity that is not transported over long distances even in industrialized countries. The manufacture of nitrogen chemical fertilizer at a production cost of 90–150 yuan per ton (ammonium bicarbonate) falls somewhere between the two extremes mentioned here.

Financial Sources

Rural areas, dominated by traditional agricultural technology, have been heavily dependent on higher levels for allocation of technology, that is, technical and organizational skills and equipment. Similarly, the financial flow from the higher levels seems to be important not only for initiating but also for sustaining rural industrial development. However, it must be noted in this context that all enterprises pay taxes and that all enterprises except collectively owned ones at commune and brigade level deliver their profits to the state budget—although an intricate system of revenue sharing has been worked out between the various administrative levels.

Small industries in rural areas are financed from national and local budgets, from enterprise accumulation, and lower-level contributions. Budget allocations are most important for the region- and county-level enterprises, while enterprise accumulation and lower-level contributions are essential for commune- and brigade-level enterprises as these hardly get any allocations from the national and local budgets. See Table 17 below. The number of region-level enterprises is very small. They usually serve as technology diffusion centers or as higher-level repair and manufacture centers for complicated machinery until the county machinery plants can take over.

Table 17. Investment Sources for Local Industries

Level	National Budget	Local Budget	Enterprise Accumulation	Lower-Level Contribution
Region	X			
County	X	X	X	
Commune	negligible	negligible	X	(X)*
Brigade			X	X

*Financing out of the teams' public welfare funds may on an average account for 20–30% of the financial requirements of the commune-run enterprises.

It seems relevant to differentiate between fixed capital and working capital since the allocation mechanisms appear to be different. Fixed capital comes from two basically different sources. First, it is allocated from national and local budgets or from accumulation funds of already existing enterprises. Second, fixed capital is provided through loans out of commune-level accumulation funds. It is then repaid as enterprise profits accumulate. The second method is not very common except for certain types of county-level enterprises, for example, chemical fertilizer plants in areas where commune accumulation funds have already been built up to a considerable level.

The dominance of national or local budget allocations can be seen from Table 18, which is an example of investment sources for local industries in northern Hopei.

Working capital also comes from two basically different sources. Part of the needed working capital is allocated along with the fixed capital allocations. Second, working capital is obtained through bank loans extended from the local branch. This would then indicate that the availability of working capital loans is partly dependent on the savings propensity in the locality—an investment-inducing mechanism.

Transfer from the national budget apparently plays an important role in establishing a county-level industrial sector. Other forms of financial transfer should also be included when discussing investment sources. Available information clearly shows that rural

Table 18. Example of Investment Sources for Local Industries.
Tangshan Region, 1971–1972
Region-, County- and Commune-Level Enterprises

1. National budget allocations	58%
2. Local budget allocations	31%
3. Accumulation funds of enterprises	11%
	100%

Source: Tangshan region industrial bureau, July 1973.

industries are subsidized in two different ways—direct financial subsidies and the financing of the technical assistance required. Financial subsidies are of two kinds:

1. Losses in enterprises with production costs exceeding ex-factory prices (transfer prices) are covered by profits from other enterprises. This rarely happens except in certain industries like iron and steel and chemicals.
2. Lower profit margins are accepted in a number of industries. This is particularly true for all industries where economies of scale are significant. It is equally true for almost all local industries in their initial stage of establishment.

Technical assistance, discussed in the following section, also involves a kind of subsidy. The development of the many small enterprises has been dependent on transfer of skills—technical, managerial, and organizational—from higher-level, more advanced industries. Consequently, production and profits in the enterprises involved in the technology transfer have suffered, which should be counted as a cost.

The iron and steel plant in Zunhua county operates at a yearly loss of approximately 100,000 yuan (1973). The loss in the county phosphate fertilizer plant, which so far only manufactures sulphuric acid, is of the same order. The losses in the iron and steel plant in the past have been considerably larger and are parallelled in a number of those localities where the approximately 430 still-existing small blast furnaces are located.

To make up for losses, light industrial enterprises yielding substantial profits have been set up in Zunhua and a number of other places. Paper and plastics factories were among those allocated to Zunhua. The planned profits of these two enterprises were 415,000 yuan in 1973, which is considerably more than the expected losses of 200,000 in the operation of the two plants mentioned above. Profits and production value as well as number of workers are given in Table 19 for a number of the county-level enterprises in Zunhua. The amount of fixed and working capital is available for only some of the enterprises.

The relocation of previously state-run production facilities to communes has been done on an extensive scale in the rural areas of big industrial cities like Peking, Shanghai, and Tientsin. This involves transfer of revenue sources as in the case of Zunhua. Prices set by the state automatically provide the commune-run enterprises with considerable profits even after industrial taxes of approximately 20 percent have been paid. This is evident from an example in Shanghai cited below. The communes, of course, have to use their own funds for the required industrial investment as national and local budget allocations only rarely are available for such purposes. But the ratio between profits and investments is usually very high.

One of the 10 counties in Shanghai rural areas is Chiating with 23 people's communes. Three of the communes (Hsuhang, Chawang, and Huating) established a bulb factory[9] in 1971. Construction was completed in May 1972. Investment amounted to 3 million yuan with another 1.2 million in working capital. Production value was 7 million in 1972. Profits were 1.95 million after the enterprise paid an industrial tax of 20 percent.

The justification for the transfer of revenue sources involved when transferring state-run industrial production to collectively owned enterprises is manifold. The regional objective of achieving a more rational distribution of industrial activity is important. Of equal importance is the objective of strengthening the communes as economic units. Further, the profits are also expected to be used for expanding rural educational and health work. And the profits of the transferred production facilities also act as a kind of seed money for further economic and industrial development in the communes involved.

Table 19. Production Value and Planned Profits in Selected
County-Level Enterprises, Zunhua County, 1973

	Production Value	Profit	Number of Workers and Employees	Capital Fixed	Working
Farm machinery 1	900,000	80,000	283		
Farm machinery 2*	438,000	3,800	147		
Electromechanic factory	720,000	120,000	225	0.22	0.70
Paper mill	530,000	140,000	97	0.23	0.065
Phosphate fertilizer	250,000	-100,000	120	0.25	0.20
Knitting mill	1,310,000	120,000	369		
Plastics factory	1,300,000	275,000	46		
Hardware factory	575,000	60,000	100	0.159	
Cement plant	920,000	50,000	307	0.80	0.20
Subtotal 1	6,943,000	748,800	1,694		
Estimates based on 1971 figures:					
Nitrogen fertilizer	1,900,000	100,000	338		
Textile mill	1,500,000	50,000	275	0.400	
Iron and steel plant	900,000	-100,000	460		
Food plant	1,000,000	100,000	230		
Subtotal 2	5,300,000	150,000	1,303		
Remaining 26 enterprises:					
	9,957,000	- 98,800	2,253		
Total	22,200,000	800,000	5,250		

Source: County industrial bureau, and enterprises—1971 and 1973.

*This enterprise is under Farm Machinery Bureau leadership. All others are under the control of the Machinery Bureau. (See Figure 13.)

The concept of rural industrial system was introduced in the discussion of models of rural industrialization. To understand fully the financial implications of an integrated approach to agricultural development and rural industrialization, it may be advantageous once more to use a diagram. Figure 13 shows the commodity flow between industrial components and agriculture. The diagram further shows which economic units at county level control the various parts of the economic system. The county agricultural-industrial

Figure 13. Administrative Control in a Rural Industrial System in China.

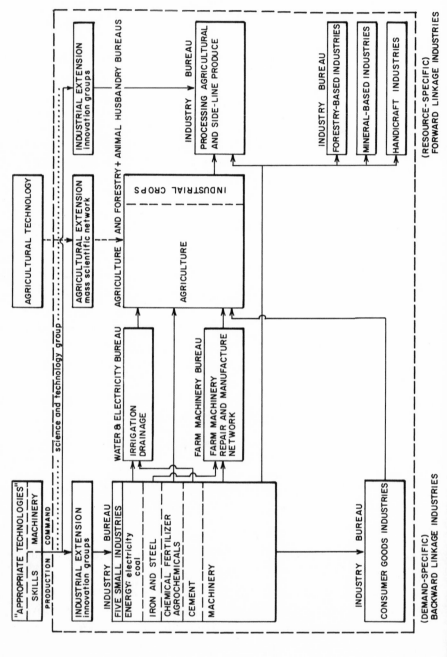

system should here be seen as one functional organization with a number of subdivisions. All the different units need not necessarily operate with a surplus. The farm machinery repair and manufacture network usually operates with little or no surplus.

The command or control of the operations of the enterprises does not lie within the single units but is vested in the *production command* of the county (left top of the figure). Under its direct control are the various economic bureaus—industry bureau, farm machinery bureau, agriculture and forestry bureau, water and electricity bureau, and so forth. The overall productivity of the system depends, aside from capital accumulation, on improvements in agriculture and industry. So it is natural to find that both industrial and agricultural extension are under the science and technology group, which is a subgroup of the production command.

Rural industrialization is in many places development-specific, which means that funds and manpower required for local industrial development cannot be obtained unless there is a general economic development, which usually must be based on increased agricultural productivity.

The Chinese news media have in the past few years published information on a substantial number of localities where there has existed a conflict between the development of agriculture and industry. In Tayeh county in Hupeh,[10] which is rich in ores, it was reported that efforts were made before the Cultural Revolution to change the backward features of the county's industry. However, emphasis on industry led to contention between industry and agriculture for manpower and funds with the result that agriculture was brushed aside, according to the report. In 1970 the new administration decided on a plan covering both industrial and agricultural production. It then worked out plans for the use of manpower, funds, and materials for both industrial and agricultural production and construction in order to control strictly the scope and speed of the local industry within the limits permitted by agricultural production. Now the county has in the past few years spent 80 percent of local financial expenditures for agricultural production including investments in those local industries that serve agricultural production.

Another county, Chaotung in Heilunkiang,[11] clearly makes
the point that agriculture is being served by saying that 39 out of
48 county-run factories serve agriculture. Further, more than 87
percent of industrial investment funds have been used for the
development of local industry in support of agricultural production.
A third county, Hanyang in Hupeh,[12] is said to have learnt a lesson
in regard to manpower. The rapid development of its local industry
since 1970 adversely affected its agricultural production, because
some of the enterprises used labor earmarked for agricultural production. Through investigations and studies it was realized that
because of the present low level of agricultural mechanization—all
the principal tasks still being done by hand—the labor force could
not be decreased at will.

So the county leadership took two important measures to
deal with the manpower problem. First, it stimulated factory
workers to increase productivity in order to economize on the use
of manpower. This was done through technical innovations, improved management, and cutting down the number of non-produc-
tive personnel. Second, it set strict restrictions on the transfer of
manpower from agriculture to commune-level and brigade-level
industries and enforced the rule that these workers must return to
work in the fields during the busy farming seasons. The different
measures meant, among other things, that a planned recruitment
of 900 workers from agriculture for a factory expansion project
could be reduced to only 119 people.

However, rural industrialization is in many counties location-
specific, which means that industrialization is primarily based on
exploitation of energy resources or other resources—for example,
minerals—which are specific to the locality. But even if this is the
case, agriculture must provide funds and manpower, which is evident from the following example.

The case of Hsingning county in Kwangtung,[13] reported in a
Peking Review article, indicates the possibility for higher levels to
obtain the kind of local industrial development they consider
appropriate. The county has considerable resources of coal and
iron ore, but before the Cultural Revolution iron and steel were

brought into the county from the outside. The *Peking Review* informs us that the county leadership appropriated large amounts of funds, equipment, and manpower to build a number of small blast furnaces, and as a consequence agriculture and light industry were adversely affected. More significant may be the fact that the county's iron and steel industry—as reported in the article—did not get anywhere. There is no further information in the article on this particular aspect, but the most likely explanation is that the county was not given access to certain critical equipment or technical knowledge. However, after a county revolutionary committee was established, it worked out an overall plan for the new arrangement of the county's agriculture, light industry, and heavy industry. It is reported that since 1969 there has been a great increase in industrial crops, forest, and side-line products. This has provided light industry, including sugar making, with abundant raw materials and thus has stimulated its quick development. On this basis, the county then went in for industry in a selective and fully planned way, it is reported. The county now has thirty-eight very small blast furnaces, and its 1971 pig iron output was about 4,300 tons. There was also a considerable increase in the output of coal. So, in localities where agriculture is the only or the dominating activity, rural industry cannot develop unless agriculture develops. It is, of course, possible initially to transfer funds and manpower from agriculture, but food production is then likely to decline as it did during the Great Leap Forward period—when rapid rural industrialization was attempted. It could be argued that a temporary decline in the production of grain and other foodstuffs would be more than compensated for by an increase later on. But the central government has not accepted this kind of argument, since it would lead to a disastrous situation if generally accepted all over the country. Consequently, the central government has on a number of occasions withheld critical equipment or industrial technology from counties that have tended to neglect agricultural production.

Chapter 3

INSTITUTIONS AND POLICIES
TO PROMOTE RURAL INDUSTRIALIZATION

There can be no doubt that localities—counties and communes
—have in the past been given a large measure of freedom in developing local industry, and not necessarily in accordance with models
previously discussed. At the same time, there can be no doubt that
the higher administrative levels—regions and provinces—have been
very influential in supervising rural industrialization programs as
they have been carried out. Furthermore, there are clear indications
that rural industrialization, in certain aspects, adheres to a national
master plan where broad principles have been laid down. It also
appears that such a master plan includes provisions for what regions
or counties should set up what types of industries, as well as approximate timing for establishing certain types of industrial activity.

The desired rural industrialization objectives have made it
necessary to forge links between the modern industrial sector and
the rural industrial sector in order to provide the needed technologies and equipment. The establishment of local technology systems
is an important and integral part of this approach. Provision for
allocating such resources must have been included in central plans
for industries directly controlled by central ministries.

The availability of services and infrastructure is essential in
setting up industrial enterprises in rural areas. Furthermore, leadership has in many places played an important role in initiating and
promoting rural industrialization. But these conditions are not
enough. Local industries in rural areas must initially be provided
with technology in the form of equipment and skills. So the transfer
of technology to previously non-industrialized areas is also very important.

Because rural industrialization is part of an overall program to
develop and modernize rural areas in China, it is dependent on an
organizational structure that can direct and control the development

75

and provide the necessary links with other sectors of the economy and with the society. It is also dependent on an incentive structure that is in general agreement with the objectives of industrialization and modernization of the country. However, within this general framework there still exist wide areas where localities—communes, counties, and regions—can decide to take or not to take action, and the quality of leadership is likely to influence greatly the speed and quality of rural industrialization programs. Furthermore, the conditions for rural industrialization are not likely to be evenly distributed, and pockets of affluence will develop if action is not taken to prevent such developments.

Technology Sources and Local Technology Systems

China is a developing country, a fact which in recent years has on many occasions been explicitly stated by Chinese leaders. Consequently, China's technology and science should be viewed in the light of the particular needs of developing countries and should not be compared primarily with already industrialized countries, even if this is occasionally justified.[1] Technology and science must serve all sectors of the Chinese economy, and it is of paramount importance to provide modernizing technology for the traditional sector (agriculture and rural industry), where the majority of the population will be found for many years to come.

The demand for technology resources arises in the following macro-sectors of the economy:

1. Modern sector
   - civilian industrial sectors
   - defense sector
2. Traditional sector
   - small and rural industry
   - agriculture

The composition of technology resources must be different for each part of the economy, and is dependent on access to technology sources, level of sophistication, societal values, and so forth. However, it must be pointed out here that rural economic development involves the rural industrial sector as well as the agricultural sector.

Unless the latter develops, the former will have less manpower, capital, and raw materials. Therefore, it is as important to increase land and labor productivity in the agricultural sector as it is to improve productivity in the industrial sector. Furthermore, agricultural development and rural industrial development should preferably be complementary. Consequently, it is not always possible to differentiate between the industrial and agricultural aspects of local science and technology.

China has since 1957 pursued a consistent policy of decentralizing industrial and economic activity. Consequently, a considerable amount of economic and industrial activity is now under the responsibility of lower-level administrations with consequences for technology and science policy. The Great Leap Forward policy attempted rapid rural industrialization through mass mobilization and the use of primitive techniques. Even if this attempt failed, decentralization was maintained and further strengthened when the Cultural Revolution started in 1966. And the economic planning has increasingly come to incorporate the development of rural areas. The desire to achieve a balanced urban-rural development is now very strong—obviously, in order to solve the food supply problem, to hinder undesired migration, and to delay urbanization, among other things. This has had far-reaching consequences for the development of technological and scientific institutions in rural areas. Before any discussion of the local technology system, it may be useful to emphasize the fact that sources of technology are by necessity different for various parts of the industrial spectrum. Nation- and province-level enterprises receive their technological inputs mainly from national R & D institutes and through imports. Lower-level enterprises are not completely cut off from these sources, but the bottom of the industrial pyramid derives its technological advancement mainly from a process of internal diffusion. Figure 14 illustrates in a much simplified way the technology flow for the various levels.

This figure further illustrates the fact that advanced science and technology are, on the whole, available mainly at higher levels. Intermediate science and technology are available for the middle

Figure 14. Technology Sources and Technology Flow

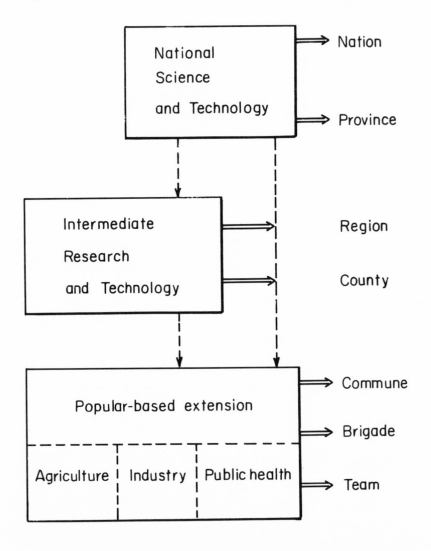

levels, while the lower levels mainly get technical knowledge to feed into a popular-based extension network, the importance of which is discussed further on. The sources of technology, of course,

Table 20. Technology Sources for Industrial Enterprises

Level	Plant Size	Technology Level	Main Technology Source
Nation	Big	Advanced	National R & D + Import
Province	Medium	Intermediate	National R & D + Diffusion
Region/County	Relatively small	Intermediate/ primitive	Diffusion (vertical/ horizontal)
Commune (city-near)	Relatively small	Intermediate/ primitive	Diffusion (vertical/ horizontal)
Commune (rural areas)	Small	Primitive	Diffusion

relate to the level of technology in enterprises, exemplified in Table 20. However, a considerable spectrum of technologies and enterprise sizes exists at each level.

A primary requirement for economic development in the many rural localities is compatibility between technology and the delivery system on the one hand and potential demand on the other. This leads to the following two secondary requirements. First, the locality must have an efficient system for introduction/delivery of technology. Second, there must be a good match between costs for products and services on the one hand and the purchasing power of the locality on the other.

The justification for a locality's having its own technology capability can be summarized in the following three points. First, conditions are rapidly changing outside and inside the locality. Second, relevant knowledge may not be immediately available. Consequently, local search (or research) must be initiated. Third, there is a need gradually to train technical forces and build up a problem-solving capability for the future.

A rural science and technology system should fulfill three objectives. First, it should contribute to the development of technologies appropriate for the locality. Second, it should also provide the means, that is, the institutional framework, to distribute new knowledge. This is a major part of the popularization aspect where the mass scientific network plays a very important role. Third, technical services should be made available to local small and medium enterprises as well as to agricultural units.

Consequently a local technology system would have the following main components:

1. "Mass scientific network." This is basically a popular-based extension network covering agriculture and related activities, public health, and rural industry. This would include formalized groups within agricultural units, rural industries, and other local production units:
   - to articulate demand for additional inputs relevant to the locality
   - to establish outward linkages into the national S & T system
   - to extend inward linkages into the extension network serving the locality.
2. Local research institutes. These would be tied in with the institutes of the national S & T system.
3. Industrial technology transfer mechanisms.

Mass Scientific Network

Popular-based extension services are a characteristic feature of the system for introduction/delivery of technology into rural areas in China. The Chinese press has since the Cultural Revolution reported that mass scientific networks have been developed in rural areas and that large numbers of people have been enrolled in them. What does this mean? What are their relations with the professional agricultural scientific system?

It may be useful to take the situation in Zunhua county in Hopei province as an example. The county has forty-three people's communes each of which has a Technology Popularization Station, which aside from commune members has at least one agricultural technician who has been sent down from a higher-level organization. These commune stations generally have experimental fields and are usually responsible for the introduction of all aspects of agricultural technology and veterinary technology, as well as farm machinery improvements.[2]

The brigades have agricultural technology groups with five to thirteen people. These are *three-in-one* groups (leadership personnel —technicians—peasants), which have at least one cadre from the brigade revolutionary committee (usually the chairman), at least one agricultural technician, and veteran peasants and educated youths for the rest. In Zunhua more than 390 brigades out of a total of 692 have experimental farms under the leadership of the brigade agricultural technology groups. Finally, the teams have agricultural technology groups with three to seven members. All production teams have three types of seed plots, very small for first stage experiments, medium-sized ones to try out selected seeds, and larger ones to provide the seeds for next year's sowing. This pattern of activity, with emphasis on demonstration of new varieties and practices and seed breeding, enables the commune to translate rapidly into actual production the findings of agricultural research.

What is, then, the total number of people engaged in this mass scientific network? If the average size of the groups is assumed to be 5 at team level, this amounts to 12,500 in the approximately 2,500 teams in Zunhua county. If, similarly, the brigades have groups with an average membership of 9, this amounts to 6,300 in the approximately 700 brigades. These two figures add up to 18,800 people. If, then, the agricultural technology people at commune level, membership in public health technology groups, and technology groups in industrial enterprises are added, the total should be roughly 25,000, according to information provided by the Zunhua County Science and Technology Group. This would mean that slightly more than 4 percent of the total population of roughly 600,000 in the county has been enrolled in the mass scientific network. The equivalent figure for the whole of Hopei province is 1,000,000, which is about 2 percent of a population of 48 million. The corresponding enrollment in rural areas in Shanghai is 70,000, which is slightly more than 1 percent of a population which was reported to be 5.8 million in 1971. Finally, it has been reported that over 10 million people now take part in scientific experiments in rural areas, which approximately corresponds to 1.25 percent of the country's population.[3]

What is the impact of the massive popular-based extension

services reported to exist in China? The information is still much too scanty for any conclusions. However, a single computation may show its potential impact. If we assume that all the 10 million enrolled work effectively two hours per week on technology problems and further assume that a man-year corresponds to 2,500 hours, their total contribution amounts to 400,000 man-years.

The efficiency of the popular-based extension services depends on selection processes, upgrading of skills, and efficient links with the national as well as local science and technology institutes. The popular-based extension services with a strength of an estimated 400,000 man-years should also be seen in the light of limited time spent on long journeys and high familiarity with local conditions.

What are the explanations for the considerable difference in relative enrollment in the mass scientific network? There are two reasons that are likely to influence the enrollment in the mass scientific network areas. First, differences in soil, water availability, and climate are relatively minor in the Shanghai region. Large parts of Hopei also have relatively uniform conditions. However, in the semi-mountainous areas north of Hopei, where Zunhua is located, the conditions may vary considerably from brigade to brigade and even between teams. Consequently, local adaptations of new seeds and new farming techniques must be carried out at brigade or even team level, which calls for a larger enrollment in the mass scientific network. Second, a scientific approach to farming is more firmly established in Shanghai rural areas where high-yielding cropping patterns have developed over a substantial number of years. This contrasts to the situation in Zunhua and many parts of Hopei, where agricultural modernization programs have only recently been introduced. A wide basis to support these programs consequently makes them more likely to succeed. Finally, it must not be forgotten that Zunhua is in many ways a model county, and consequently more emphasis may have been given to the building up of the mass scientific network which may have an inflated enrollment compared with other places.

Local Research Institutes

The successful development and use of technology and science in rural localities can in no way be self-sustained. The popular-based extension services will constantly require new ideas and new technological inputs which can only partly be locally generated. The inputs come directly from national institutes as well as local research institutes. We will again use information from Northern Hopei— from the region where Zunhua county is located—to illuminate the relations among the various levels.

In 1973 there were twenty-five research institutes in Tangshan region of which thirteen were under the regional government leadership. The remaining ones—all under the counties—are all farm machinery research institutes. Two of the institutes are integrated with companies located in Tangshan city. Another two institutes— in chemistry, in engineering—primarily serve the modern industrial sector in Tangshan city while the remaining ones are primarily serving the rural areas and are closely geared to provide inputs for agricultural development. See Table 21 for a listing of region-level and county-level institutes located within Tangshan region.

In addition to the county farm machinery research institutes, all counties in Tangshan region have the following four components of a scientific network:

1. Agricultural and forestry technology popularization station
2. Veterinary station
3. Seed station
4. Seed farm

The first three carry out experimentation and provide inputs into the extension network, while the fourth unit is mainly engaged in the production of improved seeds.

Still higher—at the provincial level—is a more elaborate structure for technology and science, which will be illustrated with information from Hopei, the province where Tangshan is located. The province has altogether a professional manpower of 7,000 in approximately 150 research institutes. Only 29 are under provincial leader-

Table 21. Science and Technology Institutes in
Tangshan Region, Hopei Province

1. Coal Mining Research Institute, an integral unit of the Kailan Coal Mine Company.
2. Porcelain Research Institute, an integral part of the "Porcelain Company" —physically located within one of the biggest of the approximately ten enterprises, which make up the Company.
3. Chemical Industry Research Institute.
4. Agricultural Research Institute, Tangshan city.
5. Agro-Reclaiming Research Institute, Paikechuang.
6. Fruit Tree Research Institute, Changli county.
7. Aquatics Products Research Institute, Chinhuangtao city.
8. Medical Research Institute, Chinhuangtao city.
9. Machinery Research Institute, Tangshan city, still under preparation.
10. Tangshan Region Farm Machinery and Tools Research Institute.
11. Tangshan City Farm Machinery and Tools Research Institute, Tangshan city.
12. Chinhuangtao Farm Machinery and Tools Research Institute, Chinhuangtao.
13. Paikechuang Agro-Reclaiming Area Farm Machinery and Tools Research Institute.
14. County-level Farm Machinery and Tools Research Institute—in each of the 12 counties.

Source: Tangshan region science and technology group (1973).

ship. Another 39 institutes are controlled by the regions and another 80 are under the leadership of the counties—usually farm machinery research institutes. It is obvious from this information that not all of the 145 counties have their own farm machinery research institutes. Furthermore, the previous discussion of Tangshan region shows that it is better endowed with research facilities than the average region in Hopei province.

However, almost every one of the 145 counties in Hopei has a set-up of "3 stations + 1 farm": agricultural and forestry technology popularization station, veterinary station, seed station, and seed farm. In the same areas of the country—for example in Shanghai rural areas—the counties may also have professional agricultural research institutes. During the Cultural Revolution a number of the counties merged professional activities with popularization work. However, many are separating the two functions again, it was reported in August 1973.

In addition, Hopei province during 1972 set up eighty-seven experimental centers and a very large number of auxiliary stations, both under joint leadership of the province or regions on the one hand, and eighteen professional research institutes on the other hand. The idea is to support mass scientific activities in agriculture and industry at commune or brigade level. Several of these centers are located in Tangshan region, and there is now a constant expansion in numbers and geographical location all over China.

An attempt has been made to sum up the formal characteristics of the local technology system in Hopei province in Table 22, which gives basic statistics of the area, details of the administrative body for science and technology, and selected information about the science and technology institutions for the three levels exemplified by Zunhua county, Tangshan region, and Hopei province.

It should be noted that, in 1973, only 25 percent of the counties in China had set up a farm machinery research institute. Few of the county farm machinery research institutes have been in existence very long. None of the region-level and county-level sixteen farm machinery research institutes in Tangshan region listed in Table 21 have been in existence for more than a few years —most of them were set up in 1972 and 1973. The same applies to most of the eighty county-level research institutes in Hopei. (See Table 22.) This, of course, does not mean that farm machinery research was not carried out before the institutes were set up, but the research was usually carried out within the farm machinery plants—possibly without much coordination. The work of the farm machinery research institutes, which includes trial-manufacture, demonstrations, selection of the best types, and commissioning models for full-scale manufacture, is of course even now partly carried out within the farm machinery plants.

What, then, are the problems that require this systematic science and technology system, which is gradually coming into existence throughout the rural areas? The change in cropping

Table 22. Science and Technology System in Hopei Province (1973)

	Hopei Province	Tangshan Region	Zunhua County
Basic statistics of the area	≈190,000 km² 48 million (1972) 10 regions 9 cities 145 counties 3,700 communes 53,000 brigades >260,000 teams	17,600 km² 6.84 million (1972) 2 cities 13 counties 1 reclamation area ≈100 districts ≈500 communes	1,640 km² 0.58 million (1972) 1 county town 10 districts 43 communes 691 brigades 2,499 teams
Administration Body	Science and Technology Commission	Science and Technology Group	Science and Technology Group
	Planning Industry Agriculture Medicine Logistics	General 4 Agriculture 3 Industry 3 Archives & data 2 Directors 2	General 1 Agriculture 2 Industry 1 Office 1
Persons	30	14	5

S & T Institutions	Province	Region	County
	150 research institutes -29 under province -39 under regions -80 under counties (Professional manpower: 7,000) + 87 experimental centers 780 auxiliary stations Most counties have the same set-up of three stations plus seed farm as in Zunhua.	25 research institutes -13 under region or above -12 under counties (Farm Machinery Research Institutes) All counties have the same set-up of three stations plus seed farm as in Zunhua.	1. Farm Machinery R I A1 Agr Technology Station A2 Forestry Technology Station B. Veterinary Station C. Seed Station + D. Seed Farm (Professional manpower: 373, incl 75 at commune level)
Mass scientific enrollment	1,000,000 (2% of population)	No enrollment figure at this level	25,000 (4% of population)

Source: Science and technology administrative units at various levels (1973).

pattern in northern Hopei is a good example. Several of the counties in Tangshan region are expanding the acreage under wheat cultivation. Zunhua was planning to expand wheat acreage to about 35,000 hectares (out of total of 60,000 hectares) in 1974, which is more than a doubling from 1971.[4] This is mainly done through intercropping with maize. This has, first of all, required substantial research in finding the appropriate timing, plant distances, application of fertilizer, and the subsequent development of the new seed varieties, which are required for intercropping. Furthermore, wheat/maize intercropping changes the whole vegetation cycle and, subsequently, upsets the supply/demand balance for agricultural manpower. So, it becomes not only necessary to develop new hand tools and tractor equipment that can be used in the new wheat/maize lands, but, furthermore, it becomes absolutely necessary to mechanize certain time-consuming tasks associated with harvesting in order to be able to carry out all other tasks. This goes a long way towards explaining the rapid development of farm machinery research institutes in northern Hopei.

Another example from Shanghai explains the situation in similar terms. A considerable proportion of Shanghai's rural areas is developing a system where three crops per year can be grown instead of the usual two. Consequently, it is essential to have new varieties of rice with a short growth period and early ripening. In order to achieve this, some places are experimenting with transplanting the rice seedlings with soil on the roots, but then it becomes impossible to use the present rice transplanters as the fine roots of the seedlings get destroyed in the machines, which considerably lengthens the vegetation period. So this problem is solved through local science and technology activities.

Obviously, all the various activities and programs discussed here must be coordinated, and for much of the work it is necessary to draw up long-term plans. Very little or no information is available on this aspect. However, it was reported in July 1973 that the Science and Technology Commission at province level in Hopei had three types of plans—annual plans, a medium-term plan geared to the present five-year plan ending in 1975, and a third more general long-term plan up to the end of 1980.

Transfer of Industrial Technology

Technology transfer is essential in order to sustain rural industrialization and other aspects of rural development. No doubt rural industries will continue to require skills and equipment from higher-level enterprises. So the transfer of technology to previously non-industrialized areas will continue to be a very important part of the policies to promote the development of rural areas. Localities which have already started their rural industrialization will continue to be dependent on technology transfer in order to upgrade their industrial capability and move into the manufacture of more complicated products. The technology transfer has initially mainly taken place between industrial centers and rural areas. However, the industrially advanced rural areas will increasingly be able to serve as sources of technology for the less advanced areas.

It is analytically useful to distinguish the following three phases or levels of technology transfer:[5]

1. *Material transfer* is characterized by the simple transfer of new materials, such as seeds, plants, animals, machines, and husbandry and management practices associated with these materials.

2. *Design transfer* is characterized by the transfer of information in the form of blueprints, journals, formulas, and books. During this phase, new plant materials, animal breeding stock, or prototype machinery may be introduced for testing purposes, or in order to copy their designs. New plants and animals can be subject to systematic tests, propagation, and selection. Machines are tested and designs modified to adapt them to local soil and climate conditions and to different tasks.

3. *Capacity transfer* occurs primarily through the transfer of scientific and technical knowledge and capacity. The objective is to institutionalize local capacity for invention of a continuous stream of locally adapted technology. Machine design becomes less dependent on prototypes developed elsewhere. Increasingly, plant and animal varieties are developed locally to adapt them to local ecological condi-

tions. As local agricultural science and engineering capacity is strengthened, both biological and mechanical technologies are invented that are precisely adapted to the ecological conditions and factor endowments of the local economy. An important element in the process of capacity transfer is the migration of individual scientists and engineers, and the building of institutions. This third phase corresponds to the creation of a local problem-solving capability—a need that now appears to be seriously grappled with by Chinese planners.

It is useful to look at the structure of the industrial system in China as a pyramid with a limited number of large national plants at the top and a broad base of very small enterprises in rural areas run by counties and communes. In between, there are layers of enterprises run by provinces, regions, and counties—decreasing in size and sophistication as one comes nearer to the base of the pyramid.

The transfer of technology—equipment and training—through the different layers has in recent years played a very important role in promoting rural industrialization. The technology transfer—vertical and horizontal—is organized to achieve a number of different objectives. Two main objectives can be clearly discerned. First, industrial bases are to be created in a large number of rural places in order to provide the necessary inputs to increase land productivity as well as labor productivity. Second, technology is transferred to provide the necessary inputs to create industrial bases and achieve their subsequent upgrading in order to supplement the modern industrial sector with intermediate or finished products and certain raw materials.

This implies two kinds of technology transfer. One is the vertical transfer of technology from provincial (or national) enterprises downwards. The other is the horizontal transfer of technology between enterprises at county level or below. Both these transfers are illustrated in Figure 15. It should be noted that these categories of transfer cannot achieve a regionally balanced industrial development at the provincial level, with the inescapable consequence that provinces with a weak industrial foundation will stay weak unless

Figure 15. Diffusion of Technology in China

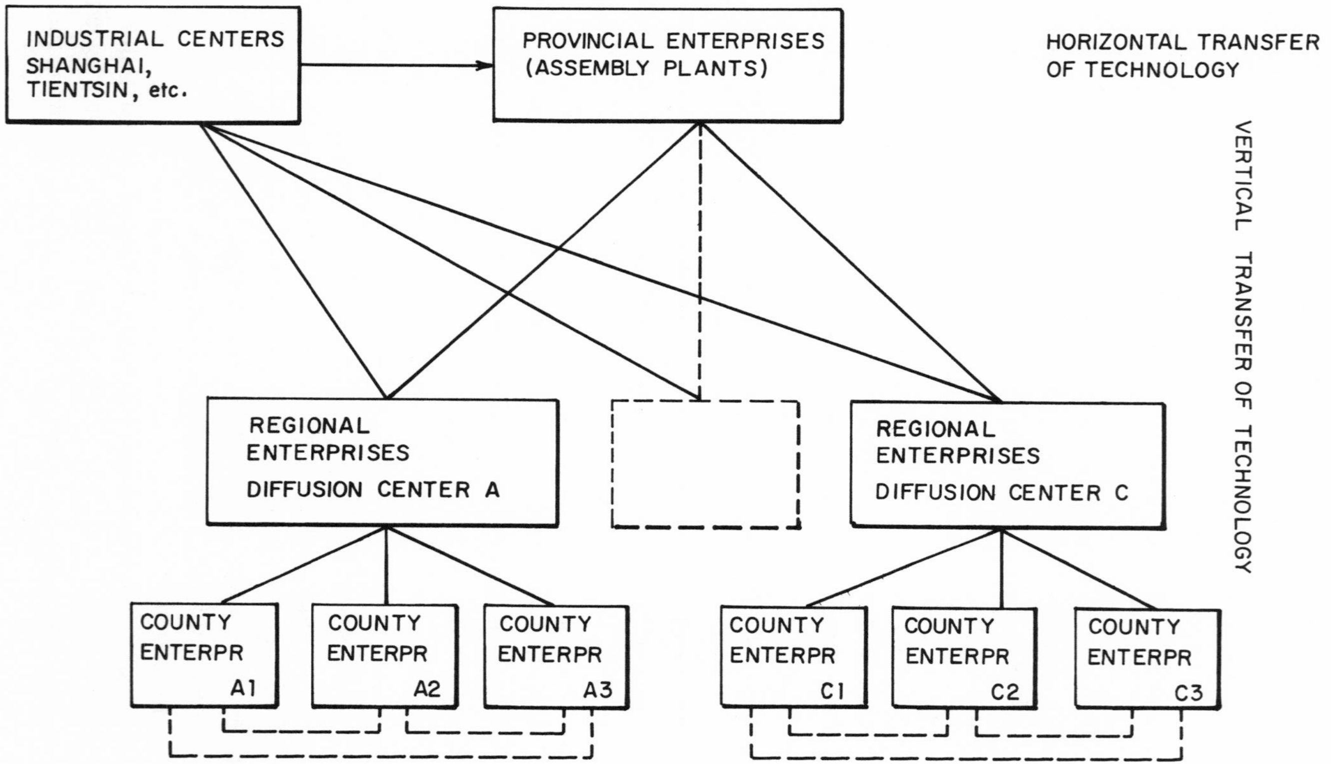

HORIZONTAL TRANSFER OF TECHNOLOGY

VERTICAL TRANSFER OF TECHNOLOGY

INDUSTRIAL CENTERS SHANGHAI, TIENTSIN, etc.

PROVINCIAL ENTERPRISES (ASSEMBLY PLANTS)

REGIONAL ENTERPRISES DIFFUSION CENTER C

REGIONAL ENTERPRISES DIFFUSION CENTER A

COUNTY ENTERPR C1
COUNTY ENTERPR C2
COUNTY ENTERPR C3

COUNTY ENTERPR A1
COUNTY ENTERPR A2
COUNTY ENTERPR A3

measures are taken to remedy the situation. This problem is discussed at the end of this chapter.

Rural development and rural industrialization have required
technology of two different kinds. First, transfer of technology
was in the early stages needed to initiate any development. Second,
it is now in a consolidation stage necessary to develop a local technical capacity, that is, a problem-solving capability.

Technology utilized in rural areas can be transferred in three
different ways. First, part of it comes capital-embodied, that is,
incorporated in equipment and intermediate goods. This approach
has been important for all of the more complex small-scale process
industries. Second, another part is human-embodied—that is,
incorporated as knowledge and experience of human resources.
This approach has in the initial stages of rural industrialization been
very important. Finally, another part is disembodied technology,
such as handbooks, product and process specifications, and so forth.
The last approach will become increasingly important as the localities build up a capability to demand and utilize this kind of knowledge.

The big urban-based industries and construction companies
have in a number of places played a surprisingly central role in
promoting small-scale industries in rural areas—examples of vertical
transfer of capital-embodied and human-embodied technology. The
assistance from the urban-based industries is provided in two
basically different ways. On the one hand, the big industries send
personnel and equipment to the places where the new small-scale
industries are to be set up. On the other hand, local personnel are
trained in urban-based plants. The first kind of assistance is exemplified in a report from the No. 1 Metallurgical Construction Company in Wuhan, which during 1971 dispatched approximately
1,200 personnel in 20 teams to various localities in three different
provinces—Hupeh, Hunan, and Honan. These teams were given two
different tasks.[6]

First, they were to help various local small iron and steel,
chemical fertilizer, machinery, and cement works with their construction. The new small-scale plants, which all fall into the category

of heavy industry, would after construction be run either by counties or regions. Second, they were also to help various communes with repair and maintenance of agricultural machinery. So the urban-based construction company has also engaged in creating and supporting parts of the three-level farm machine repair and manufacture network.

Because of unfamiliarity with industrial technology and lack of ability to interpret printed technical descriptions, it has been necessary to rely extensively on personal contacts to transmit technical knowledge. Industrial knowledge may be carried by two categories of persons. Technicians, engineers, and managers from more advanced plants travel to the sites of small rural plants to assist in all stages from planning to production and distribution. At the same time, people from the localities are sent for shorter or longer training periods to advanced industrial units and are given posts of responsibility for technical or managerial matters when they return. Further, people are transferred more or less permanently to work in rural areas. This formation of production and organizational skills in rural areas is summarized in the following table:

Table 23. Formation of Production and Organizational Skills

1. Training of personnel
   a. City-based old factories train workers recruited to rural factories
   b. Rural factories undertake training of new workers

2. Transfer of personnel
   a. Technical personnel are transferred from old to new factories
   b. Newly graduated students are allocated to new rural factories

A heavy reliance on person-to-person contacts in solving industrial problems indicates that the Chinese have found this to be the most effective method of technology transfer and that problem-solving activities cannot be successfully carried out without personal contacts in the field involving responsibilities for both parties involved.[7]

The other type of transfer may be exemplified in the case

mentioned in a report from Fukien, which specifically discusses the training of personnel for small-scale plants.[8] Here "apart from regulating the supply of materials needed in building small plants, the departments concerned of the Provincial Revolutionary Committee have also organized the technicians of the chemical fertilizer plants and chemical works in Yungchun, Changpin, Foochow, Chuanchou, Naping, Shaowu, and Soming to assist the small synthetic plants in training technicians."

There are many similar examples from other industrial sectors. The Wafang-tien Bearings Works, Liaoning, which is a large plant located in Liaoning province, has assisted in setting up twelve new bearing plants—most of them to be run by counties.[9] In order further to assist the plants, more than 1,000 technicians were trained in the big plant. Some of the small plants have an annual production of 500,000 sets of bearings, and the production plans of some county-run enterprises are now being coordinated with those of the big bearings plant under a five-year arrangement.

The No. 1 Motor Vehicle Plant in Changchun has also been instrumental in developing local industry in Kirin province through giving assistance to 135 small factories.[10] The vehicle plant—the largest in China, producing more than 50,000 lorries per year—has done so by designing and producing machine parts and by providing tools. In addition to this, the big plant has also sent skilled workers to small plants to assist in repairing machinery and overcoming difficulties.

Similarly, the big sugar refinery in Paotou in Inner Mongolia during 1970 and 1971 has helped to build eighteen small sugar refineries located in Hopei, Ninghsia, Tibet, and also in some other provinces.[11] The refinery has not only sent construction teams to the places where the small plants are to be set up, but also trained more than 1,000 skilled workers in its own plant. Apparently the big plant has also played a role in designing new equipment. The report further mentions that the Paotou refinery has devised simplified equipment for processing sugar beet. As a consequence it has been possible to further distribute beet sugar refineries, and refining can now be carried out at low cost in small-scale plants.

The assistance given by specific large plants in setting up small plants in rural areas usually forms part of a larger program. This is clearly evident in Kansu province, where in winter 1971 and spring 1972 approximately 15,000 cadres, workers, and technicians—mainly from urban centers—were organized to assist thirty-seven counties, out of a total of seventy-two counties in the province.[12] This work force was given four main tasks: to set up small industries, to produce and repair agricultural machinery, to build power-operated irrigation and drainage projects, and to train personnel.

Rural industry, once in existence, provides a further downward transfer of technology. Agricultural workers from teams and brigades are trained in local industries, for example, to repair pumps, electric motors, and other necessary equipment for the irrigation networks. In addition, other people are trained to repair farm tools and farm machinery and the techniques involved in the use of fertilizer. Further, most of the rural industries send repair and instruction teams to assist in relevant tasks within the agricultural units. Thus, the rural industrial system serves as an important training ground for local technicians. This technology transfer is exemplified in Table 24, which lists the activities used to build up repair and maintenance skills in a region in Honan province.

The importance of the farm machinery repair and manufacture network—discussed in a following section—apparently tended initially to be overlooked in a number of places in the burgeoning enthusiasm for establishing local industries. Hupeh provincial radio at the end of 1972 pointed out that it was necessary for the agricultural machinery industry to form its own network. So many factories changed their "erroneous" ideas in attaching importance to construction and ignoring repair work. Consequently they are actively manufacturing parts and spares, and some machinery-producing factories have even set up retail shops to sell spare parts —according to the report.

The training of personnel for the three-level network, which is an essential part of the base of the industrial pyramid, must, of course, be considered as important as the training of personnel for the intermediate-level enterprises previously described. From

Table 24. Formation of Repair and Maintenance Skills

1. Formal factory training
   Short-term courses are arranged in commune-level enterprises during slack farming seasons.
   Principles, structure, operation, and maintenance of machines are being taught.
2. Informal factory training
   Production teams send on their own initiative members to factories for "learning by doing."
3. Delivery training
   Commune-level enterprises send technicians to buying unit at the time of delivery.
4. Mobile repair and maintenance teams training
   People are trained on the spot at the time when repair or maintenance is required.
5. Factory repair training
   Team members accompany machinery to the repair unit.

Source: Anyang region industrial bureau (Honan).

Liaoning province it was reported by the end of 1972 that all 104 communes in Shenyang municipality had set up their farm implement repair and manufacture works. By then 3,600 experienced technicians had been sent down to various communes—apparently from the municipality—to train a technical force of approximately 9,000 *technical* workers to form a service network.[13] Another industrial city—Hantan in Hopei province—also has engaged the city's machinery plants to train more than 1,000 technicians for the communes around the city.[14] Yincheng county in Shansi reports that a network of local industries has been formed and that over 10,000 people in the county have been trained to make and repair machines and tools.[15] Linfen region reported at the end of 1970 that the enterprises within the region had trained 2,450 technicians for communes and brigades. Further, the region also had organized 141 mobile service teams to support agriculture and had sent more than 1,000 "barefoot" repair technicians—an equivalent to the paramedical "barefoot" doctors—to do on-the-spot repairs of farm machinery and tools.

Local Science and Technology Policy

In many areas of China science and technology now exist in an explicit form at county level as is evidenced by a well-developed institutional structure and substantial budget available to finance science and technology activities. The science and technology policy of a county is, of course, not directed towards advanced science and large-scale innovations, but centers rather on small improvements on machinery and production technology closely related to the immediate problems of the community and includes extension in industry and agriculture. It may be useful to take the situation in a model county, Zunhua in Hopei, as an example. The technology and science activities here cover various aspects, all more or less closely related to agriculture. The distribution of personnel can be used as a good example illustrating this fact. The total full-time employment of personnel in technology and science was reported to be 373 in July 1973, including 75 people at commune level. Of these only 45 were connected with industry—mostly with industrial enterprises serving agriculture. The remainder were engaged in agriculture, forestry, and veterinary activities, and a few in public health.

The leadership responsibility for science and technology in Zunhua rests with the Science and Technology Group, which has five full-time members. This group is one of the four sub-units of the production command, which is one of the three major county government sections directly under Zunhua county's economic-political leadership (revolutionary committee). Most provinces, autonomous regions, and centrally administered cities have science and technology groups. The groups are responsibile for science and technology activities in industry, agriculture, and medicine. Such groups also exist in most regions as well as in many counties.[16]

The Science and Technology Group in Zunhua has in its present form existed since the end of 1971, when it was set up and given the science and technology responsibilities which had previously belonged to another specialized unit. The size of the group makes it evident that the five people do not concern themselves with day-to-day activities, which are left to the specialized units and per-

sonnel being directed either by an agriculture and forestry bureau
or a farm machinery bureau, both under the production command
leadership. So the main function of the Science and Technology
Group appears to be the drawing up of relatively long-term programs, mobilization and coordination of units concerned, and evaluation of results. This is done for programs initiated in the county
as well as those handed down from the next higher administrative
level (Tangshan region) or the still higher level (Hopei province) in
more or less formal directives. The popularization of science and
technology is possibly the main area of responsibility for the
science and technology group in a county.

The budget at the immediate disposal of the Zunhua County
Science and Technology Group was, in 1973, reported to be approximately 145,000 yuan, an increase of 15,000 over the previous year.
This budget covered scientific research and experiments, training
of technicians, and the exchange of technical information. The
financial sources for the budget were in the province for provincial
projects, in the region for regional projects, and in the county for
county projects. The sum mentioned does not include the budget
for a farm machinery research institute set up at the end of 1971,
which had its own annual budget of approximately 100,000 yuan.
Nor does it include the wages and other costs for the previously
mentioned 373 full-time employees. This amounts to approximately
373,000 yuan—if one assumes a total annual cost of 1,000 yuan per
employee, which is included in the budgets of the specialized
bureaus. The major part of the amount would be covered by the
agriculture and forestry bureaus.

It should be noted that technical research within the county
industrial enterprises, which employed approximately 5,500 in
1973, is included in the previously mentioned figures only insofar
as it relates to the wages of the people in the farm machinery
institute and in the industrial enterprises—altogether 45 people—or
allocations for specific farm machinery research projects, many
carried out within the enterprises. Consequently, the figures do
not include any costs for technical research or technical innovations
that the enterprises carry out in order to improve their productive
equipment.

If the amounts mentioned above available to finance science and technology in Zunhua county are taken together, they add up to a total of 620,000 yuan. This must then be related to the level of economic activity of the county. Grain production, the main source of income, has an annual production value of approximately 50 million yuan. The income from side-line occupations amounted to 23 million yuan in 1972. The value of industrial production amounts to roughly 25 million yuan. These figures, if added, then give a total of about 100 million yuan. Consequently, the total science and technology budget previously mentioned would then amount to approximately 0.6 percent of the total production value of grain, income from side-line occupations, and industrial production value.[17] Zunhua is only used as an example because information is available from this county; it cannot be implied that other counties in China generally have science and technology activities of the level which apparently exists in Zunhua. Zunhua may, however, be taken as an example of the kind of science and technology system that China wants to develop in rural areas.

Local Engineering Industry

Earlier comments clearly indicate that the localities would greatly benefit from having their own engineering enterprises. These would then have the twofold function of manufacturing machinery and equipment appropriate to the localities and of providing timely repairs.

An important element of rural industrialization in China has been the development, in many places, of local engineering industries which can provide the locality with suitable product designs and relatively labor-intensive production methods and much of the required productive equipment. This approach permits local manufacture of goods which otherwise would have been produced in large city-based industries. At the same time, a considerable proportion of the local engineering industry appears to be located in county capitals, which thus serve as islands of industrial modernity, influencing the surrounding rural areas.

Engineering—or mechanical technology—covers a wide range

of activities. Furthermore, engineering includes two activities that cannot be easily separated—manufacture of machinery needed mainly in agriculture, and repair/maintenance of any piece of equipment directly or indirectly used in agriculture. Developing a repair capability then naturally often leads to a capability to manufacture, which has provided one of the justifications for the considerable development of relatively small engineering enterprises in rural areas. It is also important that engineering enterprises can more easily be adjusted to small-scale operation than can the process plants. Local engineering capability may also greatly influence the industrial options open to a locality.

The explanation for this is that rural industries are small in comparison with enterprises located in urban areas. If rural industries used the same machinery and the same production technology as large industries, this would in most cases mean very high production costs. Consequently, it has been necessary to adapt technology and machinery to the different conditions existing in rural areas. And this could not have been done easily without a local engineering industry, which thus plays an important role in the further development of rural industry.

The engineering industry is obviously less limited by natural resources than most other industries, and human effort, skill, and organizational ability are consequently key factors. It then appears that development efforts within the engineering sector have at least as powerful an influence on overall development as the latter has on stimulating the growth of the engineering sector. So, the "proper" level of technological sophistication for a particular locality, or the right degree of capital intensity as opposed to labor intensity, may then lose much of its relevance. The reason for this is that in a sector with rapid organic growth of skills and technology it is not the starting level of technical sophistication or of capital/labor intensity that counts, but the way these factors change over time.

If rapid economic growth is desired, preferences should be given to those sectors capable of rapid and broad advances in technology and skills, even if it is necessary to start from a very modest base. The individual engineering enterprise where the learning process takes place is a focal point for upgrading skills and technology. The enterprise can then be regarded as an actual or potential source for a number of production and training activities, such as using rudimentary techniques, manufacturing crude products, training workers in basic skills. Simultaneously, other enterprises may be pioneering in design and making technical adaptations.

Such activities are significant for development for a number of reasons. First, the activities are mutually supporting. Taken together, they can sustain themselves even though singly they would be uneconomical. Second, the sequence in which potential activities may be taken on is largely predetermined. Generally, the planning people cannot select a superior activity until a lower-level activity has already been in operation on a reasonable scale for some time. Third, the range of potential activities cannot be closely defined in advance in each of the localities. Although the transfer of technologies to the localities approximately defines the potential future activities, it is impossible precisely to foresee new adaptations, new designs, and new inventions which must be a function of local industrial activities.

The local engineering industry is basically geared to generating and manufacturing products that correspond to the immediate needs of the locality and are within the purchasing power of a large segment of the population. The immediate local needs for utility products can be divided into the following four categories: food, clothing, shelter, and transportation.

Food. Equipment is manufactured for producing, processing, and preserving food. This includes agricultural implements, irrigation equipment, and sometimes small tractors and power tillers. Drying equipment, grinders, milling machines, and canning equipment may also be manufactured locally.

Clothing. Simple spinning equipment, simple looms, and equipment for dying processes may be manufactured locally.

Shelter. Building hardware, construction equipment, and simple woodworking machinery are often made locally. Cooking stoves and simple water pumps are also made locally.

Transportation. Motorized multi-purpose farm vehicles can in many places be manufactured locally around high technology components, such as diesel engines, transmission units, and bearings, which are manufactured higher up in the industrial hierarchy.

This development of a local engineering base is very much in evidence all over China, and reports say that 96 percent of the counties have machinery plants. The local engineering industry—within a county—can be expected to go through a number of development stages according to the process summarized below for machinery for use in the fields, like plows, transplanters, and so forth.

Stage 1

Production of machinery has not yet started, and skill requirements are relatively low. The most important transformation that occurs during this stage is the gradually increasing independence for maintenance and repair of vehicles, farm machinery, and other equipment. Local repair facilities allow faster and generally cheaper service and lay the foundation of skills on which later industrial development can build.

Stage 2

The proportion of simple metal products is decreasing. Manufacture of machinery and equipment is introduced, including some electrical equipment, such as motors. Steel inputs become important, but production methods remain simple and relatively labor-intensive. There is no distinct border line between this and the preceding stage. The most important transformation is the increasing strength of the locally based technology and the appearance of small multi-purpose machine shops able to turn out most of the spare parts needed for machinery and equipment in the locality.

The manufacture of agricultural equipment and machinery becomes increasingly important. The simpler products are introduced during this stage, while manufacture of more difficult products begins in the next stage. Production usually starts with ploughs, harrows, and farm accessories, gradually extending to heavier and more sophisticated products.

The main designs are decided by central authorities, but considerable local adaptations take place. The productive facilities of the local industry will determine what agricultural equipment can be efficiently produced. Cooperation will extend outside the locality when heavy and specialized production machinery is needed.

Stage 3

The manufacture of simple machine tools plays a crucial role in this stage, since it lays the foundation for the development of a diversified base for the engineering industry. The step towards eventual machine tool manufacture is taken during Stage 1, with the establishment of repair and maintenance facilities for such tools. The importance of such facilities is considerable since the total cost of planned preventive maintenance—over the life cycle—including a major overhaul usually represents more than the original cost of a machine.

Within the metal products group, the production of items requiring markets larger than the local one, and more complex skills, is now undertaken. The proportion of simple metal products within the total output of the sector falls considerably. The manufacture of industrial machinery and equipment expands and becomes diversified. A greater number of skilled technical operators become available. The range and sophistication of locally manufactured products steadily increases, and indigenous technology develops. The local industry has now reached a sufficiently high level of sophistication for a full-scale interaction with the rest of the economy. This will become apparent in discussions of farm machinery and engineering in the next chapter.

It should be stressed that a major feature of rural industries is not their smallness of scale but their local character, which then requires that they be based on technologies that make optimal use of locally available natural resources, manpower, and equipment. In addition, rural industries are, of course, often small—particularly in their initial stages of development. This is a reflection of the limited local supply of capital as well as the limited local market for the products manufactured. As markets develop, so do the industries and the technologies utilized, so that a plant may go through successive stages of changing production technologies as long as the resource base permits it.

The technologies used in rural areas are quite often different from those that would be used in modern industrial sector or outside China. Even within the modern industrial sector, a number of technologies can be found that are different from those in the already fully industrialized countries.

The industrial technology that has been developed outside China or in the urban-based industrial sectors in China is usually not appropriate for use in small-scale industries in the Chinese countryside. Therefore central (region, province, nation) research and design institutes have been assigned the task of making designs that are appropriate for local small-scale production.

The inclusion of small heavy industries like small nitrogen chemical fertilizer plants, small cement plants, and small iron plants may be the most striking characteristic of Chinese local industrialization aside from its comprehensiveness. These three industries are basically process industries, and their economies of scale are very prominent. The Chinese plants are very small and usually serve only a county or a still smaller area. Consequently, it has been necessary to modify the processes and the equipment that go into a plant in order to be able to produce chemical fertilizer, cement, and pig iron at reasonable costs.

However, innovations in productive equipment used in rural enterprises producing or repairing machinery are largely left to the localities to enable them to make the best possible use of their combination of capital, manpower, and raw material. The manufacture and use of indigenous machines are encouraged wherever the capacity of modern specialized—and expensive—machines would not be fully utilized. Machinery and equipment used in agriculture are still a main area of rural innovation, and it has often been stressed that mass campaigns to improve farm tools and to develop semi-mechanical farm machinery could greatly improve labor efficiency.[18]

The development of appropriate[19] technology for rural industries takes place continuously as the rural industrial systems become more and more differentiated. There is an important progressive element in this, in that, as the market develops and underemployment slack is reduced, the appropriate technologies will adapt to greater scale and capital intensity. As the size and sophistication of local industry develop, so does local capacity for finding its own solutions. Thus, when development becomes partially self-sustaining and the locality becomes increasingly able to analyze its requirements for further economic and social development, the symbiotic relationship between urban-based industry and rural industry becomes important. But to function effectively the small rural industries have not only to be able to convert technique to meet standards of the modern industrial sector; they must also be able to coordinate their activities effectively and schedule production within the large industrial complex. These conversions and management skills are developed in rural areas as the local industrial systems become more and more differentiated. An industrial organization which permits the effective use of small-scale engineering industries in cooperation with modern industrial complexes seems already to have been developed in many areas in China.

Poor maintenance or inadequate repair leads to premature deterioration or destruction of productive capital. Negligence in the maintenance of buildings and structures can cause secondary damage to machinery that is not adequately protected. Since capital is scarce in developing countries, the importance of protecting capital is much greater than it would be in an industrialized country. Thus, the marginal impact on growth is likewise greater.

Consequently, it is essential to institute adequate maintenance and competent repairs as this prevents frequent breakdowns of machinery, and disruptions of the production process are avoided. It is also important to detect and repair wear and tear of machinery and to take good care of control devices, as this usually results in higher product quality.

Induced losses occur because of bottlenecks in the supply of spare parts, which may arise if their import is restricted or if their shipment is impossible without lengthy delays. Hence, many enterprises try to hold an abnormally large stock of spare parts. For the individual firm, this policy is absolutely reasonable; but for the overall national economy, it means a waste of resources. This type of loss might be avoided if the country revised its policy with respect to the supply of spare parts.

These general comments taken from a UNIDO publication[20] illuminate the Chinese approach in stressing the repair function of their local engineering system.

Repair and manufacture networks are being set up all over China. Repair services and manufacturing capability are simultaneously organized in most areas. The existence of repair facilities on the spot is likely to make them cheaper and faster than outside services and to make possible a high rate of machine utilization. Basically, all brigades should have small repair shops. Communes have larger shops which also manufacture simple tools and machinery and can carry out all medium repairs, including the overhaul of tractors. At the county level still larger shops are responsible for all main repairs and the manufacture of machinery and equipment.

The major objective of the combination of repair and manufacture is to accomplish timely repair of equipment and machinery in order to raise the utilization rate. This is achieved through a number of measures listed below.[21] A general principle is to manufacture more and repair less during slack farming seasons and reverse the priorities during the busy farming seasons.

1. Establish a three-level farm machinery repair and manufacture network.
2. Establish special groups in county-level enterprises for the repair of farm machinery
   – during work hours
   – outside work hours (there should always be people on duty)
3. Set up county-level and commune-level repair groups to go to specific areas (these groups are partly mobile)

4. Send yearly groups from county-level and commune-level enterprises for multi-purpose investigations
   - to prepare lists of damages to machines
   - to find out what machines, tools, and parts are needed so that manufacture can be planned; repair and maintenance is also planned on the basis of such investigations
   - to train technical personnel in the brigades
   - to train team members

The three-level repair and manufacture network is still under construction but has already reached a considerable level of development and sophistication, which will be evident in the discussion of local farm machinery and engineering in Chapter 4. On the national level almost all counties have at least one farm machinery repair plant. Counties in well-developed areas usually have two or three plants of which two would then usually be engaged in specialized repairs of tractors and other relatively complex machinery while the remaining one may have started to manufacture electric motors and/or simple machine tools.

Certain provinces may have farm machinery repair and manufacture stations in 80 percent of all communes. The coverage of farm machinery repair stations at brigade level drops considerably— to 50 percent—in a well-developed province like Hopei. The national coverage drops further—to close to 20 percent. More information on the three-level network is exemplified for various administrative levels in Table 25.

The initially small-scale production in most of the rural enterprises has most likely contributed to the feasibility of using old machinery and equipment. In recent years there has been a strong emphasis in economic planning in China on using, and on the advantages of using, old machinery equipment to speed up economic construction. The assumed favorable conditions for this can be traced down to the structural dualism that characterizes Chinese industry today.[22]

The enterprises of modern industry are being influenced by the expansion of the small-scale industries in two ways. First, the modern industrial sector is required to give small industries con-

Table 25. Three-Level Farm Machinery Repair
and Manufacture Network

Zunhua County

County	three farm machinery plants
District	all districts have farm machinery stations
Commune	almost all communes have farm machinery repair and manufacture stations
Brigade	90% have farm machinery repair stations

Tangshan Region

County	all counties have at least one farm machinery plant, majority have two plants
District	almost all districts have farm machinery stations
Commune	80% have farm machinery repair and manufacture stations
Brigade	≈70% have farm machinery repair stations

Hopei Province

County	all counties have at least one farm machinery plant
District	n.a.
Commune	80%–90% have farm machinery repair and manufacture stations
Brigade	>50% have repair stations

National Level

County	96% have at least one farm machinery plant
District	n.a.
Commune	n.a.
Brigade	>20% have farm machinery repair stations

Source: Industrial bureaus at the various administrative levels (1973).

siderable assistance by partly meeting their needs for technology and equipment. Second, the modern industrial sector partly loses its market when rural small-scale industries start to produce more and more of the products previously manufactured by enterprises of the modern industrial sector. This sector is then forced or given an opportunity to modernize and to specialize at an earlier stage than otherwise would have been the case.

So there are pressures operating in China's advancing modern industrial sector, as in any other industrialized country, to make machinery and equipment obsolescent before they are run-down and unusable. When a new technical process is introduced or an existing one improved, usable machines or equipment may have to be replaced by new ones which embody new or improved techniques. There are, therefore, a variety of reasons having little or nothing to do with age or usability that may make machines or equipment obsolescent. But the limited resources of the Chinese countryside almost make any machinery or equipment useful when setting up small-scale industries and machine shops in rural areas.

Used machinery is a bargain only if it will produce satisfactorily and if the transfer costs (= price) are right. The transfer costs must take into account repairs and changes needed to make the equipment operable at the required standards. In discussions about the use of second-hand equipment in developing economies, limitations imposed by repair parts are often overstated. It is often claimed that, whatever the advantages of used machinery and equipment, they are more than counterbalanced by the fact that repair parts are not usually available. But the building up of a capacity to produce machinery is an integral part of the rural industrialization program in China. In most areas there are now machine shops, some of them rather small, which are quite capable of producing almost any part likely to be found in used machinery. Difficulties may, however, arise if the proper quality of material is not easily available.

The now extensive three-level structure of engineering enterprises with their strong component of repair/maintenance and manufacture of spare parts appears to provide an institutional basis for using old machinery in China's rural areas on a much larger scale than in most developing countries.

There is no doubt that the advanced industrial sector in China must undergo considerable modernization and specialization, and this fact implies that it has too much "general purpose" equipment which needs to be replaced by "special purpose" equipment. This, of course, means that considerable amounts of "general purpose" machinery will be available to small-scale local industries which may be well suited to make use of this kind of equipment. This is not to suggest that small-scale industries should not be able—in specific instances—to make good use of modern equipment.

The transfer of used machinery involves two sides in a rather complicated transaction. On the one side, there are people who plan and run the small-scale enterprises using indigenous, rather primitive methods. On the other side there are people of the modern industrial sector who are discarding some of their old machinery. Both sides, however, are found within the same country, which, of course, makes the transaction much less complicated than transferring used equipment from an industrialized country to a developing country.

Industrial planners in rural areas may know the market potentials and production conditions of their region, but they may not know exactly what type of machinery or equipment is needed. Those who know machinery and equipment are likely to make wrong suggestions if they are unfamiliar with production and market conditions in rural areas. To overcome the disadvantages of one-sided knowledge, local planners operating the plants in rural areas must work in close cooperation with people of the plants supplying old machinery and equipment.

Electrification and Local Energy Sources

Until recently, coal has provided China with approximately 85 percent of her energy needs. Major coal deposits are relatively widely distributed in the economically important eastern and northeastern areas of the country. Furthermore, many minor coal deposits are found within these areas. The pattern of distribution of deposits has had several beneficial effects. Local domestic and industrial demand has in many places been met—at least partly—through the exploitation of local deposits. Many of the small-scale process plants in rural areas derive part of their justification from utilizing energy from local coal deposits.

However, modern forms of energy—electricity and petroleum products—are needed for every industrial activity except handicrafts. China has very rich resources of hydroelectric power and oil, but the means to exploit and distribute them are not yet well developed. Power grids for the long-distance distribution of electricity exist (except in the northeast) only in few areas in China. The railway and road transport network is one of the weakest sectors of the Chinese economy. In addition to this, China has barely started large-scale exploitation of her resources of hydro-electric power and oil; in the future, these are likely to play a very important role in the process of further industrialization.

So it is quite natural that localities far from the industrially well-developed areas have been urged or forced to look for local energy sources in order to be able to initiate and sustain a local industrialization program. In many places it has been most logical to exploit coal deposits. China is rich in coal, and small or even very small deposits are widely scattered all over the country. These deposits often fail to justify a large-scale operation, but they can be mined locally with relatively primitive methods. The use of a seasonal surplus in manpower and reduced transportation distances often makes this an economically viable alternative.

In recent years, the exploitation of water power in hilly areas has received much emphasis. There has been rapid proliferation of small and very small hydroelectric power stations wherever there is sufficient difference in water levels and sufficient water. This applies to irrigated lowland areas as well. Altogether, there are now more than 50,000 small power stations ranging from a capacity of a few kilowatts up to a few hundred kilowatts.[23] These small stations represent about 16 percent of the total of China's hydroelectric power capacity.[24]

The number of small hydroelectric stations has increased rapidly from about 9,000 stations in 1966 in areas characterized by abundant rainfall and hilly terrain and crisscrossed by rivers. This applies particularly to southern provinces like Kwangtung, Fukien, and Chekiang. Consequently more than one-third of all small hydroelectric stations are found in these three provinces.

Available information indicates that the existence of numerous small hydroelectric stations has had a considerable impact on the distribution of electricity in rural areas—particularly at commune and lower levels. The two provinces of Kwangtung and Fukien are reported to have given 95 percent or more of their communes access to electricity—which is contrasted with barely 40 percent in Hupeh. However, it should be noted that electricity reaches only 50 percent of the brigades in Fukien.

Table 26. Small-Scale Hydroelectric Stations
in Selected Provinces in China

| | | Capacity | | Electricity Coverage | | | |
Province	No. of Stations	Total	Average kw	Region Percent	Commune Percent	Brigade Percent	Team Percent
Fukien	4,600	155,000	33.7		96	50	
Hupeh				79.1	39.9	21.3	19.1
Kwangtung	9,400	300,000	31.4		95		
Chekiang	3,600						

All provinces 50,000

Source: BBC–FE/W743, FE/W742, FE/W710, FE/W749.

The average size of small hydroelectric stations—as evidenced in news items—appears to be around 30 kw. Policy guidelines have indicated that stations with a capacity of less than 500 kw. should preferably be built by counties, communes, and brigades. Consequently, a fairly substantial number of local hydroelectric stations must be very small.

The state gives necessary assistance in investment and equipment. Technicians and workers from cities often help the localities with the designing of power stations and training of electricians. It is assumed that the localities—brigades and communes—should cover the major share of the investment costs. Since 1970 most of the small generating units installed have been manufactured in county- and commune-run workshops.

The present widespread use of small generators had its precedent in the Great Leap Forward when these machines received much attention. To be able better to understand the justification of small hydroelectric stations, it is useful to look at some of the arguments brought forward in a *People's Daily* article in the summer of 1958 when one of the vice-ministers for water conservancy and electric power discussed the question of preliminary electrification.[25]

The official pointed out that the economies of scale were substantial. He mentioned that, as to the capacity of generators to be installed, the relevant factor is the unit cost of construction, which tends to diminish by 15–20 percent with each doubling of capacity, that is from 6,000 kilowatts to 12,000 to 25,000 to 50,000 to 100,000 kilowatts. So adoption of large generators is necessary and rational where there is an electricity network or where there is an established industrial area. But large generators are not suitable for regions where the industrial foundation is weak; therefore universal emphasis should not be put on such generators because China needs to adapt the supply of electricity to the demand for universal development of local industry.

The size of generators is a problem inseparable from the capacity to produce, the supply from abroad, and the specific conditions of the subscribers. In vast areas such as some of the provinces, where the industry remains undeveloped—and especially at the two levels of region and county—medium- and small-sized plants are needed. Most of the rural areas need only generators with a capacity of several kilowatts. For this reason, the vice-minister noted, the largest percentage of generators would be those destined for the medium and small power plants.

In order to achieve the desired proliferation of small power plants in rural areas, the same vice-minister promised to reinforce the cooperation and balance of technical forces between different regions. But he realized also that it was necessary for the state to provide the necessary installations, apparatus, and technical guidance. In sum, it appears that the indicated policies of the late 1950s are very similar to those now guiding the development of small rural power stations. This development is geared, furthermore, to a proliferation of relatively small rural enterprises able to manufacture simple generators and electric turbines as discussed in the preceding section.

The local character of developmental effort is clearly spelled out in reports indicating that many localities lack manufacturing skills or perhaps the capital necessary to buy a modern water turbine made of iron and steel. Instead, they have used wood as a substitute material; this is possible within certain ranges of speed, height, and water volume. A national handbook on how to construct small power stations gives detailed instructions on how to

make wooden water turbines.[26] Eventually wooden water turbines
will be replaced by ordinary, more expensive types which can be
bought when funds have been accumulated from the profits arising
from industrial activities made possible through the introduction
of electricity. Insight into local modifications is provided by the
following county report:

> Some of the equipment for the hydroelectric stations is made
> of bamboo or wood instead of iron. The fast fluctuations in
> the flow of mountain streams had to be taken into account.
> Foreign technical literature says that power stations should
> not be built on such streams, but the peasants of Fokang
> County reduced the weight of the rotor of the water turbine
> by substituting wood for iron, modified the angle of the rotor
> blades so that the rotor was turned even by a small flow, and
> made three kinds of rotors with different blade angles to suit
> the different flow in various seasons to ensure that the stations
> operate the year around.[27]

Sometimes the locality has constructed first only the water
wheel (without a generator) which then powered only local
machines on the spot, the generator being added at a later time.
But the distribution of electricity even within a locality remains a
problem for two different reasons. First, the distribution involves
substantial capital expenditure. Second, the transmission lines
require copper or aluminum, and China's production capacity of
both metals is very limited. In order to overcome both problems,
but particularly the second, many localities have adopted the
principle of one-wire distribution with the earth-ground substi-
tuting for the second. There are disadvantages (the lessening of
safety being one), but the system appears to be widely used; some
places report that their two-wire distribution lines have been
stripped of one of the wires in order to extend the network.

Wood is a scarce commodity, and cement poles are used
throughout the country instead of wooden poles; this has considerably added to the demand for locally manufactured cement.

Some places also report that they have extended considerably the distance between poles in order to reduce the costs involved in setting up the system for the distribution of electricity. It is not clear, however, if this has been made possible through the introduction of the one-wire system.

A variety of energy sources is exploited, although coal and hydroelectric power remain the prominent ones. There are places where wind-powered machines are common. In one of the Shanghai counties and also further down the coast, there are some small tidal power stations, most of which appear to operate in both directions of tidal flow. In other places natural underground hot water is used to power small generators; natural gas is reported also to be used to meet local energy requirements.

Yet there is no indication of a revival of the former campaign to build small refineries using locally available oil shale to produce petroleum products. Reports indicate that simple methods of producing marsh gas (methane) have been widely popularized. A provincial report from central Szechwan province has mentioned that a mass campaign to operate with marsh gas has been vigorously promoted since 1970.[28] Marsh gas seems in some areas to have solved the peasants' problems of lighting fuel and to have saved coal and paraffin. Every district and commune within a particular county has a leadership group for the popularization of marsh gas, and the county has set up a special office for this work.

Another (national) report discusses the use of locally produced marsh gas, saying that communes in many parts of China are adapting simple methods for using marsh gas as fuel. A national meeting on the subject was organized by the Chinese Academy of Sciences and the Ministry of Agriculture and Forestry in a Szechwan county in 1972. Rural communes in more than a dozen provinces are now using marsh gas produced by (among other methods) fermenting grass or straw in sealed pits. The gas is used principally for cooking, but marsh gas lamps are becoming increasingly popular. The method is said to have spread to many areas remote from the electricity system.[29]

The extension of a biogas program depends heavily on official policy, but it can only be viable if costs are sufficiently reduced, operation is made simple, and the return on resources spent (capital and labor) is sufficiently rewarding to those engaged in farming.[30]

A New China News Agency report clearly points out that "because of the leaders' attention and personal participation, use of marsh gas has also been quickly developed in some counties and communes." The same report clearly indicates that meetings such as the national conference in Szechwan to exchange experience on the exploitation and popularization of marsh gas—organized in mid-1975 by the State Planning Commission, the Chinese Academy of Sciences, and the Ministry of Agriculture and Forestry—play an important role. However, more pertinent information may be found in the following sentences. "In recent years, construction of marsh gas containers has become simpler and cheaper. The amount of cement used for making one container has been reduced to less than 300 catties (150 kg.) from about 800 catties (400 kg.) in the past. Some containers are made entirely of concrete. The cost of building a container has also dropped to some 40 yuan now from more than 100 yuan before." This may be a major reason why "over the past few years, over 410,000 marsh gas containers have been built throughout the province (Szechwan)." (FE/W834/A/14.)

Leadership and Infrastructure

A rapid development of local industry in rural areas appears to be essential for further development of agriculture, but in many areas it is also a consequence of the favorable development of agricultural production in recent years. Improved seeds and their popularization through agricultural scientific networks have, together with increased irrigation and more fertilizers, considerably increased yields per acre in many areas. This has two important consequences. First, increased grain yields have made it possible to expand the acreage available for industrial crops, thus supplying industry with more raw material. Second, through increased agricultural production, purchasing power and the potential for savings and investments have increased. The peasants can thus buy more agricultural inputs, such as agrochemicals and machinery, which in turn will further decrease labor intensity.

The initial development of agricultural production would then appear to be an important prerequisite for starting rural industries. However, such development has not been evenly spread, and it has been reported from Hengtung county,[31] for example, that, since leadership paid attention to progressive units only and disregarded giving specific assistance to backward communes and brigades, the 13 comparatively backward communes in the county did not undergo a major transformation, although production developed greatly in the remaining 26 communes. The county then sent about 1,250 cadres to stay at 853 production teams in 101 brigades in the relatively backward communes. The people sent included political and administrative as well as technical personnel. As a result, it was reported, the backward communes and brigades were quickly trans- formed. The strengthening of leadership in these areas resulted in an increase of total grain production in the county of 29.8 percent in 1970 over 1969. According to the same report, improvement in the leadership of backward brigades was carried out on a wide geographical basis. Since the beginning of 1971, it was said that leading cadres of counties, districts, and communes in the Hengtung region had led about 6,000 office cadres to stay at a total of 1,453 rather backward brigades which constituted one-third of the total brigades in the region.[32] They gave education in ideology and politi- cal line for basic-level cadres and commune members, and these units were said to have improved remarkably in only a short period, with grain output increasing 15–30 percent over 1970.

China's success in agricultural development has, to a large degree, been based on the tremendous authority of the central political leadership. This leadership has had the power to lead land reform and collectivization, to reorient industrial development so that it emphasizes agricultural inputs, to define the broad incentive system, to orient many bureaucrats to serve better the needs of people in rural areas.[33]

The introduction and acceptance of new rural industries and new technologies often seem to require a special type of leadership, even though some mechanisms can be devised to encourage their automatic acceptance. Conscious decisions to promote rural industries and to foster technologies appropriate to rural areas take a vast amount of political will on the part of government and party leaders, because of the strong urban bias which has apparently been a serious problem in China. Furthermore, the type of technological development chosen will play a large part in determining the nature of the society that emerges. This point is relevant to Mao Tse-tung's Cultural Revolution letter of May 7, 1966,[34] where he points out:

> While the main task of the peasants in the communes is agriculture . . . they should at the same time study military affairs, politics, and culture. Where conditions permit, they should collectively run small plants . . . Where conditions permit, those working in commerce, in service trades, and Party and government organizations should do the same.

This directive has usually been interpreted as an indication of Mao's fascination with the issue of creating a "new man" in China. However, it may be appropriate to look at those instructions as a tool, one among many, to create more relevant knowledge and attitudes for a development strategy which, to a considerable extent, must be based on local interdisciplinary planning.

Attempts to delegate planning authority to local communities have, in many countries, produced unsatisfactory results. This has partly been due to lack of technical skills or resources, or both, but the failure is basically a political one. It appears that an important consequence of the Cultural Revolution in China is that skills and resources are more quickly developed in the countryside to enable local overall planning than would otherwise be the case. While broad strategies and policies must be centrally determined, wide authority has been delegated to the localities to plan for themselves. But to make the decentralized approach work, the central planners—at all levels—must have a full understanding of the relevance of local developments. Similarly, diversification in the countryside means that more and more people are moving into new activities, and consequently peasants need the knowledge and attitudes appropriate to their new tasks.

At the same time, urban-based industry is increasingly drawn into interaction with rural industry. If these relations are to develop favorably, the people in all sectors must have a thorough understanding and knowledge about each other's conditions and activities which can only be obtained through a combination of study and experience. Thus, Mao's directive of 7 May 1966 may be seen primarily as a measure designed to foster attitudes and create knowledge that are interfunctional in character and appropriate for the present stage of development in China. The necessity to know all sides of multi-sector planning applies, of course, still more to officials at all levels. The need for a better understanding of the countryside's requirements was, of course, recognized long before the Cultural Revolution, which is evident from the following *Peking Daily* editorial in 1960:

Acceleration of the pace of agricultural development is the central link in the proportional development of the whole economy at high speed. The organization of the flow of cadres between cities and the countryside, first of all the organization of a number of urban cadres to go to the countryside by turns to give aid and support to technical transformation of agriculture, is a new kind of development for the revolutionary tradition of the party ... *As a result* of the selection of cadres for dispatch to the countryside, the *different aid-giving units are able to understand the needs of agriculture better,* and are therefore able to give better aid and support to agriculture in all kinds of work ... The flow of cadres between cities and the countryside is also a political measure for further strengthening the alliance of workers and peasants.[35] [italics added]

Rural industries in China are part of a comprehensive effort to achieve economic, social, and political development of rural areas all over the country. Consequently, policies to extend appropriate services have been necessary and have formed integral parts of the rural development programs in China. In the earlier discus-

sion, it became clear that the multi-level local science and technology system is an important tool for a rapid introduction of new
agricultural technology. Similarly, it was shown that the multi-level
engineering sector in rural areas functions as a network of industrial extension services, which enables a rapid introduction of
industrial technologies. Furthermore, the availability of electricity
is also a prerequisite for almost any industrial activity.

In addition to services already mentioned, the following are
also important for a variety of reasons:

1. Education
2. Public health
3. Communications
   — postal network
   — telephone and telegraph network
   — wirebroadcasting network
4. Physical transportation
   — lorry services (goods)
   — bus services (passengers)

In comparison with the large cities, rural areas were neglected in
the development of such services which are important in themselves
in providing equal opportunities for the rural population. On the
assumption that a majority of the Chinese population will have to
stay in rural areas for a considerable period of time, it was for political reasons necessary to reduce the differential between urban and
rural areas.[36] At the same time, the kind of pattern of rural industrialization previously discussed is hardly possible without integrated
development and expansion of services. Young people must have a
fairly comprehensive education in order to work with relatively
complex technologies in agriculture and industry, and the education
must be to a certain degree adapted to the local needs. The labor
force must be freed from malnutrition and disease in order to be
efficient and in order to reduce nonattendance due to illness. The
communications and transportation services are no doubt necessary
for providing efficient links within the locality, but also for an
efficient interchange of ideas, instructions, and goods with the
outside.

But the localities have been lacking in the resources required for establishing the necessary services. Initially, the central government—and the cities—have in different forms subsidized the setting up of services in rural areas. This may be particularly true for education, public health, and agricultural and industrial extension services.[37] But the managerial responsibilities for most of the services have been transferred to the counties. The further expansion has to a large extent been made dependent on local recruitment of personnel and extensive use of paratechnical personnel in almost all the services. This has considerably reduced costs for training and for wages, and has made it possible for rural areas to support financially services which would not have been possible if they had been based on previous city-based practices.[38]

Certain characteristics of the public health, agricultural extension, and machinery repair services are listed in Table 27. An important feature—based on the use of paratechnical personnel—is the pyramid structure of services. This makes it possible to treat large numbers of patients and take care of the large numbers of problems at low-level units, where average costs of treatment per illness per person or average costs per problem solved are generally much lower than in the more specialized—and more distant—units higher up in the hierarchy.

Another very important consideration is that improved education, improved public health, and improved communications and transportation are all desired by the local population. The introduction and development of such services come simultaneously with the introduction of new agricultural technologies and rural industrialization, and the services promote directly or indirectly the productivity in both the agricultural and industrial sector. Thus, the localities provide the financial capability to further improve their services and this consequently represents an important part of the incentive structure.

Industrial Coordination and Regional Balance

The pattern of distribution of capital, industrial knowledge, and services has far-reaching consequences for income distribution

Table 27. Characteristics of Some Infrastructure Services
in Rural Areas in China (at county level and below)

	Public Health	Agricultural Extension and Seed Selection	Machinery Repair and Manufacture
Main feature	Preventive medicine	Local adaptions	Preventive repair and maintenance
Structure	Pyramid—3 levels — county — commune — brigade	Pyramid—4 levels — county — commune — brigade — team	Pyramid—3 levels — county — commune — brigade
Problem-solving	Network Minor cases treated within brigade. Complex ones transferred upwards	Network	Network Minor repairs within brigade. Complex ones transferred upwards
Personnel	Paratechnical training Local recruits (barefoot doctors) and sent-down specialists	Paratechnical training Local recruits and sent-down specialists	Paratechnical training Local recruits (barefoot technicians) and sent-down specialists
Technology	Capital-saving		Capital-saving
Wages	Local wages—work points	Local wages—work points	Local wages—work points
Other cost factors	Less transportation "Cheaper and faster" Use of locally grown medicinal herbs	Earlier introduction	Less transportation "Cheaper and faster"

in rural areas and is likely to have further consequences for the
political and social structure of the country. So it is of interest to
find out if it is an objective to achieve a regional balance in rural
industrialization and, if so, the means for achieving this. It has
already been suggested that the existence of strong local political
leadership is of great importance in initiating economic and indus-

trial development. But leadership in isolation is not sufficient to check regional differences.

No doubt, local initiative has been much stressed in Chinese rural economic planning. This may have favored the development of areas already well-developed, particularly in the initial stages of local development. However, there are means at the disposal of the center (meaning region, province, or nation) to guide the distribution of industrial activity and thus the distribution of income. There can be no doubt that the question of regional balance and regional variations, because of its political implications, has received serious attention.

China is today developing a high level of machine labor skills and factory discipline in previously nonindustrialized areas. A pool of experienced engineering and technical skills is gradually being developed in many localities. The use of old machinery is often— initially—both the justification for this approach and the necessary training ground. The transfer of used equipment from large and modern to smaller and more primitive enterprises has been quite substantial in recent years and is likely to be an important factor in explaining the fairly rapid development of industrial skills in many places in rural China.

The rural areas in China have in recent years greatly benefited from the creation of formal networks for different purposes, and technology transfer takes place within these networks. The machine-building network in Hopei which, it is proposed, will be organized as in Figure 16, can be taken as an example.[39] The province has two different networks, one for the production of complex products like diesel engines, tractors, and vehicles for use in rural areas, and one for the repairing and building of farm machinery and other products almost exclusively used within the counties. The two networks interlock at the county levels, as Figure 16 indicates. The services and products provided from the networks are important in influencing the productivity and consequently income distribution of a locality.

The more advanced rural industries appear to play an increasingly important role in industrial networks where a larger number

Figure 16. Machine-Building Network

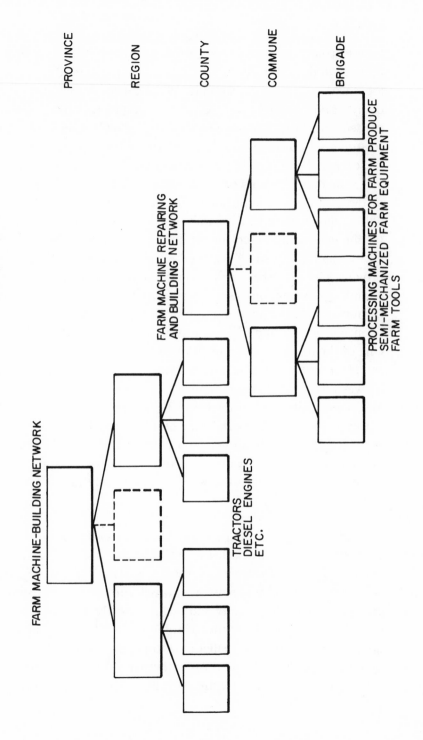

PROVINCE

REGION

COUNTY

COMMUNE

BRIGADE

FARM MACHINE-BUILDING NETWORK

FARM MACHINE REPAIRING AND BUILDING NETWORK

TRACTORS
DIESEL ENGINES
ETC.

PROCESSING MACHINES FOR FARM PRODUCE
SEMI-MECHANIZED FARM EQUIPMENT
FARM TOOLS

of enterprises are coordinated for specific industrial projects. Thus, in industrially developed areas, rural industry is able to participate in up-to-date, high technology levels of industrial production. In areas with a relatively weak industrial foundation the same type of coordination enables rural industry to raise its technical level. As a consequence, many small enterprises are quickly drawn into close relations with other units of a network, and in this process manufacturing adaptation and management skills are developed.

The coordination concept is used for the manufacture of different types of complicated machinery and equipment, which will be shown through a number of examples. The coordination technique is mainly used for comprehensive production, and the motor vehicle industry[40] is a good example of this. Hitherto, most provinces have not been able to manufacture motor vehicles because complete sets of equipment and advanced techniques were required throughout the production process. However, today more than twenty provinces and municipalities can produce cars and trucks. One of the important factors in the development of the motor vehicle industry in China has been the extended use of coordination between large numbers of plants. On the basis of the experience in mass coordination when the Great Leap Forward began in 1958, automobile repair shops, machine building factories, and other small and large plants formed a coordinating network within a province or within a large municipality. The network appears usually to be made up of enterprises which are geographically fairly concentrated.

The networks for the manufacture of trucks may still not be very important when their production capacity is compared with the four or five big truck plants in China. But it should be remembered that a few of the new relatively big plants started in a similar way as the now existing networks, which provide a basis for upgrading production capacity and quality. Furthermore, once a coordination network for the manufacture of vehicles has been set up in a province or in a smaller area, the network provides a knowledge pool which can be used for a number of purposes. The following examples may illustrate different possibilities of the network concept.

China reported in September 1970 that the policy of the simultaneous development of national and local industry has given great impetus to the local motor vehicle industry.[41] Most provinces, municipalities, and autonomous regions, the report stated, are now making motor vehicles of various capacities. A number of towns and administrative regions in Kiangsi, Shantung, Fukien, Yunnan, and other provinces had at the time successfully produced vehicles suited to the local needs. Local motor vehicle industry was in many places able to make basic components such as engines, gear boxes, front and rear axles, chassis and bodies, and 80–90 percent of the accessories. In Yunnan 80 factories were organized to pool part of their resources in order to produce vehicles. At the end of 1970 Yunnan Motor Vehicle Works had built 141 Kunming trucks. Before 1970 no motor vehicles had been built in the province— according to a report. Provincial departments in Yunnan had organized the manufacture of components and parts in various localities.[42] The development of a motor vehicle industry in Chinghai —a province with a weak industrial foundation—was pursued along similar lines. At the end of 1969, 37 factories started to cooperate in the manufacture of motor vehicles—Chinghai Lake trucks.[43] As a consequence, the first heavy-duty truck was produced in the province in spring 1970—without a special plant being built for that purpose.[44]

A provincial report from Chinghai later on pointed out that, since the serial production of the Chinghai Lake truck started, it had become necessary to further develop the technical potential of the commune-run and brigade-run industries and to further promote an exchange of technical information and industrial experience.[45] Some of the small plants which had been organized for serial production—of components and parts—had run into difficulties due to a lack of machinery. But this problem had been solved after the larger plants provided the small enterprises with badly needed machinery.

Another example is that of Szechwan where the production of two new types of tractors through the combined effort of ninety-three factories was initiated in 1970.[46] A similar example but on a smaller scale is reported from Chengchow city in Honan, where, in

1970, small farm trucks were trial-produced which later led to serial production through the cooperation of more than 30 small- and medium-sized factories.[47] Similarly, the same city has organized serial production of a 12-hp. power tiller—involving a much smaller number of enterprises.

All the regions in Honan—eight in all—were by the middle of 1971 able to make diesel engines by interfactory cooperation.[48] In a region in another province—Shantung—forty-eight small industrial units were organized for the manufacture of a small diesel engine— type 195.[49] In a number of places the manufacturing capability for diesel engines and small tractors is found within the counties, which is the case in many places in Kiangsi. In yet another province— Hopei—there appears to be an emphasis on using certain enterprises for subcontracting instead of integrating them into the cooperative network. In 1970 a total of thirty-five industrial enterprises in ten regions were commissioned to manufacture components in order to increase output of Tungfeng trucks being produced in the province.[50]

The coordination of a relatively large number of enterprises to produce complicated end-products is not limited to the manufacture of trucks, tractors, and diesel engines. Shanghai, for example, has organized more than a hundred factories for a joint effort for the manufacture of high-capacity generating units.[51] Similar coordination has also been organized in the cities of Peking, Tientsin, Harbin, and also a number of other cities and provinces. In provinces and cities which are industrially less advanced, the same approach has been used for producing small and less complicated equipment. The Provincial Revolutionary Committee in Kiangsi, for example, organized twenty-four factories in 1970 to coordinate the manufacture of hydroelectric equipment.[52] In certain provinces where power-generating industry has developed rapidly—like Kwangtung—the majority of counties can independently produce small power-generating equipment.

Another interesting example is the gradual diffusion of the capability to manufacture complete equipment for small-scale fertilizer plants. Shanghai was at the beginning of 1970 assigned to make the major equipment for small chemical fertilizer plants. But the dozen factories specializing in making chemical engineering equipment were fully engaged for a couple of years. But then a large number of industrial units—a total of over 400—were coordinated to make the equipment for small-scale fertilizer plants.[53] The following year it was reported from Kiangsu, which borders on Shanghai, that by far the greater part of the equipment for the small fertilizer plants was produced by local engineering plants. Under the unified planning of the Provincial Revolutionary Committee, dozens of general machinery works cooperated in producing equipment for the chemical industry. Kiangsu has also set up twelve specialized machine-building plants and trained large numbers of designers and building workers for the purpose.[54]

Honan also reported in 1971 that in the course of developing chemical fertilizer industry it had developed the capability to make production equipment locally.[55] Since locally run small works had experienced difficulties in building production equipment, the Provincial Revolutionary Committee had organized factories and communes. As part of this coordination many small works had accepted the task of making valves and other machine parts. And the province had over a period of two years turned out over fifty sets of chemical fertilizer manufacturing equipment and basically met its needs in building small chemical fertilizer works. Similarly, several other provinces have also developed a capability to produce complete sets of equipment for the small-scale fertilizer plants.

The use of the coordination concept in the manufacture of complex equipment appears to be justified on a number of counts. First, China wants to use the industrial bases primarily geared to the needs of agriculture in order to achieve a dispersal of industrial activity, which better corresponds to the distribution of population and natural resources than is the case at present. Second, China may also want to achieve a geographical dispersal of industrial activity to make the country less vulnerable in case the main urban centers were to be attacked by an enemy. Third, it appears that reduction of manufacturing scale and the use of local engineering enterprises make it possible to reduce the contents of imported equipment going into a plant. Fourth, it is likely that China wants to substitute labor for capital whenever possible. It should be noted that the production of vehicle parts usually is undertaken in multi-purpose subcontracting units. This makes it possible to achieve flexibility in the use of manpower and equipment. The manufacture of different parts can be assigned to the unit best qualified and equipped for the task of choosing among a large number of units. Thus the use of a coordination network may enable substitution of labor for capital.

There may be other important reasons for choosing the coordination approach in manufacturing vehicles. If comprehensive vehicle plants were built with modern automatic machines, it is possible that demand might be inadequate in relation to the high initial output of modern technology plants. The coordination approach enables a gradual development of vehicle design and a gradual development of productivity equipment and of the necessary raw material supply system. And the coordination also enables a fairly flexible interaction of production factors. Thus it becomes easier to strike an appropriate—and changing—balance between the use of capital and labor in decisions regarding equipment, manpower, and raw material.

A further reason for the coordination approach is the elimination of the risk that knowledge is monopolized within comprehensive industrial units. The coordination concept requires that knowledge relating to designs and manufacturing technologies be shared whenever needed. This may, however, require new management techniques where long-term political and economic goals are more important than short-term economic or technical performance of an individual enterprise. Some of the changes of enterprise management during the Cultural Revolution may partly be explained on this basis.

For further industrialization, it is essential that quality standards be set and standardization encouraged so that local industrial systems can eventually fit into the national industrial structure. The local distribution of industrial products—from local manufacturing units—within a geographically small area is likely to make feedback mechanisms work efficiently to improve the quality of poor products. But coordination networks are essential for drawing a number of small enterprises into working relations with quality- and standardization-conscious enterprises. It also appears that the center encourages the development of strict standards through placing orders with county-run and commune-run enterprises for products at prices which enable local enterprises to make a profit.

There are also a number of other instruments the center (region, province, or nation) can use or is using to achieve a balanced economic development. The center will continue to control the admission of students to institutions of higher learning and is also likely to control the allocation of highly skilled manpower. As more and more sophisticated skills are needed for local industrialization in communes and counties, the center will be able within certain limits to use the admission of students and the allocation of skilled personnel as a means to guide local development.

Another equalization mechanism appears to play an important role. Income above a certain level will to a considerable extent be spent on consumer goods which—if the definition is stretched—can be termed luxury goods. The pricing of these consumer goods has been designed to achieve a considerable surplus at the higher levels of the rural industrial-economic hierarchy. The surplus is—among other things—used to expand services and industrial activities, including those at the lower levels. Consequently, members of the economically more advanced units will subsidize the development of productivity-increasing services in the less advanced localities.

The distribution of skilled manpower and equipment may also present means by which the center coordinates central and local planning. A county industrial system is never likely to manufacture special alloy steels or specialized bearings, but such products will be increasingly needed in the future. These, and other similar items, are likely to be manufactured only by some of the national enterprises at the top of industrial hierarchy. As specialized equipment is demanded by local industry, the localities will become increasingly dependent on the center for the allocation of certain critical equipment. It should also be remembered that the center is in control of imported technology, which for a number of purposes eventually will be required in local industries.

The control of investment funds may, however, be one of the more important means of controlling the geographical distribution of industrial activities. Investment in new local process plants, such as iron plants or chemical fertilizer plants, and the expansion of such plants is usually of a magnitude beyond the capacity of the local level. Similarly, the distribution of electricity and the provision of feeder lines from the main networks can become another way of forcing coordination between local and central planning. Despite this possibility of subsidization, however, the general policy is that local industry should be built on a sound technical and economic basis. But the effect of widely differing conditions for starting local industry on the level of investment and planning is clear in this remark from Hunan province:

> Some counties have developed agriculture comparatively rapidly and have surpluses and ample raw materials, so more industry is run there; where that is not the case, not so much industry is run. Some counties have a rather weak industrial foundation and so the region builds more factories there. Some counties have industries run by the center or the province, so the region runs none at all or not many factories there.[56]

It is evident that certain measures have been taken to achieve a more equal distribution than otherwise would have been the case. It is also evident from the comment that there exists—in this particular area—a positive correlation between agricultural development and opportunities to establish local industries.

A further illustration of at least an intent in implementing a policy for more equal distribution of industrial activity comes from Kiangsu in the south bordering on Shanghai which, with one percent of the population, covers about 10 percent of the total industrial production in China.[57] "Kiangsu industrial departments are putting emphasis on building new industrial enterprises in various counties, particularly in the North part of the province which was short of industry in the past."

But it is not always possible to promote a wide geographical distribution of industrial enterprises when the objective conditions are not available. This problem was discussed in a *Red Flag* article on relations between agriculture and industry which stated: "As for those small industries which failed to follow the correct orientation and whose raw materials, fuel, and electric power were not definitely available, they were not allowed to continue their building."[58]

The availability of fuel and electric power can certainly be influenced in the long run. Measures to influence conditions affecting the feasibility of rural industry have been discussed in the section on technologies. There are also examples among the Chinese reports on rural industrialization indicating that the raw material situation can be influenced. Tangshan region informs us that "an overall arrangement has been made to coordinate iron mines and plants in production and in providing counties and communes, which have shortages of mineral resources, with raw materials for producing farm tools."[59] A critical problem for a large number of the plants will still be the availability of capital. This applies to all the small-scale rural enterprises that fall into the heavy-industry category. An important aspect of this problem is stated in the earlier mentioned report from Hunan: "The development of iron and steel, chemical fertilizer, and farm machinery industries needs a lot of investment and produces little profit. For a short time, they may even run at a loss."[60] However, the operation of rural industrial system has to be seen as a whole and some plants may have to run at a loss.

Chapter 4

EXAMPLES OF SMALL-SCALE PLANTS
IN SOME IMPORTANT INDUSTRIAL SECTORS

The lower end of the industrial spectrum—the small industries in various sectors—is justified for a number of reasons. The main ones are foreign currency savings, transportation savings, improved raw material utilization, resource mobilization, and the industrial training impact for changing the mentality in rural areas to support future industrialization.

The justification varies from sector to sector even if the various reasons each have some importance in most sectors. An attempt will be made to illustrate some of the reasons which have been most pronounced in five sectors—chemical fertilizer, cement, farm machinery and engineering, iron and steel, and paper.

The present stage of production technology for small plants has been reached through a gradual process. Central research and design institutes are likely to have played an important role in the initial stages, but local plants are now an important source for improvements and incremental innovations. Very small process plants may not be set up in the future, as the country's economic development would remove or change constraints with regard to limited availability of equipment, market size, and the necessity to utilize local raw materials which today favor the small plants.

Small nitrogen fertilizer plants have been justified because of foreign currency constraints in combination with constraints resulting from the relatively undeveloped engineering capability for large process plants. Small cement plants, on the other hand, appear to be justified mainly because of transportation costs, a reflection of the still undeveloped capability to manufacture more efficient transport equipment and road-building equipment. In both sectors, the impact on employment and the training of large numbers of people in technical and organizational skills provide further justification.

133

Mechanical technology covers almost every aspect of industrialization. However, small-scale plants appear to be justified for two major reasons. First, certain machinery and equipment is more easily provided by small local plants. Second, the badly needed combination of deliveries with service and maintenance can most easily be achieved with an industrial structure consisting of many small local plants.

Iron and steel production in small-scale plants is today becoming less important because of the rapid expansion of medium and very large plants. Small paper plants are more important for raw material utilization than is the case in chemical fertilizer and cement production. This, of course, relates to a desire to minimize foreign expenditure for buying pulp and paper.

Chemical Fertilizer[1]

The number of small-scale chemical fertilizer plants was in early 1974 around 1,800 of which approximately 1,000 were producing nitrogen fertilizer and the others phosphate fertilizer. This discussion will be limited to the role of small nitrogen fertilizer plants.

Small-scale chemical fertilizer plants were first set up during the Great Leap Forward in the late 1950s. Most of them were, however, at least temporarily closed down because of economic difficulties. After the rehabilitation of the economy in the early 1960s, the central government again started to pursue a policy of decentralization of fertilizer production by encouraging the construction of very small fertilizer plants with an annual production usually of less than 10,000 tons of ammonia. Almost all now-existing small nitrogen fertilizer plants produce ammonia as an intermediate product, which is then converted into ammonium bicarbonate (NH_4HCO_3).

When coal is used, typically the raw material for small nitrogen fertilizer plants, the main production stages are as follows:

1. Gas generation—steam and air alternatively blown over burning coal
2. Separation of carbon oxide and hydrogen

3. Compression of hydrogen
4. Refining
5. NH_3 conversion
6. Conversion into solid fertilizer (carbon oxide utilized)
7. Packing

The plants of the late 1960s and early 1970s are similar to those first built in the late 1950s and early 1960s. At that time, the technology was not sufficiently good to make them a successful venture. Another serious hindrance may have been the unavailability of trained manpower. The conditions during the late 1960s were much better and made it possible for the plants to be constructed in large numbers and to operate with reasonable efficiency.

Consequently the share of the small-scale plants has increased rapidly from about 12 percent in 1965 to 54 percent in 1973 of a total nitrogen production of 15 million tons with nutrient content of roughly 20 percent.[2] The share of small-scale plants may continue to increase for another year or two and will then drop drastically for reasons that will become apparent in the following discussion. The small-scale plants stand for a considerably larger share of phosphate fertilizer production with around 75 percent in 1973. Economies of scale are less pronounced for the types of phosphate fertilizer usually produced in small-scale plants in China today. The development of the small-scale phosphate and nitrogen fertilizer plants—as shares of total production in recent years—is available in Table 28.

The small plants differ considerably in size. The idea of small nitrogen fertilizer plants originated in the new economic planning of the late 1950s which manifested itself in two different development approaches. First, that counties and regions should establish their own relatively larger small fertilizer factories. Second, that fertilizer production and almost any industrial activity should be located in the people's communes established in the autumn of 1958. The latter approach was thought to justify a considerable smaller plant—with an annual production of 800 tons of ammonia. Technical deficiencies and the very high costs of production led to the closing down and redesign of these very small plants. With very few exceptions small plants were also transferred to county-level

136

Table 28. Estimated Chemical

Year	Total Nitrogen and Phosphate	Nitrogen	Phosphate
1965			
1966			
1967			
1968			
1969	9.68		
1970	14.00[a]		
1971	16.83[a] (+20.2%)[b]	9.67	7.16
1972	19.88[a] (+18.1%)[c]	11.93 (+23.4%)[c]	7.95 (+10.9%)[c]
1973	25.00 (25.8%)	15.00	10.00
1974			

Source: The underlined figures and percentages have at various times been published by
Chinese news media but are somewhat ambiguous. All others are estimates based
on the reported information. The estimates are, furthermore, based on the assumption that the production figure in 1971--14 million tons—as reported by premier
Chou En-lai to Edgar Snow in 1971 is more or less correct. However, others using
the same figures may be able to construct a different table—but not very much
different.

a. "Between 1970 and 1972, the rise in China's chemical fertilization industry averaged
3.4 million tons annually." (*Peking Review*, May 18, 1973).
b. *Peking Review*, January 14, 1972.
c. FE/W756/A/15. ("Production of phosphate-fertilizer also expanded rapidly. It made
up some 40% of China's total chemical fertilizer output.")
d. "Total production in the period January–November 1973 was reported to be 25.8%
higher than in the corresponding period of 1972" (New China News Agency, December 12, 1973).

control. The other two basic designs of the Great Leap Forward
period have also undergone changes.[3] The smaller one has been
expanded to a standardized unit of 3,000 tons capacity. A plant of
this size is usually expanded to an annual production of 5,000 tons
ammonia as soon as the demand develops and the technical problems have been overcome. Considerably larger plants with an annual
production capacity of 10,000–15,000 tons are today found mainly
in counties that are economically well developed and cover relatively larger areas—which is the case in certain places in the Kwangtung province in the south, and in rural areas of Shanghai. The
different plant sizes are listed in Table 29.

Information in Table 28 shows that the average size of the

Fertilizer Production in China (in metric tons) (Table 28, *continued*)

Small-Scale Production

Nitrogen and Phospate			Nitrogen			Phosphate		
Total	Per-centage	No. of Plants	Total	Per-centage	No. of Plants	Total	Per-centage	No. of Plants
			1.38^g	$\underline{12^i}$				
10.00	$\approx 60^e$		4.15^g	$\underline{\overset{\approx 40^j}{43^k}}$	<700	≈ 5.85	≈ 82	
11.93	$\approx 60^f$	$\approx 1.400^f$	5.97	$>\underline{50^c}$	$>800^m$	≈ 5.96	≈ 75	≈ 600
15.50	62		8.00^h	$\underline{54^l}$	$\approx 1.000^n$	7.50	$\underline{75^o}$	

e. "New Leap in China's National Economy" (*Peking Review*, January 14, 1972).
f. FE/W723/A/9.
g. FE/W673/A/5. ("Small synthetic ammonia enterprises . . . production last year [1971] was more than treble that of 1966.")
h. Production of nitrogen chemical fertilizer in small-scale plants for the period January 1–November 24, 1973 was reported to be 33% higher than in the corresponding period of 1972 (FE/W762/A/15).
i. New China News Agency, December 27, 1970.
j. FE/W642/A/2.   m. FE/W740/A/7, FE/W748/A/11.
k. FE/W698/A/16.   n. FE/W756/A/15.
l. FE/W756/A/15.   o. FE/W748/A/12.

small plants producing ammonium bicarbonate has increased during the past few years. The average production which in 1971 was somewhat above 5,500 tons had in 1972 increased to almost 7,500. In 1973 it was 8,000 tons. The increase in the annual production of small plants reflects a number of different contributing factors. All new small plants now have a designed capacity of 12,000 tons ammonium bicarbonate. Many of the older plants with an annual capacity of 3,200 tons or 8,000 tons of ammonium bicarbonate are still being expanded, one by one. Finally, the overall efficiency of the plants is increasing all the time. So further production increase in the small plants will result from improved efficiency, expansion of existing plants, and the building of new plants.

Small-scale nitrogen fertilizer plants are today found almost everywhere in China. A few plants may even have been located where raw material is not available, where the technical base does

138

Table 29. Small-Scale Nitrogen Fertilizer Plants

Size (annual produc-
tion of ammonia)

800 tons	Great Leap Forward design for commune-level plants
2,000 tons	Standard design in 1958 for county-level plants
3,000 tons	Standard design in 1960s and 1970s for county-level plants
5,000 tons	Modified version of the 3,000-ton plant (expansion is usually carried out in a second stage)
8,000 tons	Standard design in 1958 for region-level plants

not exist, or where other necessary conditions for an efficient use are absent. However, small plants appear, on the whole, to have been well located. The setting up of new plants now requires a careful screening procedure at provincial level after the national authorities have made their allocation of plants to the various provinces. All the following points are usually taken into account when the provincial authorities decide if a particular county should set up a small nitrogen fertilizer plant or not:

1. Size of the county (= market)
2. Need rapidly to increase agricultural production (potential results)
3. Availability of industrial knowledge in order to guarantee production
4. Availability of (irrigation) water to guarantee efficient use
5. Access to electricity and process water
6. Access to transportation for raw materials and finished products
7. Ratio between cultivated area and population. A high ratio usually gives priority because of difficulties in providing sufficient amounts of manure.

The policy of decentralization of fertilizer production has had the effect of reducing cost to the central government and placing some of the burden on the rural areas from where part of necessary finance was obtained. The policy of small-plant construction was formulated in order to utilize local resources to an increasing extent and to relieve the transport system of as much fertilizer material as feasible. The plants were to produce simple fertilizers such as ammonium bicarbonate, ground rock phosphate, or fused phosphate and to require a minimum of raw materials from elsewhere. Their construction, of course, involved the use of equipment manufactured in more or less centralized workshops and the services of technicians from elsewhere but, once the staff was trained and the plant started up, the new production facility was expected to be run by local people, using local raw materials. In the main this policy appears to have been followed, and there is little doubt that it has—like many of the other small-scale plants—greatly stimulated local initiatives in the development of the country's resources.

The proper choice of raw material is a critical factor in minimizing the burden on the transport system and maximizing the use of local resources. Consequently, the small-scale fertilizer plants have been designed for different raw materials such as coke, brown coal, and coke oven gas which were the traditional raw materials in the late 1950s and early 1960s. Most of the early small plants were designed to use coke, which must be viewed in the light of the very rapid proliferation of local coke ovens, a movement tied in at the time with the local manufacture of iron and steel. However, the design has been modified to accommodate high quality coal and eventually coal powder and low qualities of coal available in the south. Without these design changes the small plants would have become dependent on raw materials from the outside with resulting increased production costs. The rapid development of the petroleum industry is once more changing the raw material situation. A number of small-scale fertilizer plants located near refineries are now contemplating the switchover to petroleum feedstock.

The choice of raw material has consequences for investment costs and consequently for production costs. It appears—in the absence of petroleum feedstock—that coke would give the lowest investment per ton finished product. A plant producing 2,000 tons ammonia or 8,000 tons ammonium bicarbonate per year would require an investment of 295 yuan per ton of finished product if based on coke. The investment per ton would be 388 yuan if the production were based on brown coal. See Table 30 for further information on raw material and fuel consumption, number of workers, and production per worker in small-scale plants of different sizes and using different raw materials. This information is taken from a handbook on industrial planning published in 1963 but mainly based on figures relating to the situation in early 1958.

The Chinese planners quickly realized that *very* small plants were uneconomical—even if all external benefits were considered; they are consequently not included in this handbook. The figures still show that economies of scale are not unimportant for the larger plants. The investment figure drops from 295 yuan per ton for a plant producing 8,000 tons of ammonium bicarbonate to 239 yuan per ton for a plant producing 40,000 tons per year—if production is based on coke. The figures are 388 yuan and 299 yuan respectively if production is based on brown coal. Investment figures for process industry for plant sizes with a ratio of 1:5 would in other countries usually differ much more than the Chinese figures given here. There may be two not mutually exclusive explanations for this. First, the pricing of the equipment for plants of different sizes may in China have been done in such a way that the small plants are subsidized. Second, the engineering and construction enterprises may in the past have been less able than their counterparts in Japan, the United States, and Sweden to utilize the inherent economies of scale in process industry. Such a fact—if true—would then clearly have helped to tilt the balance towards a choice of producing chemical fertilizer in relatively small plants.

The rather small differences in investment per ton finished product for plants of different sizes are further documented in Table 31. The figures here show that the investment per ton ammonium sulphate drops from 360 yuan for a plant producing 7,600 tons to 235 yuan for a plant producing 210,000 tons per year—which is almost 30 times as much. The ratio for investment costs per ton is then 100:65. Production of ammonia is in this case based on coke. Table 31 further gives the investment figures for production based on brown coal as 457 yuan and 270 yuan respectively, which gives a ratio of 100:59. There can be no doubt

Table 30. Production of Nitrogen Fertilizer (NH_4HCO_3) in Small-Scale Plants

Annual Production	Raw Material		Fuel Consumption (coal) (tons)	No. of Workers	Investment			Production Per Worker (tons)
	Type	Amount			Total (million)	Per Ton	Per Worker	
8,000	coke	3,400 tons	3,300	193	2.36	295	12,228	41
40,000	coke	16,100 tons	17,400	327	9.54	239	29,174	122
8,000	brown coal	9,200 tons	3,300	193	3.10	388	16,062	41
40,000	brown coal	36,400 tons	14,500	420	11.96	299	28,476	95
40,000	coke oven gas	3,000m³/h	7,300	430	10.46	262	24,326	93
40,000	coke oven gas (refrigerated)	6,000m³/h	4,400	400	10.46	262	26,150	100

Source: *Site and Transport Planning for Industrial Enterprises*, compiled by Peking Industrial Construction Planning Bureau, Ministry of Construction and Engineering, Peking, 1963.

that the ratio for process plants with a production capacity range of almost 1–30 would have been much greater in any other industrial country. These figures relate to the early 1960s and by necessity reflect the conditions of the industrial base in China at the time. However, it may be safe to assume that the capacity for China to manufacture large process plants in the early 1960s and even later has been rather limited and that this continues to be at least partly reflected in the pricing of equipment for process plants.

It must then be relevant to find out the relationship between investment costs and production costs. Relatively little information is available, and fragmentary information from a small plant visited by the author on two occasions—in December 1971 and July 1973 —has been used here as an illustration. The figures relate to a small plant with a designed capacity of approximately 12,000 tons of ammonium bicarbonate. Actual production was slightly less— 11,000 tons in 1973. Ex-factory price is 150 yuan per ton. Total coal consumption was reported to be 9,000 tons at a price of 25 yuan per ton. (Coal is supplied at a state uniform price of 17 yuan plus transportation costs.) Electricity consumption has been estimated and costs calculated at the reported price of ¥0.09/kwh. Number of workers and average wage level were reported as well as tax and profit rates. These cost components then cover 57.3 percent of total production costs calculated as production times ex-factory price (= transfer price). The remaining costs, which mainly cover depreciation and maintenance and most likely capital charges, amount to 42.7 percent which equals 25 percent of a total investment cost of 2.8. Consequently costs relating to the investment consist of almost one half of total costs for the standard size small nitrogen fertilizer plants.

There are now a number of economies of scale. First, the number of workers and employees increases much more slowly than the size of plant. (See information in Tables 30 and 31.) The thermal balance can more easily—at least in theory—be improved in large plants, which then lowers coal consumption. If total investment costs and consequently investment costs per ton finished product can be reduced, this also has an immediate impact on pro-

Table 31. Production of Nitrogen Fertilizer—Ammonium Sulphate—in Plants of Different Sizes

Annual Production (tons)	Raw Material		Fuel Consumption (coal) (tons)	Electricity (capacity) (kw.)	No. of Workers	Investment (in yuan)			Production Per Worker (tons)
	Type	Amount				Total (million)	Per Ton	Per Worker	
210,000	coke	88,500	72,500	19,800	1,413	49.40	235	34,961	149
38,000	coke	16,100	20,300	3,500	450	10.12	266	22,489	84
7,600	coke	3,700	4,000	800	267	2.74	360	10,262	28
210,000	brown coal	200,000	63,800	25,000	1,450	56.60	270	39,034	145
38,000	brown coal	36,400	17,400	4,100	470	12.55	330	26,702	81
7,600	brown coal	9,200	4,000	1,100	298	3.47	457	11,644	26

Source: Site and Transport Planning for Industrial Enterprises, compiled by Peking Industrial Construction Planning Bureau, Ministry of Construction and Engineering, Peking, 1963.

duction costs. As argued earlier, pricing of equipment is such that production cost savings due to the size of plants are considerably less than they would be in other industrialized countries.

However, there can be no doubt that economies of scale play a role. For example, the plant for which production costs are displayed in Table 32 was at the time of the last visit planning to undergo an expansion which would raise the annual production of ammonia from 3,000 tons to 5,000 tons and the designed production capacity for ammonium bicarbonate from 12,000 tons to 20,000 tons per year. Total investment costs for this expansion were reported to be approximately 700,000 yuan. Further, it was reported that production costs would after the expansion be approximately 135 yuan per ton, a reduction which more or less completely appears to result from the reduced costs for depreciation, maintenance, and capital charges. A still larger ammonium bicarbonate plant in Shanghai in 1971 reported a total investment cost of approximately 8 million for a plant producing 60,000 tons of ammonium bicarbonate. The production costs were then around 90 yuan per ton. These figures clearly indicate that the economies of scale are more important for production costs than has been revealed by the industrial handbook figures of the early 1960s.

What are the options that have been open to the Chinese planners in providing agriculture with nitrogen fertilizer? Before a discussion of the choices of nitrogen chemical fertilizer, it should be noted that a considerable amount of the nitrogen intake comes from non-chemical fertilizers. It is virtually impossible to quantify the contribution of non-chemical fertilizers to total nutrient intake, but it seems likely that it at present probably exceeds, on average, the amount provided by chemical fertilizers. However, as the amount of organic manures is already near the possible limit, any expansion of inputs must be achieved by the use of chemical fertilizers, and it is for this reason that so much attention is paid to the development of the domestic industry and to the importing of chemical fertilizers. A steady increase in the total availability of nutrients is essential to maintain the food supplies of the nation and to ensure the increased availability of industrial crops for the use of its own industry and for export.

Table 32. Estimated Production Costs in
Small-Scale Nitrogen Fertilizer Plants*

Example from Lin County, Honan Province
Installed Capacity: 3,000 tons of synthetic ammonia per year
       12,000 tons of ammonium bicarbonate
Actual Production: 11,000 tons of ammonium bicarbonate
Price: ¥150/ton
Production Value: ¥1.65 million per year
Total Investment: ¥2.8 million

1. Coal 9,000 tons × ¥25.00	¥225,000	14%
2. Electricity 4.0 million kwh × ¥0.09 installed capacity: ≈1,000 kw	¥360,000	22%
3. Wages 285 × ¥45 + 25%	¥160,000	10%
4. Tax 3% of ¥1.65 million	¥ 50,000	3%
5. Profit 8-10% of ¥1.65 million	¥150,000	9%
	¥945,000	58%
Remaining Costs: 25% of 2.8 million — depreciation — capital charges (?) — maintenance	¥705,000	43%

TOTAL PRODUCTION COSTS   ¥1,650,000 101%

*The reader must bear in mind that these fragmentary data may
have been misunderstood and/or misinterpreted by the author.
Furthermore, the underlying principles for cost calculations are
not known. After more visits to small-scale plants and on the basis
of detailed statistics provided by the Chinese, it will eventually be
possible to arrive at a clearer understanding of the present economic
and social justification of the small plants.

  The small-scale industry delegation sent to China in summer
1975 by the National Academy of Sciences under the chairman-
ship of Dwight Perkins reports that their data for the same plant
are slightly different but broadly consistent with the figures presented here. The production costs were ¥130 per ton ammonium
bicarbonate in 1975, which is consistent with the predicted costs
after the expansion which is discussed above.

It appears that China has four main options. First, fertilizer can be imported. Second, large plants for making fertilizer can be imported. Third, China can manufacture her own large-scale plants for producing nitrogen fertilizer. Fourth, China can continue to construct small-scale plants to be spread all over the country. Some of the characteristics for the four different options are listed in Table 33. All four options have been exercised in the past.

Table 33. Alternatives for Providing Nitrogen Chemical Fertilizer

	1	2	3	4
Product origin	foreign	domestic	domestic	domestic
Plant origin	—	foreign	domestic	domestic
Plant size	—	large	large	small
Plant location/Market	—	central	central	local
Technology	—	modern	modern	modern

China has in the past imported very large quantities of nitrogen chemical fertilizers, which is evident from Table 34. The country has been the single largest buyer of chemical fertilizer in the world market. The figures below indicate that China's consumption of nitrogen fertilizer in 1970–1971 was covered through imports to approximately 50 percent. In view of the shadow-pricing of electricity and equipment for plants, it has been very advantageous for China to supply certain areas of the country—mainly in the coastal provinces and areas which could be reached by railway or accessible by water transportation. Chemical fertilizers have in the world market been available at very low prices—roughly US $40 (f.o.b.) per ton of urea for example. However, the cost of petroleum feedstock has since the beginning of 1973 raised production costs by about 150 percent. Furthermore, the present imbalance between demand and supply has pushed the price much higher—and urea presently (June 1974) sells at approximately US $300 per ton.[4]

The second alternative in providing agriculture with increased amounts of chemical fertilizer is to import complete plants. This option has been exercised in the 1950s when plants were bought from the USSR and again in the mid-1960s when plants were bought from Western Europe. The situation the planners have to deal with

Table 34. China's Fertilizer Imports in Recent Years

Contracts for 1970/1971	1,785 million tons nitrogen
Contracts for 1971/1972	1,601 million tons nitrogen
Contracts for 1972/1973	1,153 million tons nitrogen

Source: *Review of the Fertilizer Market in the People's Republic of China*, The British Sulphur Corporation Ltd., London 1972 or 1973.

has once more become ripe for the importing of chemical fertilizer plants. Several factors appear to have contributed to the new situation. First, the rapid price increase for chemical fertilizer in the world market has made the importing option the least favorable one. Second, availability of domestic petroleum feedstock in relatively ample quantities has tilted the balance in favor of large-scale modern plants which—in the short run—could only be obtained through imports. Third, the prospects for increased foreign exchange earnings may possibly have improved considerably in recent years—through the development of the petroleum industry and through the more mature industrial base that now exists in China. Fourth, the country may experience an urgent need rapidly to increase agricultural productivity in order to provide more raw materials for domestic industry and exports.

As a consequence of deliberations which can, at present, only be vaguely indicated, China has since the beginning of 1973 contracted ammonia/urea plants with a total annual production capacity of 3.78 million tons of ammonia, which more than equals the total domestic production of nitrogen in 1973. The total cost for these plants amounts to US $442 million (see Table 35). All the plants are very big—among the biggest built anywhere in the world today —each with a daily production of ammonia of approximately 1,000 tons or more, which more or less equals 100 small plants. When these plants go into production starting from 1976, the share of production coming from the small-scale fertilizer plants is going to be considerably reduced even if total production in the small-scale plants continues to increase.

Investment costs have important consequences for production

costs, as shown earlier. How do the small plants compare with the imported ones in this respect? The average price for one of the 1,000-tons-a-day ammonia plants is US $36.3 million. If this amount is converted into Chinese currency at the official rate of exchange and calculated per ton of nitrogen, the cost is 322 yuan per ton.[5] The corresponding cost for a 2,000-ton ammonia plant of the late 1950s is 1,740 yuan per ton, which for a more recent, modified plant with the designed capacity of 5,000 tons of ammonia per year is reduced to 1,030 yuan per ton (see Table 36). Then it must be remembered that the cost recorded for the foreign plants does not cover site construction and certain peripherals included in the domestic alternatives. Additional cost for the imported alternative may then be estimated to be in the region of 80 percent—leading to a total investment cost of approximately 575 yuan per ton nitrogen against 700 yuan per ton for the best small-scale alternative. With limited foreign exchange earnings this difference may have been compensated for through the existing shadow-pricing.

However, it must be noted that the plant equipment and technology now imported not only lead to considerably lower investment costs per ton of nitrogen—at an official rate of exchange —but to lower production costs through a drastically reduced consumption of electricity, which has a high price in China. The uncertain thing is then the cost of petroleum feedstock, which in the past has been priced considerably higher than the equivalent amount of coal. If this price differential for raw material—reflecting raw material scarcity—is maintained, the costs for the finished product may differ less than expected.

This very tentative reasoning indicates that in the past—with limited foreign exchange reserves to buy foreign technology and very limited domestic capability to build large fertilizer plants at low costs—small-scale fertilizer plants have been a good alternative in providing nitrogen fertilizer. Further, it is not likely that small-scale fertilizer plants will be closed down in any larger numbers since the fertilizer they produce is still badly needed. And it is even likely that a number of small plants will continue to be built in areas where conditions are favorable.

Table 35. China's Imports of Nitrogen Fertilizer Plants

Product	Company	No. of Plants	Capacity Each (tons)	Capacity Total (tons)	Costs Total (million $)	Costs Each (million $)	Completion
Ammonia	M. W. Kellogg	3	300,000	900,000	70	23.3 }	1976
Urea	Kellogg Continental	3	486,000	1,458,000	34	11.3 }	
Ammonia	Kellogg Continental	5	300,000	1,500,000	130	26.0 }	1976
Urea	Kellogg Continental	5	486,000	2,430,000	56	11.2 }	
Ammonia	Mitsui Toatsu (Japan)	1	300,000 }	300,000	42		1975–1976
Urea	Toyo Engineering Corp.	1	486,000 }	486,000			
Ammonia	Heurty Industries (France)	2	350,000	700,000			
Ammonia/Urea	Heurty Industries	1	380,000/ 616,000 }	380,000/ 616,000	110		1976–1977
Totals:							
Ammonia		12		3,780,000 }	442*		
Urea		10		4,990,000 }			

Source: Information in this table and the following one (Table 36) has been compiled on the basis of data in the *U.S. China Business Review*, Vol. 1 (1974), no. 1.

*Investment cost per ton urea (plants only): $ 76.0   (excluding the French plants)
 Investment cost per ton ammonia: $121.6

149

150

Table 36. Comparison of Investment Costs in Indigenous Small-Scale and
Imported Large-Scale Nitrogen Fertilizer Plants

| | | Plant Production | | Nitrogen | | Investment | | Investment Per |
Origin	Product	Amount	Content %	Amount	Plant	Total	Ton Nitrogen
Foreign	Urea	480,000	≈46	220,000	US $36.3 = ¥70.8*		¥322 (excludes site construction)
Chinese	NH₄HCO₃	8,000	≈17	1,360		¥2.36	¥1,740 (includes site construction)
Chinese	NH₄HCO₃ (modified)	20,000	≈17	3,400		¥3.50	¥1,030 (includes site construction)

*According to an estimated average exchange rate of 1.95 RMB to US $1.00 (June 1974).

For a final comparison it may be useful to look at the alternative to providing 3,000,000 tons of synthetic ammonia—in 1,000 small plants with the alternative of manufacturing the same amount in 10 large imported or domestically fabricated plants. The small-scale alternative makes it possible to distribute the effects of industrialization much more widely through location of plants in almost half of the county capitals all over China. Distribution of the product can then be carried out by local means of transportation, and no elaborate distribution network is required. Further, sources of technology are domestic, and equipment has been manufactured in province-level or lower-level enterprises. Consequently, this kind of expansion of nitrogen fertilizer production has required very small amounts of foreign currency. The smallness of the plants and the relatively low investment sums involved have made it possible to rally the communes which were to benefit from the supply of fertilizer to partly finance the plants through contributions from their accumulation funds. Employment considerations are also important. The small-scale alternative provides employment for approximately 250,000 people against roughly 2,000 in the large-plant alternative. This has had the consequence that China has trained a large number of technicians and workers in relatively advanced industrial skills. This trained labor force is now an industrial asset in itself but is also an important force in changing the mentality in the rural areas where traditional attitudes have to be changed. Moreover, the large number of small plants has required the plants and the industrial bureaus concerned to build up a

Table 37. Development Strategy Characteristics—
Nitrogen Chemical Fertilizer

	Alternative 4	Alternative 2-3
Production volume (synthetic ammonia)	3,000,000 tons	3,000,000 tons
Number of plants	1,000 units	10 units
Production capacity (synthetic ammonia)	3,000 tons	300,000 tons
Location	Small towns	Cities
Distribution	Factory depot + horsecart	Distribution network (railway + truck)
Technology source	Domestic	Foreign
Engineering	Provincial	Foreign/national
Foreign currency consequences	Low import content	High import content
Resource mobilization effect	Considerable	Negligible
Construction period	Short (< 1 year)	Long (several years)
Total employment (factory)	250,000	2,000
Training		
—technical skills	Significant	
—organization skills	Significant	
Relative production costs (ex-factory)	Higher*	
Capital/output ratio	Higher	

*It has among certain industrial engineers been argued that the small-scale plants have an extra advantage in developing countries over the very big plants because a considerable period of time is generally required before full capacity is reached. In the meantime production costs may be 100%–150% over planned costs because the large component of capital costs greatly increases production costs as soon as the plant is operated below capacity. However, the share of capital costs in total production cost is also very high for small-scale nitrogen fertilizer plants—as shown earlier. Furthermore, the process technology of a small nitrogen fertilizer plant might be just as complex in a rural setting as that of the very large plants is in the urban setting of a major city. And available information indicates that it has taken considerable time to make the small plants operate at full or near full capacity. In summing up, the small plants may have a slight advantage over the big ones on this particular issue—even if it is considerably less than some industrial engineers would like to think.

substantial foundation of organization skills which has relevance
not only for fertilizer production proper but also for any other
advanced economic and industrial activity.

An attempt to list the different characteristics for the two
main alternatives in providing chemical fertilizer to agriculture in
China is recorded in Table 37.

All positive factors mentioned above have to be weighed
against the disadvantages of higher investment costs per unit of
finished product and higher production costs. Available information indicates that the Chinese planners have made a good choice
in the past. However, they have never argued that small-scale plants
should be an aim in themselves. And it now appears that conditions
are changing, and that the time has come to emphasize fertilizer
production in units that in already fully industrialized countries
are calculated to be more economic. Nitrogen chemical fertilizer
production would then provide an example of a sector where the
two-leg policy has worked and where a new industrial strategy is
gradually taking its place.

Cement

The most striking feature of the Chinese cement industry is
the recent and rapid introduction of vertical-shaft technology used
in most small-scale cement plants.[6] The number of small cement
plants in rural areas has increased from about 200 in 1965 to 2,800
in 1973.[7] The production capacity of the small plants has during
the same period increased from roughly 5 million tons to an
estimated 19 million tons. So the average size of the plants has
decreased considerably—from about 25,000 tons per year in 1965
to 6,800 tons in 1973. Consequently, most of the plants must be
very small, as a number of relatively large small cement plants have
continued to be built during the period. However, available information given in Table 38 indicates that the average size is increasing
and may now be approaching 10,000 tons per year.

The annual production of cement has more than doubled in
the period 1965–1973 and now stands at an estimated 38 million
tons. The share coming from small rural plants has during the

Table 38. Estimated Production in Small Cement Plants in China

Year-end	No. of Plants	County Coverage Percent	Total Million Tons	Small-scale[m] Percent	Small-scale[m] Total Million Tons
1949			0.7		
...					
1957			6.9		
...					
1965	≈200[b]		15.0		≈5.1[l]
...					
1969					7.9
1970			25.9	40[h]	10.4
1971[a]	1,800[c]	60[f]	30.2	44[i]	13.3
1972	2,400[d]	70[g]	36.9	48[j]	17.7
1973	2,800[e]	80[e]	39.8	50[k]	19.9
1974			41.8	>50[n]	21.7
1975	>2,800[o]	>80[o]	49.6	57[o]	28.3[p]

a. "Total cement production increased in 1971 by 16.5%" (*Peking Review,* January 14, 1972).
b. "In 1972 there were 12 times as many (small-scale) plants as in 1965" (*Peking Review,* January 11, 1974).
c. 600 new ones (small cement plants) appeared in 1972 alone (*Peking Review,* No. 49, 1973).
d. FE/W707/A/13.
e. FE/W762/A/18.
f. *Peking Review,* No. 3, 1972.
g. New China News Agency, November 25, 1972.
h. New China News Agency, December 16, 1970.
i. *Peking Review,* No. 39, 1972.
j. *Peking Review,* No. 49, 1973.
k. New China News Agency, December 18, 1973.
l. "In 1972 there were 12 times as many (small-scale) plants as in 1965, and output was 3-4 times as high" (*Peking Review,* January 11, 1974).
m. "From 1970 to 1973 an average annual increase of over 3 million tons was achieved" (*Peking Review,* January 11, 1974).
   "Yearly increase in small-scale plants since 1969 (-1972) was reported to be 31%" (New China News Agency, December 28, 1972).
   "Output was (in 1973) 12.2% more than in the corresponding period of 1972" (*Peking Review,* January 11, 1974).

The production figures for cement manufacture in the small-scale sector for 1969, 1972, and 1973 have been calculated in the following way:

$P(1969) = X$

$P(1972) = X + 12/1.112$

$P(1973) = X + 12 = 1.31^3 \cdot X$

Consequently the production from the small-scale plants in 1969 turns out to be 7.88 million tons. The average plant size in the small-scale sector is assumed to be same for the two years 1971 and 1972. The production figure for 1971 can then be calculated. Further, the increase in total cement production in 1971 was given as 16.5 percent over the preceding year (*Peking Review*, No. 2, 1972)—which amounts to 25.9 million tons. The small-scale plants contribute 40%, which is 10.4 million tons. The figures for total production in 1949 and 1957 are taken from *Ten Great Years* while the production figure in 1965 is a rough estimate.

n. The figures for 1974 are based on the assumption that total cement production increased by 5% and that the share of the small plants increased to 52%. The only information available for cement production in 1974 has been released from NCNA and says "China's small cement works . . . accounted for over 50% of the national total." (BBC Summary of World Broadcasts FE/W814, February 19, 1975.)

o. The figures for 1975 have been derived from the following information contained in a NCNA release. "China's small cement plants fulfilled their 1975 production quota 2 months ahead of schedule, with an output increase of more than 30% over the same period of 1974. The quality of cement showed further improvement. Over 80% of the counties in China now have small cement plants, the number of which exceeds 2,800. These account for 57% of the national cement output." (BBC Summary of World Broadcasts FE/W854, November 26, 1975.)

p. It should be noted that other observers, basing themselves on U.S. Government estimates of 31.6 million tons of cement in 1974, arrive at figures which are considerably lower: 21.3 million tons and 37.3 million tons respectively. The argument about total national production in various industrial sectors in the PRC, however, cannot be easily resolved until the Chinese authorities more freely release their production statistics.

period increased from roughly 35—50 percent. Some more information—mostly estimates—on this development is provided in Table 38.

Three basically different technologies—dependent on size—are used for the sintering process which is the core process in the manufacture of cement: rotating horizontal kilns, vertical-shaft kilns, and ground-level chambers. Some of the characteristics of the different kiln types are given in Table 39.

Table 39. Types of Cement Plants

Level	Plant Size (tons/year)	Technology	Mode of Operation
Nation/Province	>150,000	Rotating kiln(s)	Continuous
Region/County	10,000–50,000	Vertical kiln(s)	Continuous[8]
County	<15,000	Ground-level chambers	Intermittent
Commune	200–5,000	Vertical kiln(s)	Intermittent

The development in recent years differs from the development of small-scale nitrogen chemical fertilizer in several important respects. The average size of nitrogen plants has increased considerably since 1965, while the average size of the small cement plants has decreased quite considerably. There are a number of reasons for this. First, economies of scale most likely play a more important role in the manufacture of nitrogen fertilizer than in the manufacture of cement. Second, it is easier to control the quality of cement in a small primitive plant than in the manufacture of nitrogen fertilizer.[9] Third, much of the investment for the very small cement plants has been accomplished with scrap and idle equipment with very low opportunity cost, an approach which is ruled out for chemical fertilizer plants. The use of such equipment requires less investment, as transfer prices are considerably lower than if the required equipment had been brand new and obtained from state-owned engineering enterprises which would be supplying at uniform prices. Finally, it appears that localities—collective units at county level and communes—have been given a relatively free hand in setting up their small cement plants, and no strict national supervision like the one for small chemical fertilizer plants has been enforced. It should also be noted that most of the very small cement plants are probably owned by people's communes. They are then run intermittently and serve only a small localized demand.

Much experimentation[10] is still going on, both to find technologies appropriate for rural industrialization efforts, and to find in each locality the appropriate combination of industrial activities.

In this two-pronged experimentation it is often necessary to start from scratch, and many of the small plants set up and run by counties and communes should in their initial stages be viewed as pilot plants.

The pilot-plant approach is necessary for a number of reasons. The availability of workers with industrial training is in most places limited, and many workers come directly from agriculture. A transitional training period is required for these people to become accustomed to industrial technology, which may be quite complex even if indigenous methods and equipment are being used.

The question of product quality and adaptation of products to users is also related to industrial training. The use of native methods of production and indigenous equipment may need a certain period of adaptation in order to achieve the desired quality with the available raw materials. Setting up cement plants, for example, must be preceded by proper planning of mining activities. The quality and quantity must be guaranteed before cement plants and other process industries can go into full operation.

Another important consideration may be the fact that the initial smallness of a plant enables the capacity of the plant to grow with local demand, which may make overall costs lower than if a large-capacity plant had been set up from the very beginning. The production costs in the very small plants are fairly high, but usually are considerably reduced when plant size is increased and the technique is fully mastered.

This is illustrated in Figure 17 which shows the changing costs in a county-run plant in Honan province. The cost has dropped from ¥134.00 per ton when the plant was originally set up in 1958 to ¥36.00 per ton in 1970 at an annual production of 17,000 tons. The information in the figure refers to a plant in a locality where the price had been set at ¥47.00 per ton.[11] The Chinese press reports that a plant with an annual capacity of 100,000 tons would produce at ¥31.00 per ton.[12]

What, then, are the main reasons for the rapid proliferation of the small and very small cement plants which apparently still continues? Meeting a localized demand with a production based on

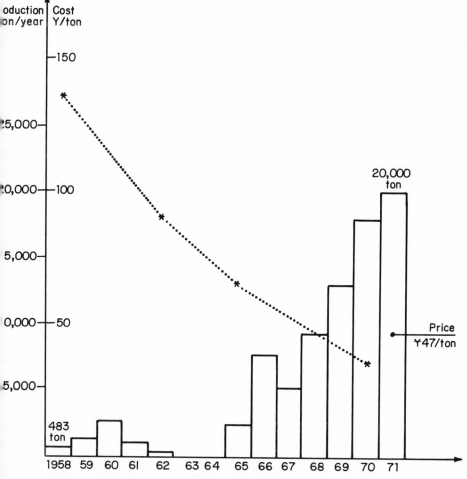

Figure 17. Development of Annual Production and Production Costs at a Small Cement Plant (Lin County, Honan Province)

Source: Information provided by chairman of revolutionary committee, chairman of the enterprise in 1971.

local resources may be important. However, it is likely that the training objective is more important than the objective of increasing production through setting up the numerous very small plants. First, large rural plants require already trained personnel when they start production. Such personnel can be trained in small and very small plants and later on transferred to the bigger plants—still in rural areas. Second, cement plants may be one of the categories of industrial enterprises where rural workers can be trained in industrial discipline and organization at low costs. Finally, it should not be ruled out that many of the very small plants should be seen as pre-investment studies in finding out if local resources and other conditions justify the setting up of a large-scale operation.

Nitrogen chemical fertilizer is produced with the sole objective of providing agriculture with more fertilizer inputs, except for relatively small amounts of synthetic ammonia, the intermediate product, used for other industrial purposes. Cement, however, is used in both rural areas and cities. This characteristic may possibly have influenced the proliferation of small cement plants. The reasoning would then be as follows.

The rural demand for cement has in the past partly been met by deliveries from urban-based cement plants. As a consequence of increased self-sufficiency in rural areas, that production in urban places previously allocated for rural consumption has now to a considerable degree been reallocated for urban projects. Consequently, the expansion of the rural cement plants has partly had the effect of making more cement available for urban projects without corresponding investments in the urban-based sector of the cement industry. And most of the small cement plants have been built by counties or people's communes which have raised funds, procured equipment locally, and trained technical personnel locally.

The industrial handbook referred to in the discussion of costs for small-scale nitrogen fertilizer plants also lists investment costs for cement plants of different sizes. The investment cost is reported to be 1.2 million yuan for a plant with a designed annual production of 32,000 tons, the standard design for small cement plants in the same way that the 3,000-ton synthetic ammonia plant is the standard design for the small nitrogen fertilizer plant. This requires an investment of 37.5 yuan per ton. The larger plants with rotating horizontal kilns require investment of 19.5 yuan and 17.6 yuan per ton for plants producing 492,000 and 709,000 tons per year respectively. (See Table 40 for further information.) It should also be noted that the large plants produce a cement of higher quality and that the product in the larger plants is likely to be of a more even quality.

Investment costs reported from visits to small cement plants in 1971 and 1973 indicate that costs for the 32,000-tons-per-year plant may be slightly lower than the figures quoted. Coal consumption per ton of cement does not differ significantly for plants of different sizes.

What consequences do the different investment costs per ton of cement have on the costs of the finished product? The pricing of cement is ambiguously dependent on the purpose it is used for. The ex-factory price is around 70 yuan per ton when taxes and planned profits are included. If depreciation and maintenance charges and possible capital charges are calculated to 25 percent of the investment costs, this would then amount to 9.4 yuan per produced ton in the 32,000 ton plant and 4.4 yuan for the largest of the two mentioned plants using rotary kilns. There are, of course, other economies of scale. The wage costs are becoming relatively less important with increasing plant size. Coal consumption per ton cement does not differ significantly for plants of different sizes and there is no reason to believe that electricity consumption would be significantly higher per ton cement in a small plant than in a big one.

In the field of cement manufacture China is also contemplating using foreign technology to its advantage—but not complete plants. According to a business report, the Machinery Export-Import Corporation has been discussing the importation of certain critical equipment for a cement plant with a production capacity in the range of 1.0–2.0 million tons per year. The total investment costs for a plant with an annual capacity of 1.0 million tons per year

Table 40. Production of Cement in Plants of Different Sizes

Annual Production (tons)	Number and Type of Kilns	Coal Consumption			Employment	Investment			Production Per Worker (tons)
		Cement Quality	Total (tons)	Per Ton		Total	Per Ton	Per Worker	
32,000	2 vertical	400	7.6	238 kg	358	¥ 1.2.10⁶	37.5	3,350	89
492,000	2 rotary	500	126.0	256 kg	810	¥ 9.6.10⁶	19.5	11,850	607
709,000	3 rotary	500	168.0	237 kg	972	¥12.5.10⁶	17.6	12,860	729

Source: *Site and Transport Planning for Industrial Enterprises*, compiled by Peking Industrial Construction Planning Bureau, Ministry of Construction and Engineering, Peking, 1963.

Table 41. Comparison of Investment Costs in Indigenous Small-Scale and Large-Scale with Imported Large-Scale Cement Plants

Origin	Plant Size (million tons)	Cement Quality	Investment		Investment Per Ton	
			Plant	Total (million)		
Foreign	1.0	>500	US 35.0 million	¥70.0	¥70.0	(incl site construction)
Chinese	0.032	400		¥ 1.2	¥37.5	(incl site construction)
Chinese	0.79	500		¥12.5	¥17.6	(incl site construction)
Chinese	0.492	500		¥ 9.6	¥19.5	(incl site construction)

would be US $35.0 million (1975).[13] If this amount is converted into yuan at the official exchange rate and is calculated as costs per ton of cement, it amounts to 70.0 yuan per ton including costs for site construction and all peripherals.[14]

It should be noted that investment costs per ton of cement differ much more widely between large and small plants than for plants producing ammonium bicarbonate and ammonium sulphate. This fact should be seen as an indication that the Chinese engineering industry at an early stage was able to make use of the economies of scale inherent in the plant manufacture. An obvious explanation for this is that the production technology required for the manufacture of cement plant equipment is much simpler than nitrogen fertilizer plant equipment—even for very large plants.

In decisions involving location, size, and technology for cement plants, it appears that transportation costs are much more important than investment costs per ton of finished product. That is to say that economies of scale due to reduced investment costs per ton cement for large centrally located plants rarely compensate for the increased transportation costs in comparison with widely distributed smaller plants. Production costs depend on the efficiency of the plants, and many of the small plants are, of course, initially much less efficient than the larger plants. However, because of the lumpy character of the large plants, the demand may not immediately match production capacity. A lowered utilization of capacity would then immediately lead to higher production costs.

Local manufacture of cement can, according to available reports, be achieved in a small plant of standard design with a capacity of 32,000 tons per year at approximately 40 yuan per ton. A substantial number of China's more than 2,000 counties have all the necessary raw materials for producing cement. And press reports from China now mention that small cement plants have been set up in 80 percent of all counties. There can be no doubt that the high transportation costs—in the absence of railways or waterways—have been a significant factor in the Chinese emphasis on local manufacture in relatively small plants where the plant capacity has been chosen in order to match the market requirements of a county or part of a county.

To understand this fully, it is necessary to look more deeply into the question of transportation costs. The transportation system is, compared with industrialized countries, underdeveloped in many parts of China. Railway transportation or cheap water transportation is not generally available. A majority of the more than 2,000 counties have to rely on small trucks, horsecarts, or still more primitive means of transportation. The relative transportation costs in the early 1960s in Hopei province, where Peking is located, are given in Table 42. The apparently high costs for transportation by truck may reflect the use of small-capacity vehicles, poor roads, and also a conscious shadow-pricing of this means of transportation—as indicated earlier.

Table 42. Transportation Costs in Hopei Province

Railway	¥0.010/ton km	(100 km coal)
	¥0.015/ton km	(100 km pig iron)
	¥0.017/ton km	(100 km cement)
	¥0.018/ton km	(100 km steel)
	¥0.027/ton km	(100 km steel products)
	¥0.045/ton km	(100 km fertilizer)
Truck	¥0.24/ton km	(flat rate)
Horsecart	¥0.41/ton km	(11–15 km)

The influence of transportation costs can more easily be understood through looking at two different alternatives for meeting an assumed annual demand of 32,000 tons in each of nine counties. It might be assumed that an average region with nine counties would cover approximately 22,500 km². The general policy today is that each county where raw materials are available should have its own cement plant. The centralized alternative would be to build a rotary-kiln plant producing 9 × 32,000 tons annually. To minimize transportation costs, this would then be located in the center of the region. See Figure 18.

The average increased transportation distance (alternative 1) for sending cement to the county centers—before redistribution—would be:

$$\frac{4 \times 50 + 4 \times 70}{9} = 53 \text{ km}$$

Figure 18. Centralized and Decentralized Transportation Pattern

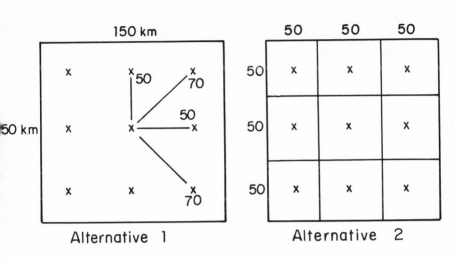

Alternative 1   Alternative 2

In the absence of cheap railway or waterway transportation the cement produced centrally should then be manufactured at a cost which is at least

$$53 \times ¥0.24 = ¥12.70$$

lower than cement produced in the county centers if transportation takes place with trucks. If transportation is carried out with horse-carts, the transportation costs of the central plant must be at least

$$53 \times ¥0.41 = ¥21.70$$

lower in order to compete with cement produced locally in the counties.

It is likely that the cost difference between big rotary kilns and small vertical kilns is not sufficiently great for centrally located plants to be built for meeting the counties' needs for cement, particularly not when other factors—favorable to the smaller local plants—are also taken into consideration.

It should be noted that certain counties in some regions are covered by railways or waterways, which both provide cheap transportation. On the other hand, there are many regions in urgent need of cement where transportation costs are much more in favor of local cement plants than in the example discussed above.

However, it should also be noted that cement produced in small local plants must be consumed locally for the reasoning above to be valid. And the influence of transportation of raw materials should be neutral. Furthermore, the quality in terms of strength of the locally produced cement is lower than cement produced in large rotary kilns. The quality of the locally produced cement is on the whole likely to be uneven. This leads to the conclusion that the localities will have to "import" cement of higher qualities for projects where higher quality is required.

It is apparent that, once a county center is reached by railway, transportation costs no longer provide the same justification as before for building small local plants. However, the investment cost per ton of cement may still be lower than for big plants if idle equipment with low-opportunity cost can be used. Aside from the transportation considerations, the impact on employment and industrial training may have been considered very important in the regional context.

The scanty statistical information available indicates that the production of cement in small-scale plants in China has increased from roughly 5 million tons in 1965 to approximately 19 million tons in 1973. Consequently, the total increase in the small-scale sector amounts to 14 million tons.[15]

A small plant producing 10,000 tons per year employs around 200 persons. The total increase in industrial employment in small-scale cement plants would then correspondingly be at least 140,000 persons. A substantial number of rural plants are smaller and more labor-intensive than in the example cited here.

Thus, it can be safely assumed that the total direct employment effect from rural cement plants (manufacturing only) would amount to at least 250,000. This number is at least ten times higher than employment in a small number of modern large-scale cement plants producing the same quantity of cement using a rotating kiln with an annual capacity of roughly 500,000 tons.

There are other important labor force considerations aside from the employment effect. First, a large number of people are being trained in industrial process technology. Second, a sizable number of people have, inside production units, received training in organizational skills. A smaller number, but still sizable, have been trained in administrative skills related to the procurement of machinery and raw materials, distribution of products, and coordination with other industrial units.

It appears that local small cement plants—aside from farm machinery and local engineering—provide one of the most successful examples of using alternative technologies for rural industrial development. The question immediately arises why this approach has not been duplicated in any other developing country.[16] However, the feasibility of small cement plants has been studied in the Indian context. In the early 1970s the chairman of a working group on small-sized plants requested a group of three persons to:

1. assess the comparative costs of setting up different sizes of cement plants along with the costs of raw materials and other inputs required;
2. make suggestions regarding location of small-size plants;
3. find out the possibility of supplying a package plant including nodulizer, shaft kiln, and other components;
4. prepare a cement map of India giving details regarding size and location of existing cement plants.

A number of small plants have been set up on an experimental basis,[17] all of which were evaluated by the group. A detailed examination of the existing four experimental plants revealed that economic viability could not be ascertained for two of them. Certain doubts were also expressed about the quality of cement. Available technical and economic data from the remaining two plants enabled the working group to conclude that "depending upon the availability of mineral deposits, installation of . . . cement plants of 30-ton and 100-ton per day capacity can be deemed appropriate." This size range would most likely include the major part of the cement produced in small plants in China.

The group further argued that the location of small-scale cement plants in different regions of the country depended on the availability of basic raw materials and that transport costs need not be a constraint if the cement is produced where the market is. Furthermore, as vertical-shaft kilns are utilized for producing limited quantities of cement, the marketing would not be a main constraint. Consequently, small-scale, vertical-shaft-kiln cement plants can be located in areas where communication and transport facilities are not well developed but where limestone and coal are available in limited quantities sufficient to sustain the plant for about twenty to twenty-five years.

On the basis of these criteria the group prepared a list of approximately thirty-five locations suggesting that plants of 30 ton per day and 100 ton per day should be set up in these places. It was further suggested that a phased program should be initiated and that seven primary locations should be chosen so that their experience could be used in the remaining plants to be set up later on. However, no such program has been initiated, and there are a number of factors which have hindered a duplication of the Chinese approach in India. First, the plant designs and process technology may not have been fully developed. Consequently, economic and technical data may not have been sufficient to convince either central planners or local entrepreneurs. Furthermore, it must not be overlooked that many proven existing mineral resources for the manufacture of cement have been leased to established cement manufacturers who have obtained industrial licenses for their activities.[18] This reduces the number of possible places for small cement plants; furthermore, the national cement enterprises can hardly be expected willingly to give up part of their market to small-scale manufacturers. It has also been suggested by observers in India that the technical requirements for strength, setting time, soundness, fineness, and so forth which follow international standards[19] for all cement marketed in India have hindered the establishment of small-scale cement plants there.

Even though it has not been proven without doubt that small-scale cement plants are feasible in India, it appears that the country could provide conditions for setting up of a relatively large number of small vertical-shaft kilns in a number of locations. However, a number of constraints—some of which have been mentioned—hinder this development.[20]

Farm Machinery and Engineering

A gradual development of the capacity for manufacturing farm machinery is an important ingredient of the Chinese approach to rural industrialization. In 1973 there were more than 1,000 factories in China producing farm machinery. Most of these were relatively small, a substantial proportion county-level enterprises. The factories can be divided into two categories. First, the so-called backbone factories, which are big factories under central control. These manufacture all tractors and approximately 30 percent of small diesel engines. Second, the small and medium factories, most under local control. While the products of the first category are distributed all over the country, those of the second are distributed only within the localities where the factories are situated. However, those localities which are highly developed transfer some of their local production to less developed areas.[21] Great differences in soil, cropping, and climatic conditions are among the main factors explaining the dominance of the small-scale manufacture of farm machinery. Thus it is possible for a locality to decide for itself what machines should first be produced, and how they should be produced, even if types and models are roughly decided by the central authorities.

A substantial number of the relatively small, county-run machinery plants, however, have come to play an increasingly important role in the manufacture of a wide range of products within the Chinese machine-building industry. The local manufacture of electric motors, generators, and transformers with a capacity of up to 100 kva., and electric welding machines is one example of this development. A considerable number of counties have started to manufacture machine tools like bench drills, simple lathes, planers, and cutters, which are supplied to county-run enterprises and to other units of the three-level farm machinery repair and manufacture network. There are also a number of counties which have been commissioned to start the manufacture of small diesel engines—usually standard engines of 10 or 12 hp or complete power tillers ("walking tractors") for which the engines are used. Similarly, a number of counties have already established a production capacity for rolling bearings.

A survey of the BBC Summary of Chinese broadcasts over a period of three years—from March 1970 up to February 1973— revealed that more than 150 counties, out of a total of approximately 2,000, were mentioned as having started manufacture of advanced machinery of the types mentioned above. It is most likely that the total number of counties manufacturing advanced machinery is considerably larger. This is evident from information pertaining to regions stating that a number of counties—not mentioned by name—within the region are engaged in this kind of manufacture. It can also be assumed that not all counties having production of advanced machinery would figure in the broadcasts during the period surveyed.

The geographical distribution of county-run machinery production appears to be dependent on the complexity of the product involved. The production of more complex machinery like rolling bearings, is less widely distributed than the production of simpler equipment like electric machinery. Table 43 shows that the production of electric machinery was reported for 91 counties located in 23 provinces or autonomous regions. However, the manufacture of rolling bearings which was reported for 34 counties was limited to 11 provinces.

Even if planning authority has been largely delegated to the county administration in matters relating to the manufacture of industrial inputs for agriculture, it is clearly evident that the manufacture of the industrial categories mentioned above could not have been initiated without approval from provincial or national decision-making bodies. Trial-manufacture may, however, have been initiated by the localities, but production—even on a small scale—would require allocation of copper, certain critical equip-

Table 43. County Machine-Building Industry

	Reported for	Located in
1. Electrical machinery	91 counties	23 provinces
2. Machine tools	41 counties	17 provinces
3. Diesel engines (or small tractors)	34 counties	14 provinces
4. Rolling bearings	34 counties	11 provinces
5. Electronics	15 counties	10 provinces

Source: *BBC Summary of World Broadcasts, The Far East— Weekly Economic Report.*

ment, and transfer of production technology, which are likely to be centrally controlled. So the pattern of county-run enterprises engaged in the manufacture of advanced machinery can clearly be seen as a reflection of national or at least provincial policies for overall industrialization. The geographical distribution of counties reported to have engaged in manufacturing electrical machinery, machine tools, diesel engines (or small tractors), and rolling bearings has been plotted on Figure 19 where the dots indicate the locations of county capitals.

Figure 19 shows rather heavy clusters for electrical machinery in Shansi (around Sian) and in Kwangtung and Yunnan. The appearance of clusters may reflect the fact that a larger number of counties were reported for the manufacture of electrical machinery than for any other category. Other explanations are that plants producing electrical machinery were allowed to proliferate without much central control, or that certain areas have been designated as future centers for the production of electrical machinery. The clusters would then be the visible nuclei for the future centers.

All production lines—except rolling bearings—appear to be located in counties spread relatively evenly all over the country, which may be an indication that a pattern of wide diffusion is followed when counties are encouraged or chosen to upgrade their industrial capabilities. Even the counties reported to have started manufacture of rolling bearings are widely spread, but it is evident that they are mainly found in the industrial areas in the north.

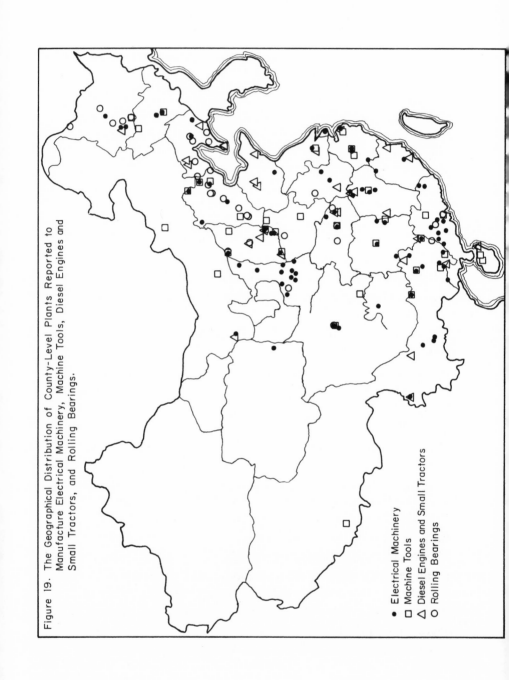

Figure 19. The Geographical Distribution of County-Level Plants Reported to Manufacture Electrical Machinery, Machine Tools, Diesel Engines and Small Tractors, and Rolling Bearings.

• Electrical Machinery
□ Machine Tools
△ Diesel Engines and Small Tractors
○ Rolling Bearings

There is a high correlation between counties producing machine tools and counties producing electrical machinery. Sixty percent of the counties producing machine tools were also reported to produce electrical machinery. This high correlation may primarily be attributed to the fact that both production lines were reported simultaneously. Another explanation may be that, once the technique required for making electrical machinery like generators and motors is mastered, the next logical step on the industrial ladder would be the production of relatively simple machine tools primarily intended for the local market. The manufactures of diesel engines and rolling bearings which could certainly not be mastered until considerably later do not show any correlation with the manufacture of electrical machinery.

A surprising feature of the geographical distribution is that Szechwan with approximately one-tenth of China's population hardly figures in the BBC county sample of 1970–1973. There are, of course, several possible explanations for this which are not mutually exclusive. First, the reporting principle may vary from province to province. Second, the favorable conditions for agricultural development in this province may have led to a certain "neglect" of rural industries at county level. Third, the province may have a substantial small-scale industrial base which has not yet manifested itself in plants manufacturing relatively advanced machinery.

Small Diesel Engines

The significance of an industrial base becomes evident when one looks at the expansion in the manufacture and use of small diesel engines. The existence of an industrial base has been important for spreading the manufacture of small diesel engines to a large number of places. It has enabled the diffusion of the manufacture of replacement parts still further. Equally important is the fact that a wide—even if thinly spread—base has facilitated the training of a large number of mechanics in villages where the diesel engines are to be used.

The annual production of small diesel engines was 5.7 million hp units in 1972 against only 900,000 in 1965.[22] The figure for 1972 corresponds to approximately 500,000 units of model 195 (1-cylinder, 95 mm bore), which is by far the most common model manufactured in China. Approximately 50 percent of the small diesel engines were in 1972 manufactured in three provinces— Hopei, Shantung, and Honan. The annual production in 1972 was between 70,000 and 100,000 in each of these provinces. Hopei is reported to have increased its annual production to 140,000 units in 1973, and the number of such diesel engines in operation in this particular province increased to 290,000 at the end of 1973.[23]

Chinese planners realized in the late 1950s that the country needed a small tractor to supplement the big tractors (imported or produced in a Soviet-built plant) and in certain areas (for example, paddy fields) to substitute for the use of big tractors. Another important objective was to develop small tractors well suited to not-yet leveled and consolidated holdings and subsequently relevant for the labor-intensive (garden-like) Chinese agriculture. At the same time, rural areas, which in many places lacked a well-developed electric power grid, were in urgent need of mobile power units. A primary requirement was then that the *small tractor* which must be *versatile* should be equipped with a *power unit* which could be used for *multiple purposes.* The eventual outcome was a design for a water-cooled, relatively light (150 kg), high-speed (1,800–2,000 rpm), and relatively powerful (10–12 hp) diesel engine which was to be used for water pumping, threshing, and as a power unit for a two-wheel tractor which was designed and equipped to carry out a considerable amount of transportation.

The initial steps in developing the Chinese power tiller industry have been described by Professor Shigeru Ishikawa based on an analysis of relevant articles of Chinese agriculture machinery journals in the mid-1960s.[24]

A first step was to obtain imported samples through one of the import corporations for which the directive was given by the ministry concerned. A second step was to direct a number of units to work out designs on the basis of structural analysis of imported samples. The units involved were the National Tractor Institute, the Shanghai Internal Combustion Engine Institute, and a provincial Agricultural Mechanization Institute (Fukien). The design was developed in close cooperation with units responsible for trial-manufacture and field experimentation. Designers participated in all three activities, and design revisions were made on the basis of tractor users' opinions as well as workers' opinions.[25]

The next step was to authorize a more or less final design relevant to Chinese needs and production capability. The power rating made at the time has been only 5 hp. A number of places were then authorized to manufacture the power tiller—among them Shanghai, Wuhan, and Shenyang. In most places the manufacture was organized as a joint effort of three parties—a major assembly plant, a plant producing the engine, and a number of cooperating factories making various components for the tiller as well as for the engine itself. Further design changes were made to increase the power rating and to suit farming practices of the area in which the tillers should be used. The various steps and cooperation network are illustrated in Figure 20.

Small diesel engines have been especially important for provinces like Hopei, Shantung, and Honan, which have depended in agriculture on tube-well irrigation and which have not had sufficient electric coverage to allow the use of electric motors. Chinese small diesel engines were first manufactured in a few large industrial cities. Shanghai appears to have been the most important place and was already in 1963 manufacturing the model 195 engine in limited numbers—at a cost of more than 2,000 yuan per unit against less than 500 yuan in 1973.

Another important requirement was *decentralized manufacture* for the power units as well as for tillers. The present annual production (1973) of more than 500,000 power units comes from an estimated fifty to a hundred localities involving a considerably larger number of enterprises through subcontracting. An estimated one-fourth to one-third of the power units are used in power tillers estimated to be manufactured in approximately 30 localities distributed all over the country.

The production of the model 195 small diesel engine appears

Figure 20. Stages in the Development of the Chinese Power Tiller Industry.

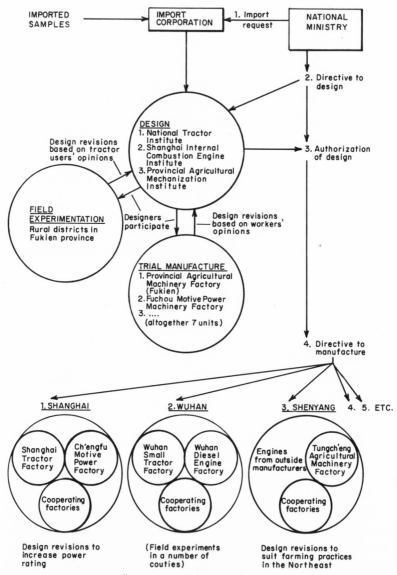

IMPORTED SAMPLES

IMPORT CORPORATION

1. Import request

NATIONAL MINISTRY

2. Directive to design

DESIGN
1. National Tractor Institute
2. Shanghai Internal Combustion Engine Institute
3. Provincial Agricultural Mechanization Institute

Design revisions based on tractor users' opinions

3. Authorization of design

FIELD EXPERIMENTATION
Rural districts in Fukien province

Designers participate

Design revisions based on workers' opinions

TRIAL MANUFACTURE
1. Provincial Agricultural Machinery Factory (Fukien)
2. Fuchou Motive Power Machinery Factory
3. ....
(altogether 7 units)

4. Directive to manufacture

1. SHANGHAI

Shanghai Tractor Factory
Ch'engfu Motive Power Factory
Cooperating factories

Design revisions to increase power rating

2. WUHAN

Wuhan Small Tractor Factory
Wuhan Diesel Engine Factory
Cooperating factories

(Field experiments in a number of couties)

3. SHENYANG   4. 5. ETC.

Engines from outside manufacturers
Tungch'eng Agricultural Machinery Factory
Cooperating factories

Design revisions to suit farming practices in the Northeast

Source: Adapted from "Chinese Method for Technological Development – Case of Agricultural Machinery and Implement Industry," by Shigeru Ishikawa, paper presented at OECD Symposium on Science, Technology and Development in a Changing World, Paris, April 21-25, 1975.

in many provinces to be based on regions, of which China has 200. Provincial enterprises are then drawn into the organization only for the manufacture of some of the key parts which go into the assembly of the engines. The machine-building department of the First Ministry of Machine Building of the central government in Peking is the highest supervising body for this development. A diesel engine office in the machinery bureau of the regional administration is usually assigned the coordination task. Planning responsibilities at the county level are given to the industry bureau.

The manufacture can be organized in two different ways. First, a comprehensive factory can be responsible for the manufacture of almost all parts except rolling bearings and possibly the fuel pump. Second, one factory is assigned the task of manufacturing certain heavy and critical components while relying on a large number of subcontractors for the manufacture of all other parts which in the earlier alternative were manufactured in the comprehensive factory. Hopei province, for example, has sixteen works producing small diesel engines located in various places all over the province. Total investment in these factories is reported to be 30 million yuan. Most of these appear to be organized as comprehensive factories. However, there are examples of industrial networks involving up to twenty-six different small factories.

A representative of the industry bureau in Anyang region, Honan province, commented on the choice of the main plant in the local manufacture of small diesel engines through cooperative efforts. In the choice of the main plant many different alternatives were considered. An important constraint was that a higher level enterprise should not be incorporated. A major reason for the actual choice—a plant already in the service of agriculture through the manufacture of seeders—was the fact that the factory had a sufficiently large site. Not mentioned but probably equally important was the evaluation that the technical level was sufficiently good for large-scale expansion. The network concept—involving a number of enterprises—had to be chosen for the manufacture of small diesel engines in this locality as in many other places. There was hardly any other possibility if production were to start quickly.

A very large number of enterprises have been drawn into the manufacture of the small diesel engines. Almost all of the approximately 150 counties in Hopei have been given the assignment to produce certain parts for the diesel engines which are assembled in different places in the province. Selection of counties is done on the basis of the required quality of the part and the technical level of the industrial system of the locality. The cooperative networks for the production of diesel engine networks have in a few cases been replaced by single-factory production. This is not likely to happen in many more places since the required skills have now been well developed in a number of places.

Production costs, of course, differ from plant to plant. Already well-developed plants are able to manufacture the model 195 diesel engines at a cost somewhere between 500 and 600 yuan, which appears to require a production of at least 5,000 units per year. Hunan province reported that production costs for the model 195 engine in one of its plants ran as high as 1,370 yuan per unit, which should be compared with the ex-factory price of 800 yuan. However, the production was then as low as 146 units. Available information indicates, however, that at an annual production of 5,000 units the manufacture can, with reasonable efficiency, be carried out in single factories as well as in cooperative networks consisting of a relatively large number of enterprises. Some more information is provided in Table 44 for five different locations where the model 195 engine is manufactured. Only the two first in the list—Shanghai and Tangshan—carry out the manufacture in single factories.

The small tractor is mainly manufactured in large enterprises but in some places in relatively large county-level enterprises. Earlier plans indicated that a considerably larger number of counties should be allowed to start local manufacture of tractors. The following two conditions should then be fulfilled. First, the localities must guarantee that repair and maintenance work for farm machinery would not suffer when the county and commune enterprises started to manufacture the components that go into tractors. Second, the counties concerned must, of course, have the necessary production

Table 44. Manufacture of Diesel Engine 195 in
Different Machinery Plants
(planned production in 1973, price: ¥800 per unit)

Location	Production (units)	No. of Workers	Production Costs (¥ per unit)	Production Value (million)	Capital Fixed	Working
Shanghai	21,800	1,320	490	17.4	8.29	2.63
Tangshan (Hopei)	18,000	1,060	n.a.	14.0	3.80	4.50
Sulu county (Hopei)	5,000	510	546	3.3	1.10	1.00
Anyang (Honan)	5,000	>1,000	730	n.a.	n.a.	n.a.
Kaocheng (Hunan)	146	n.a.	1,370	n.a.	n.a.	n.a.

Source: Information provided on visits to the enterprises, except for Kaocheng (BBC–FE/W731).

capability. Apparently, the Shanghai planning agencies had almost decided to transfer the manufacture of small tractors to three of the ten counties which make up the rural areas of Shanghai. However, further investigation proved that the very large number of components involved would make it difficult for the counties concerned to undertake the task, and production still remains within the Shanghai Tractor and Truck Industrial Company.

A third requirement was that the *repair and maintenance* (including manufacture of certain replacement parts) should be *integrated with the local engineering workshops.* There were two major reasons for this. First, local nearby repair can be quickly done (not only for power units and small tractors) and cut down idle time due to breakdowns, and consequently contribute to a higher rate of farm equipment utilization than would otherwise have been possible. Second, combining repair with manufacturing also enables a higher machine utilization in the local workshops.

A large share of diesel engines will be used for pump sets in wells. Consequently, it is essential to organize repair and maintenance in an efficient way in order to achieve a high rate of utilization. This requires spare parts and mechanics. Hopei has solved the first problem through organizing 280 small factories—many of these at county level. Further, the industrial departments of the province in 1972 helped the communes and brigades train more than 45,000 mechanics.[26] This apparently means that almost every brigade has a mechanic, since the province has 53,000 brigades.

It is obvious that it would not have been possible to achieve the decentralized production of power units and small tractors if considerable design modifications had not been made and if local training and cooperation programs had not been initiated. It was necessary to adapt the design to suit local manufacturing capability and local repair skills. This involved changes in the use of materials as well as changes in production technology. For example, the amount of aluminium casting differs quite considerably from one place to another. The decentralized approach also proved to be beneficial since it apparently became easier to modify tillers to suit different soil and climatic conditions in different parts of the country.

Furthermore, it became necessary to waive national requirements for standardization and interchangeability of parts until such regulations could be enforced without hindering the development of the local engineering system. This does not appear to be a disadvantage for the time being, since components and replacement parts are manufactured locally except for certain items like bearings. In addition it was also necessary to make design changes in order to suit larger or smaller subcontracting networks.

The localities chosen for the manufacture of power units and/ or tillers were given special attention for developing necessary skills and manufacturing capability through programs for cooperation with larger enterprises or enterprises already well established in the manufacture of power units and tillers. These programs have been executed by local planners in close cooperation with national agencies.

Rolling Bearings

The manufacture of rolling bearings is another example,[27] among many, which demonstrates that Chinese planners have used county-run enterprises for the kind of machine building which in

most other countries would have been the sole responsibility of
large plants. This approach is the continuation of a policy initiated
in 1958-1960 to meet the local demand for relatively simple bearings needed for agricultural machinery and for carts used for long-
distance transportation, and so forth. However, very few of the
enterprises set up in 1958 have remained in operation. There were
two main reasons for this. First, there was no effective demand for
low-grade bearings until the recent development of local industry.
Second, the necessary cumulative skills, equipment, and capital for
setting up small bearing factories were not available until recently.
To understand the present, relatively cautious approach, it may be
useful to recall the early beginning of local manufacture of rolling
bearings.

The local rolling bearing industry was an integral part of the
Great Leap Forward approach.[28] Honan appears to be the province
where local ball bearing activities started. It was reported in *People's
Daily* in August 1958 that the ball bearing industry in that province
came into being in March and April that year, which suggests that
this development started a few months before the Great Leap
Forward was officially announced in May 1958.

Ball bearings were to be manufactured in great quantities in
rural areas of China to be fitted to farm tools, vehicles, and irrigation
machinery. In August 1958 it was clearly stated that the movement
for mass production of ball bearings had come into being very
quickly in order to enable the manufacture of machinery to make
up for the shortage of manpower experienced in agriculture. A
People's Daily editorial stated that the government was giving every
encouragement to local plants to make ball bearings.

Inner Mongolia set up a number of plants expected to produce
150,000 sets per year. Hopei province pledged that, before October
1, 1958, every county, town, and village would have its own ball
bearing plant. Shantung, Chekiang, and Anhwei figured prominently
among provinces which had started to mass-produce ball bearings.
In a number of places, not only the counties but also hsiangs and
small cooperatives were going to produce bearings—apparently
without having access to any specialized machinery or knowledge.

180

However, there seem to be certain hints of more careful planning. The Tientsin Department of Commerce reported that it was going to supply each county with a complete set of machines for making ball bearings so as to replace handicraft production. A ball bearing exhibition jointly sponsored by Shansi, Hopei, Shantung, Honan, Shensi, Kiangsu, Anhwei, and Peking opened at the end of July and was later transferred to Peking. "The exhibition is held for the purpose of exchanging experiences in developing a ball bearing industry through the efforts of the masses. It is held for the purpose of achieving the goal of equipping all the means of transportation in the countryside with ball bearings," the *People's Daily* reported at that time.

What were the ball bearings like which apparently were produced under very primitive conditions? An American correspondent in Peking, Anna-Louise Strong, who visited Honan in the autumn of 1958, reports visiting a commune, Kushing, where ball bearings were being made. She mentions that she was intrigued to find that in the workshops

> they actually made ball bearings by hand and had put ball bearings during the summer on all their 1,169 mule-carts as well as all wheelbarrows... In Peking I had seen exhibitions of these home-made ball bearings in all kinds of material: steel, iron, glass, porcelain. Szechwan even made ball bearings of bamboo for the casings and round acorns for the balls, and these were said to hold a weight of half to three-quarters of a ton. Very round acorns are a peculiarity of Szechwan oaks.

> All this I had seen in Peking. Now in Kushing commune I saw them making the bearings in a couple of sheds in a backyard ... they got thin iron rods and cut these into small cubes, about a quarter-inch in size. Each cube was put in a mould and hammered by hand until it was roughly round. It went through several processes ... The cases were also handmade, and fitted to the carts. By this tedious process Kushing Commune had put all its carts and barrows and water-wheels on ball bearings, and thus more than doubled the load they would handle.[29]

The campaign to produce ball bearings apparently had a tremendous momentum and Shantung province was reported to have established some 60,000 small bearing plants by the beginning of September. And a report from Hopei said that 123 counties and cities had fitted all their revolving tool parts with ball bearings. The whole province had by then produced 3.6 million sets of ball bearings. At the same time, it was mentioned that Kwangtung province planned to produce 25 million sets of ball bearings by the end of the year. Kwangsi with barely any industrial base at all had in September 62 counties producing ball bearings.

The exaggerated reports disappeared and the claims became more modest. NCNA reported at the end of November 1959 that the county-run enterprises in Hopei had, since the beginning of the year, produced 94,000 sets of ball bearings.[30] Another attitude was already apparent when an assistant researcher of the Research Institute of Geography, Chinese Academy of Sciences, in January 1959 pointed out that "hsien [county] and qualified people's communes should establish ball bearing factories and immediately start planning the production of machine tools." Evidently every county should not have a ball bearing plant, and this appears to be more or less the present policy for the local manufacture of ball bearings.[31]

Why did this whole movement to produce ball bearings in rural areas start? It is not possible to give a full explanation. However, it is apparent that at least a few workshops in Honan, and maybe also in other provinces, had been able to produce small batches of ball bearings which could be used for slow-moving vehicles and machines. On this scanty evidence it was then postulated that almost every village all over the country would be able to do the same—and on a massive scale. It should be remembered that at that time China had just a fledgling rolling bearing industry. The Loyang rolling bearings plant had been completed in 1957. The Harbin plant had been expanded on the base of a small Japanese plant. The Peking plant was not to be completed before 1959. The total annual production of bearings is likely to have been less than 10 million sets, which should be seen in relation to the claim by Kwantung to produce 25 million sets before the end of 1958. So it was hardly possible to draw on an established ball bearing industry for providing the necessary technology. It was then evident that it would not be possible for the large number of small workshops to master the necessary techniques in—among other things—surface grinding and heat treatment.

There were also misconceptions involved. Ball bearings are likely to have been much too advanced for a number of purposes for which they were intended to be used. Many short-haul vehicles did not really require ball bearings. And when the locally made ball bearings, which were acceptable for low-speed purposes, were used in machines revolving at high speeds, they naturally broke. It appears that the processes involved in making bearings in rural areas were very time-consuming, with the result that many local productions of bearings proved to be costly. In sum, the local manufacture of ball bearings was at the time not quite feasible.

But the manufacture of rolling bearings in rural areas is once more very much in evidence in China. China now has many small bearing plants run by counties and communes. Most of existing enterprises have been established since 1966 and particularly in the late 1960s and early 1970s. These enterprises are usually fairly small, with between fifty and a few hundred workers. Initially the production of bearings in such plants is usually only one of the activities in multi-purpose repair and manufacturing enterprises. Such production has in many places started with the repair of bearings, the necessary replacement parts being supplied from elsewhere or gradually manufactured within the unit. Available information indicates that a number of these enterprises will eventually develop into small specialized bearing factories, producing a rather limited number of varieties.

The number of county-run enterprises manufacturing rolling bearings is likely to approach 100 units, and probably there are also a substantial number of commune workshops producing rolling bearings. Today the rolling bearing industry consists of enterprises at all the five administrative levels—nation, province, region, county, and commune. Very little information is available on ball bearing manufacture at region and commune levels. So, based on available information, the industrial pyramid for manufacturing rolling bearings would basically look like Figure 21.

But if we look at the distribution of production capacity between national, provincial, and county-run enterprises, we find an inverted pyramid like the one in Figure 22. This would then indicate that the county-run enterprises particularly are of little significance. However, this would be to overlook the dynamic aspect of the development of county-run enterprises manufacturing rolling bearings. In a similar diagram showing the distribution of production capacity a few years ago, the county-run enterprises would hardly have been seen at all.

When a new plant is set up, technology is usually transferred from other small bearing plants as well as from provincial or national bearing plants. A relatively large number of workers usually go to study in other plants for periods of a few weeks up to six months or more. Technicians from higher levels are also assigned, at least for a while, to lower levels. Very little equipment in small plants is new, and specialized old machines are taken over from provincial or national bearing plants.[32]

Two of the large national ball bearing plants in Liaoning and Honan have been reported during 1971–1972 to have assisted more than twenty small rolling bearing plants in establishing production.[33] Some of these small county-run enterprises are reported to have an annual capacity of about 500,000 sets per year. If all other county-run enterprises should be similarly expanded, they would play a considerable role in this sector of the Chinese machine-building industry.

What is, then, the significance of this plausible expansion of the county-level rolling bearing plants? First, it enables a wider distribution of industrial activity, which means that the local bearing plants in their turn can transfer industrial technology further down in the industrial pyramid—within their particular area of responsibility. Second, the expansion may be a reflection of a national division of labor between small and large plants, assuming that labor is less costly in the small plants and that more labor-

CHINESE ROLLING BEARING INDUSTRY

Figure 21. Number of Producing Plants

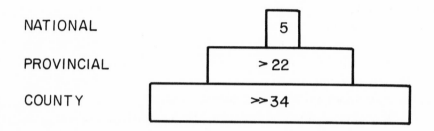

NATIONAL   5

PROVINCIAL   > 22

COUNTY   >> 34

Figure 22. Annual Production Capacity 1973 (estimates)

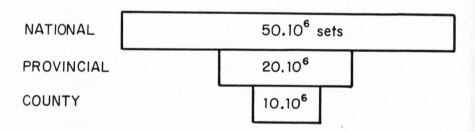

NATIONAL 50.10^6 sets

PROVINCIAL 20.10^6

COUNTY 10.10^6

Source: Author's estimates

intensive methods of production can be used. That the latter is the case appears to be evident. Available information indicates that single-spindle machines are used for making the outer and inner rings. The initial processing of the rings is in many places based on a hot forging process which is both material-saving and machine-saving for the later processes.

There may be two possibilities in achieving a division of labor between small and large plants. First, the small plants can take over the manufacture of specialized bearings. Second, they can take over some of the bread-and-butter production lines from the large plants. The former is, for technological reasons, not feasible. So it is likely that the latter approach is being used. What, then, is the significance of the expansion of small bearing plants? First, the manufacture in small plants is likely to lead to fewer demands on that part of the machine-building sector which produces specialized machinery. Second, it may be possible to utilize manpower in the countryside which is paid local wages related to the relatively low productivity of land and not to the national wage scale in state-run enterprises.

Small bearing factories may be able to take over the production of a considerable proportion of the intermediate-size ranges where quality requirements are not so stringent. Some small enterprises are already able to manufacture bearings used for simple machine tools, electric motors, and probably many of the bearings used for farm machinery. There are already places where small plants have started to manufacture bearings for motor vehicles. If quality can be improved and quantity increased in the small plants, the large national enterprises can concentrate more of their resources on high-quality bearings. The transfer of used equipment from large to small enterprises may also mean that large enterprises will be able to modernize earlier than otherwise would have been the case.

Iron and Steel

Small iron plants represent a fourth main category of small plants and were the mainstay of rural industries during the early Great Leap Forward. Since then the sector policy for the production of pig iron in small plants has undergone great change; the design of a small blast furnace may still be partly indigenous but the production technology is modern in order to be able to maintain necessary quality standards. Equipment allocated from central sources is based on standard blast furnaces of 8, 13, 28, 50, 100, and 120 m³. The smallest of these is much bigger than the backyard furnace of 1958 and gives an annual production of approximately 2,000 tons of pig iron. It should be noted that it is only in the blast furnace that a modern, up-to-date process is used. The casting of ingots, production of coke, sintering of iron ore, and internal transportation are usually all done with indigenous labor-intensive methods. Basically these plants are modern and small only in the core process. A number of smaller blast furnaces set up in 1959 with a blast furnace volume of 6.5 m³ or less have been restored. Furthermore, reports during the past two years have increasingly mentioned that communes in a small number of provinces have set up blast furnaces with volumes as small as 0.5 m³, reminiscent of the backyard furnaces of the Great Leap Forward. Apparently there are places in China where the quality of the iron ore and the high level of local skills may justify these very small furnaces.

China's production of steel in 1972 was reported to be 23 million tons. The production of pig iron is considerably higher, as the amount of steel scrap is very low—as in all developing countries. Consequently, almost all steel comes from the conversion of pig iron. And pig iron is also required for a number of other purposes. So it is assumed here that pig iron production in 1972 must have been in the region of 29 million tons.

Iron and steel are manufactured in a spectrum of plant sizes.[34] The majority of pig iron and steel is produced in very large iron and steel complexes located in Anshan, Shanghai, Wuhan, Peking, and a few other places. There are also a relatively large number of medium-sized works, each with an annual capacity of between 50,000 and 100,000 tons or more. In addition, localities—usually counties—operate more than 430 small pig iron plants each producing over 1,000 tons annually. Further, it should be noted that even smaller iron melting furnaces—down to volume of 0.5 m³— still exist in a number of localities. Their production capacity is negligible in the national context.

Table 45. 1972 Distribution of Iron and Steel Production in
Enterprises of Different Sizes (in metric tons)

Product	National Total (million)	Big Total	%	Medium Total	%	Small Total	%
Steel	23	20.2	88	2.8	12	negligible	
Pig iron	29	21.2	73	6.7	23.1	1.1	3.8

In 1972 the steel output of the *medium-sized and small works*
represented 12 percent of the country's total. Their output of pig
iron was in the same year 27 percent. Table 45 shows the distribution of iron and steel production in enterprises of different sizes.
The figure for pig iron production in the small plants—3.8 percent
—is based on the assumption that the average annual production is
2,500 tons. This gives a total annual production of approximately
1.1 million tons. It may be less or slightly higher. It is also evident
from available information that small plants today play an almost
negligible role in the national production of steel.

Small iron plants were once the mainstay of the Great Leap
Forward strategy.[35] What, then, are the reasons for their limited
role today? To understand this, it is necessary to recapitulate the
thinking of the iron and steel industry in early 1958. Based on the
assumption that coal resources existed in 1,500 counties and iron
ore resources in 200 counties, it was envisaged that approximately
1,000 small iron plants should be set up all over the country. These
plants were to be scaled-down versions of the big plants but with
considerable modifications.

Table 46 lists some selected characteristics for the early small
and medium blast furnaces ranging from 8 m³ to 100 m³ and an
annual production capacity of from 3,000 tons to 200,000 tons of
pig iron. The small pig iron plants which are still in operation
usually have a blast furnace of 8 m³ or 13 m³. The medium-size
iron plants today usually have blast furnaces of 250 m². Table 46
clearly shows that investment costs per ton are more or less the
same for the whole range of sizes, which should then be seen as an

Table 46. Production of Pig Iron in Small Furnaces
Without Hot-Air Blast

Iron content of ore: 45%

Annual Capacity (tons)	No. of Furnaces (m³)	No. of Workers	Investment Total	Per Ton	Per Worker
200,000	4 × 100	332	3,900,000	¥19.5	¥11,747
49,000	2 × 55	140	780,000	¥15.9	¥ 5,571
12,500	1 × 30	79	233,000	¥18.6	¥ 2,949
5,000	1 × 13	43	98,000	¥19.6	¥ 2,279
3,000	1 × 8	30	59,500	¥19.8	¥ 1,983

Source: *Site and Transport Planning for Industrial Enterprises,* compiled by
Peking Industrial Construction Planning Bureau, Ministry of Construction and Engineering, Peking, 1963.

indication of the then still relatively undeveloped capability to
manufacture equipment for large plants at low costs.

The investment for a 13 m³ blast furnace is given as 98,000
yuan in Table 46. This sum should be compared with the 450,000
reportedly needed for a pig iron plant of the same size in 1971
(Lin county, Honan province). Consequently, the blast furnaces
in Table 46 must be of a very simple design.

Apparently, they would not have a hot-air blast. It was quickly
realized that these plants would still have considerably higher costs
than the large plants. As a consequence, the primitive, very small
iron melting furnaces—"backyard furnaces"—were promoted. These
should only melt iron which would partly be used for local manufacture of equipment needed in agriculture, partly be converted
into steel in modern steel plants.

The widespread proliferation of "backyard furnaces" did not
consider transport costs, availability of manpower in agriculture,
or quality of the product. These shortcomings were realized after
only a few months. The remedy chosen then was to concentrate
the primitive furnaces around certain steel-making centers. However, even this was not a realistic alternative in terms of costs and

product quality. Most of the primitive furnaces were consequently abandoned.

A number of very small "backyard furnaces" and small modernized enterprises have continued to operate throughout the early 1960s, and there has been a considerable expansion since the mid-1960s, even if their share of total production still is very small. A reason for this is the comparatively high costs in the small-scale plants. Table 47 shows that only raw materials and wages are likely to exceed the ex-factory price of pig iron. Still higher costs are reported for other small plants. An important reason for the high costs is apparently the high consumption of coke, which may be three times higher than in the very big plants.

Table 47. Production Costs in Small-Scale Iron Plants (1973)
(Example from Lin County, Honan)

Cost Category	Alternative 1 Using Coke	Alternative 2 Using Coal
Iron ore		
3 tons at ¥20–30	¥ 60–90	¥ 60–90
Coke		
1.5–1.7 tons at ¥80	¥120–136	
Coal		
1.5–2.5 at ¥30–40 per ton		¥ 45–100
Wages per ton	¥ 20	¥ 20
Subtotal	¥200–246	¥125–210
+		
Electricity		
Other raw materials		
Depreciation		
Maintenance		

Total production costs: in excess of ¥200
Delivery price to consumers: ¥110–160

Small iron plants do not seem to be a realistic alternative for expanding production capacity—except in localities where very favorable conditions exist. Small plants must not compete with large plants for raw materials. This has two consequences. First, high-grade ores are generally reserved for the big plants. Second, coke or coal of appropriate quality is often not provided on a long-term basis. The question of iron ore quality can be solved through ore dressing which, however, considerably raises investment costs. This in turn greatly influences depreciation and maintenance charges to be levied per unit of output.

The quality of the product and the efficiency of the plant can often be assured only if a hot-air blast is used in the process. This greatly increases required investments with considerable cost consequences for the product.

There is no reason to doubt the claims that a number of small plants compare favorably in terms of efficiency and production costs with the very large plants in Anshan, Wuhan, and Peking. But these small plants—limited in number—are likely to operate under very favorable circumstances which cannot be easily duplicated in other places. One likely explanation is that such small iron plants have access to high-grade iron ore deposits which are sufficiently small and/or inaccessible not to be required by national planning agencies. Further, it may be assumed that such plants are also favored by provisions for coke or coal and the locality has been able organizationally and technically to train a high-caliber labor force. Where these conditions exist, the small plants are likely to continue to be in existence for quite some time.

Paper

The lower end of the industrial spectrum—the small-scale plants using intermediate or primitive technology—are found in almost all industrial sectors. This is true also for the manufacture of paper. Table 48 gives some of the characteristics of paper plants of different sizes using rice/wheat straw[36] or bamboo as raw material. The plants range from an annual capacity of 350 to 42,000 tons—only the smaller plants designed to utilize rice/wheat straw. The investment costs per unit of production do not indicate any sizable economies of scale and are therefore consistent with the information available for the process industries discussed earlier.

Table 48. Paper Manufacture in Small Plants of Different Sizes

Capacity (tons)	Raw Material*	Quality	Coal Consumption		Electricity		No. of Workers	Investment (¥)			Production Per Worker (tons)
			Total	Per Ton	Total (kwh)	Per Ton		Total	Per Ton	Per Worker	
350	Rice/wheat straw	Printing	420	1.2	184,000	526	43	62,520	179	1,454	8.1
700	Rice/wheat straw	Printing	700	1.0			45	133,400	191	2,964	15.6
1,750	Rice/wheat straw	Printing	830	0.47	900,000	514	68	389,600	223	5,721	25.7
3,500	Bamboo	Book	3,800	1.09	1,400,000	400	200	1,170,000	334	5,850	17.5
10,500	Bamboo	Book	11,000	1.05	5,300,000	505	385	3,800,000	362	9,870	27.3
21,000	Bamboo	Book	22,000	1.05	12,000,000	571	534	7,530,000	359	14,101	39.3
42,000	Bamboo	Book	41,000	0.98	18,000,000	429	800	12,220,000	291	15,275	52.5

Source: *Site and Transport Planning for Industrial Enterprises*, compiled by Peking Industrial Construction Planning Bureau, Ministry of Construction and Engineering, Peking, 1963 (first edition).

*The ratio between raw material and finished product is 2:1. The ratio in production is usually higher.

Small paper plants produce for the local market as do small chemical fertilizer and cement plants. But there are distinct differences in the justification for setting up small paper plants, and one is the utilization of scarce raw material resources. The previous two types of small plants are based on raw materials—coal and limestone —which are not really scarce in China. However, traditional raw materials for paper manufacture *are* scarce in China and large quantities of pulp and paper are still being imported.

There are also other important differences. The quality of the product in small plants manufacturing cement and chemical fertilizer is comparable to the products from big plants—even if the cement quality usually is somewhat lower and uneven. The small or at least the very small paper plants, however, manufacture only low-grade paper and are not expected to produce any paper qualities similar to the ones coming from the big plants.

Small paper plants are meeting a real demand through utilizing local raw material resources. This has two important consequences for the upper end of the industrial spectrum in this sector. First, the raw material base is expanded, and less pulp and paper have to be imported in order to meet a certain demand. Second, the production capacity in the small plants releases capacity in the big modern plants which then can increasingly be used for the production of higher quality paper. This, of course, is likely to reduce the demand for imported high-quality paper and/or the equipment to manufacture high-quality paper.

Small-scale plants play another important role in many localities related to the financing of local industries which operate at a loss. Certain industries, particularly heavy industries like pig iron manufacture and chemical fertilizer plants, are operated at a loss in certain localities. The central authorities have often allocated light industries—like paper manufacture—to such places in order to provide profits which can compensate for losses on other industrial enterprises. The reasoning behind this runs as follows. The difference between production cost and price is quite considerable for paper manufacture, which is evident in Table 49. A small county-level plant in Hopei with an annual production of 600 tons was

Table 49. Paper Production in a Small Plant,
Zunhua County, Hopei, 1973

	Costs (¥)	Percentage
Raw material (wheat straw) 3 × 600 tons × ¥60	108,000	20.3
Coal (estimate) 600 tons × ¥50	30,000	5.7
Electricity (estimate) 600 × 500 kwh × ¥0.09	27,000	5.1
Wages 97 × 12 × 33 × 1.25	48,000	9.1
Depreciation + maintenance 25% of 230,000	58,000	10.9
Tax	53,000	10.0
Planned profit 400 tons × ¥200 200 tons × ¥300	140,000	26.4
Subtotal	464,000	87.5
Unaccounted for	66,000	12.5
Total	530,000*	100.0

*Value at ex-factory price
Printing paper: 200 tons × ¥1.150 = ¥230,000
Wrapping paper: 400 tons × ¥750 = ¥300,000

expected to make a profit of 140,000 yuan in 1973. It was indicated at the time of the visit that this particular county had been allocated the plant in order to compensate for losses sustained on the iron and steel plant.

Chapter 5

TANGSHAN REGION AND ZUNHUA COUNTY
IN HOPEI PROVINCE

Zunhua county in Tangshan region in the northeastern part of
Hopei has in recent years received much coverage in the Chinese
press and broadcasts because of its rapid local industrial development.[1] There is no doubt that Zunhua is being presented as a model
and that its local industrial development has basically taken place
in recent years—most of it after the Cultural Revolution—even if
some of the enterprises set up during the Great Leap Forward continued their operation throughout the period when most other
small local enterprises were closed down.

Tangshan region, where Zunhua is located, consists of two
municipalities, twelve counties, and one agriculture and reclamation
area with state farms. The names of the principal administrative
units are listed in Table 50. The two cities and the county capitals
can be identified on the map in Figure 23, which also shows other
county towns (market towns) in the region as well as the main
roads and the railway line from Peking to the northeast. It should,
however, be noted that a railway link from Tangshan to Zunhua—
passing through the county capital of Fengrun—was completed in
1972. Road construction may also have taken place on a considerable scale since the basic information for the map was collected
some time in the late 1960s.

The total area of the region is 17,600 sq. km. and the population was reported to be 6.84 million at the end of 1972. The
population of the regional capital amounts to approximately
1,000,000, which includes around 400,000 in about twenty
people's communes, which are also part of Tangshan municipality.
The city has approximately 150,000 industrial workers. Industrial
employment in county-level and commune-level enterprises was in
1973 reported at 70,000.

195

Table 50. Principal Administrative Units in
Tangshan Region, Hopei Province

Location	Population	No. of Communes	No. of Brigades	Year
Tangshan city	1,000,000[a]	≈20		
Qinhuangdao	310,000			
Fengrun county	600,000	48		1970
Fengnan county				
Luan county	430,000	31		1971
Luannan county				
Leting county		34		
Changli county	420,000	37		1969
Funing county	416,000	46		1971
Lulong county	320,000	34	557	1968
Qianan county	450,000			1970
Qiansi county	280,000	36	≈400	1971
Zunhua county	580,000[b]	43	≈691	1972
Yutian county				
Baigezhuang agriculture and reclamation area				
Total	6,840,000	≈500		1972
Tientsin city	3,500,000			

Source: Most of the figures in this table are taken from *Travels in China, 1966–71*, by Rewi Alley, Peking, 1973.

a. Urban population is approximately 600,000.
b. The population was reported to be 485,000 in autumn 1966.

There are altogether about 500 communes in the region. Because of the large average number of communes per county, the counties have been subdivided into districts, of which there are approximately 100. The district offices are manned by officials sent down from the county governments. The districts are often the centers for county-run hospitals, tractor stations, and other units where the county is considered to be too large and the communes too small areas to be served.

Some pairs of counties previously used to form a single unit. This was the case for Fengrun/Fengnan, Luan/Luannan, and Qianan/Qiansi in the 1950s. Changli used to be the regional capital until the administration moved to Tangshan. Tangshan region lies just south of the Great Wall. The topography is characterized by mountainous, semi-mountainous, waterlogged, and plain coastal areas. The region is rich in natural resources such as iron ore, coal, bauxite. There are also certain other resources of nonferrous and nonmetal minerals. Some of the counties in the coastal areas in the south have rich salt resources. The cities Tangshan and Qinhuangdao have a number of large enterprises including metallurgy and machinery companies.

Specific information is at present available to the author only for a single county–Zunhua–located in the northern part of the region. Zunhua county has an area of 1,640 sq. km. and the population was 0.58 million at the end of 1972. There is one county town, and the county is subdivided into 10 districts. There are altogether 43 communes, 691 brigades, and 2,499 teams.

In December 1971 an official of the county industrial bureau reported that there were 39 county-level plants and another 71 units run by the 43 communes. This included iron and steel, cement, chemical fertilizer, and a number of machinery plants. Total industrial employment in county-level enterprises was 5,500 at the end of 1971. The commune-level enterprises had 2,500 industrial workers, and there were about another 5,500 in brigade-level enterprises.

Rural industrial enterprises are found at brigade, commune, and county levels. It appears, not only in Zunhua but all over the country, that the county and brigade levels are the most important ones, at least in terms of employment. Hsipu Brigade in Jianming People's Commune is one of the three main model brigades in Zunhua county; Table 16 has clearly indicated the potential for industrial activities at brigade level.

Farm machinery stations exist in all communes in Zunhua county and are the most important industrial units at commune level. However, a considerable amount of mining in Zunhua is

carried out by commune-level units. Jianming People's Commune
Farm Machinery Repair Station may exemplify the industrial
activity at commune level. The total number of employees was 58
in July 1973. The activities of the station are seasonally adjusted
in accordance with the peak labor demands in agriculture, but outside the station usually involve machinery repair and not farm
work. Main products are water pumps, water valves, water buckets,
small farm tools, and steel hammers. The mixing of phosphate
chemical fertilizer had recently been added to the responsibility
of the station—but most likely only on a temporary basis. The
station also has considerable carpentry section and had two sections
out of nine engaged in repair.

In press reports and information given to visitors it has often
been pointed out that agricultural production in Zunhua—and most
likely in the whole region—had been more or less stagnant during
the period 1958–1969. The average grain production in 1969 was
3,000 kg. per hectare, which increased by 25 percent by 1970.
Development of side-line occupations including mining has become
increasingly important. The income of these made up approximately
50 percent of the value of grain production in 1972. It is not clear
if the recent rural industrialization was triggered by a rapid increase
in agricultural productivity or vice versa. However, increased agricultural productivity and rapid rural industrialization have come
more or less simultaneously and are now mutually supporting. That
rural industry is to a considerable extent geared to agriculture is
evident from the development of the three-level agricultural
machinery repair and manufacturing network. In December 1971
this consisted of 7 county-level units, 37 commune-level units, and
407 units at brigade level. This meant that most of the communes
and about 60 percent of the 691 brigades had their own farm
machinery units for repair and manufacture. A year and a half later
there were more than 600 brigade-level units, which amounts to a
coverage of 90 percent. There were 44 commune-level units, which
amounts to one in each of the 43 communes plus one additional
unit which serves the agricultural area included in the county
capital. County-level farm machinery repair and manufacturing

units were at the same time reported to number 7, said to be located in 7 of the 10 districts into which the county is divided. The remaining 3 districts, located around the county capital, were said to be served by the 3 central county-level farm machinery plants located in the county capital.

Many of the county-level industrial enterprises are listed in Table A2-1 in Appendix 2, which also gives some information on the school and public health systems as well as the administrative structure as reported in December 1971 and July 1973. No new factories were set up during this period with one single exception. A carpet factory based on a previous pilot loom making use of waste in the textile mill has now been set up as a separate unit. However, there was a new element in the objectives of the industrial system in Zunhua, which had not been there eighteen months earlier. At least three county-level industrial units were producing export items. Among these were the carpet factory, which was still making use of textile waste but also producing carpets using high quality raw materials. Furthermore, the hardware factory produced two types of 2–3-inch polished nails for export. This production had started in May 1973 and was going to expand into more varieties. It was also reported that the clothing factory produced padded children's jackets for export. Similar examples were also found in Sulu county, Shihchiachuang region, where it was reported that one of the machinery enterprises manufactured engine tops to be exported to Southeast Asia. However, it may be generally assumed that only relatively few of the county industrial systems in China have reached such a degree of sophistication to have been assigned export tasks.

It is fairly obvious that county-level enterprises are on the whole either directly or indirectly serving agriculture or based on agricultural products that are locally available. This may not always be the case for the mines where at least some units have been set up to serve national enterprises located outside the county. However, when this happens, the mines provide the locality with income which can be used for investments in agricultural development.

At the end of 1971 there were indications that the county

industrial system was to be still more diversified and drawn into closer contact with the modern industrial sector. This may have been premature, and it was said that a certain consolidation of the industries in Zunhua had taken place. Overall industrial employment was more or less the same in July 1973 as in December 1971. Employment figures were slightly higher in some enterprises but lower in others. At the same time, it was planned that the total industrial production value of county-level enterprises would increase by about 25 percent in 1973 with scarcely any increase in industrial employment.

The consolidation of the rural industrial sector has, among other changes, also meant that rural industry was given a clearer orientation of serving agriculture than might have previously been the case. Certain production lines were discontinued in Zunhua from December 1971, among them the diversification of chemical production in the sulphuric acid plant. Further, the decision to produce ball bearings in addition to the roller bearings already in production had not been followed up. The equipment for a new 13 cu. m blast furnace which had partly arrived eighteen months earlier had not yet been installed, and it also appeared doubtful that sugar refining would be continued in the food processing plant.

There were also other changes in Zunhua, all indicating the importance given to agriculture. For example, a relatively small cement plant run by the county construction company had been closed down. A new cement plant with a designed annual capacity of 30,000 tons, directly under the county industrial bureau, had started production in 1972. A considerable part of the output from this plant was now to be used for irrigation projects.

The number of tractors had increased from approximately 150 at the end of 1971 to more than 400 in mid-1973—the majority being power tillers. The tractor repair plant had recently been given state grants in the form of specialized precision machine tools needed for the overhaul of large tractors. This included a gear hobbing machine from Shanghai, a crankshaft grinder, and another specialized grinding machine. Consequently, the plant could undertake more of the necessary specialized repairs and had been able to improve the quality of repair work and considerably reduce repair costs. The relevant tractor parts had previously been sent to Fengrun county, a tractor repair center serving the whole Tangshan region. The other two county-level farm machinery enterprises were now able to turn out, among other things, more simple lathes to be used in the communes' repair stations, more electric motors and pumps, and, at the same time, product quality had been improved.

The industrial bureau, which is responsible for all the county-level industrial enterprises except the tractor repair plant and the county-level brick kiln, had been reorganized at the beginning of 1973, and the staff had increased to thirty, ten more than at the end of 1971. At the same time, a new group for technology had been made a permanent feature of the industrial bureau. The Zunhua Electromechanic Factory, which is one of the three county-level machinery plants in Zunhua, had at the beginning of the year introduced a new system for quality control, which meant that specialized personnel were given the responsibility of supervising product quality. In this enterprise much emphasis was also given to the technical training of personnel both during working hours and in workers' spare time. The strengthening of leadership, as well as the attention given to technology and quality matters, had led to a considerable reduction in the rate of rejects for most products.

In Zunhua plants as well as in other farm machinery plants, a "three guarantee" system was now firmly being implemented. This means that the buyers—communes and brigades—are guaranteed repair, replacement, or even refund within a certain period of time—usually six months—if the product delivered is not up to specifications. This system is likely to have existed for a number of years in most places, but its rigid implementation may be a new thing. These changes are, of course, not confined to the county-level and even brigade-level enterprises, and there is no doubt that agriculture is benefiting from the strengthening of central management and technology matters in enterprises which serve agriculture.

Zunhua county has no doubt reached a more advanced stage in the development of the three-level farm machinery repair and manufacture network than many other parts of the country. This is evident from the information given in Table 25 (p. 107), which also shows that the whole of Tangshan region basically shared in this favorable development. However, at regional level, more than 10 percent of the communes lack farm machinery repair stations and about 30 percent of the brigades have no stations either.

Is the rural industrialization in Zunhua specific, or has the county only shared in a widely spread favorable development in Tangshan region? It appears from available evidence that the whole region has in recent years had a relatively rapid and favorable development of local industries—mainly serving agriculture. As a tentative conclusion, it is suggested that Zunhua is only slightly ahead of the development in the region.

The relatively rich resources and the big enterprises apparently have provided a very good base for local industry. In July 1972 it was reported by NCNA[2] that Tangshan region had set up more than 1,200 small plants and mines—most of them since 1969. These small plants were scattered all over the plains as well as in the mountainous and coastal areas. More than 2,000 different products were said to be produced by the local small industries including iron and steel, cement, chemical fertilizer, caustic soda, insecticides, grinders, threshing machines, water pumps, diesel engines, ball bearings, transformers, electric motors, machine tools, and a large number of industrial products for daily use.

In 1972 there were altogether 570 small mines producing coal, iron, copper, gold, mica, limestone and other minerals—usually run by counties and communes. Iron and steel industries existed in the two municipalities and in four counties—including Zunhua. There were then 30 small cement works run by counties or municipalities. Furthermore the region had 15 chemical fertilizer plants (nitrogen and phosphate)—one of which was run by the region itself, the rest by counties or municipalities.

At the same time it was reported that twenty-one small coal pits had been opened in the region supplying about a million tons

of coal per year for domestic and industrial use. Most counties—
among them Zunhua—had been allocated their own small coal pits
near the big Kailan coalfields in Tangshan city. Furthermore, an
overall arrangement has been instituted to coordinate iron mines
and production plants and to provide counties which have shortages
of mineral resources with the necessary raw materials for producing
farm tools.

The rapid development of local industries is said to have
brought about an enlarged farm machinery repair and manufacture
network serving counties, communes, and brigades within the
region. The network comprised at the time of the report 24 county-
level farm machinery repair and manufacturing plants, 400 commune-level farm machinery repair and manufacturing stations, and
2,000 brigade-level farm machinery repair and assembly points.

In addition to developing heavy industry, the region had
developed light industries for two different reasons. First, to provide people with daily necessities. Second, to provide heavy industry
and units engaged in agricultural mechanization with the necessary
funds for expansion. Many of the counties in the region have used
the funds and equipment of their existing factories and handicraft
cooperatives for establishing and running light industry factories or
workshops and for expanding and diversifying their production.
For example, sugar beets have been cultivated in at least five
counties.

Further evidence that the region has shared in an overall development of small local industries can be gained from looking into
the sources of technology for a number of plants that Zunhua had
set up since 1969. If local industrial development had been specific
to Zunhua, the two municipalities—Tangshan and Qinhuangdao—
would with their industrial bases have been the dominant sources
of technology for establishing new industries in the county. When
leading personnel in a number of county-run plants were interviewed
in December 1971 and July 1973, it became evident that Zunhua
had relied heavily on the industrial experience of counties—within
the region—where similar types of industrial production had already
been initiated. Some of the more important technology transfer

links used for setting up industries in Zunhua county have been illustrated in Figure 23. This indicates that neighboring counties were—aside from the two cities—major sources of manufacturing technologies.

Technology transfer involves transfer of equipment but consists basically of training provided in the donor's plant or by people from the donor plant in the new plant. Figure 23 is, of course, not comprehensive but indicates some of the technology sources utilized for initiating fairly complicated manufacturing tasks. It is clear that relations with Tangshan city, which is a major industrial city, were more important than those with any single county. But Changli county had been a major source of technology when setting up the iron and steel works, the rolling bearing manufacture, and the paper mill. Two neighboring counties had played an important role when Zunhua started to manufacture electric motors. Figure 23 also indicates that Zunhua had usually relied on a number of different technology sources for each new line of production. However, it is surprising that Qinhuangdao, which is both a port and an industrial city, did not figure as a major source of technology, except for the plastics factory, in any of the county plants surveyed. It should also be noted that sources outside the region were of considerable importance in setting up plants for which there was insufficient knowledge within the region. This appears , for example, to have been the case when Zunhua decided to set up a sulphuric acid plant which was to become a nucleus for a small chemical complex.

A major railway runs through Tangshan region, passes through one county capital (Changli) and touches two other county capitals. See Figure 23. There is no doubt that railway transportation will be beneficial for further industrialization of the region, but from earlier information it does not appear that the railway in itself has played a very significant role in the overall rural industrialization efforts carried out within the region. However, construction of a new railway link began in 1971 from Tangshan to Zunhua and passes through Fengrun county. This was said to reduce considerably the costs for coal transported from Tangshan—70 kilometers

Figure 23. Some Important Sources of Technology Used in the Setting Up of Selected Industries in Zunhua County, Tangshan Region, Hopei Province

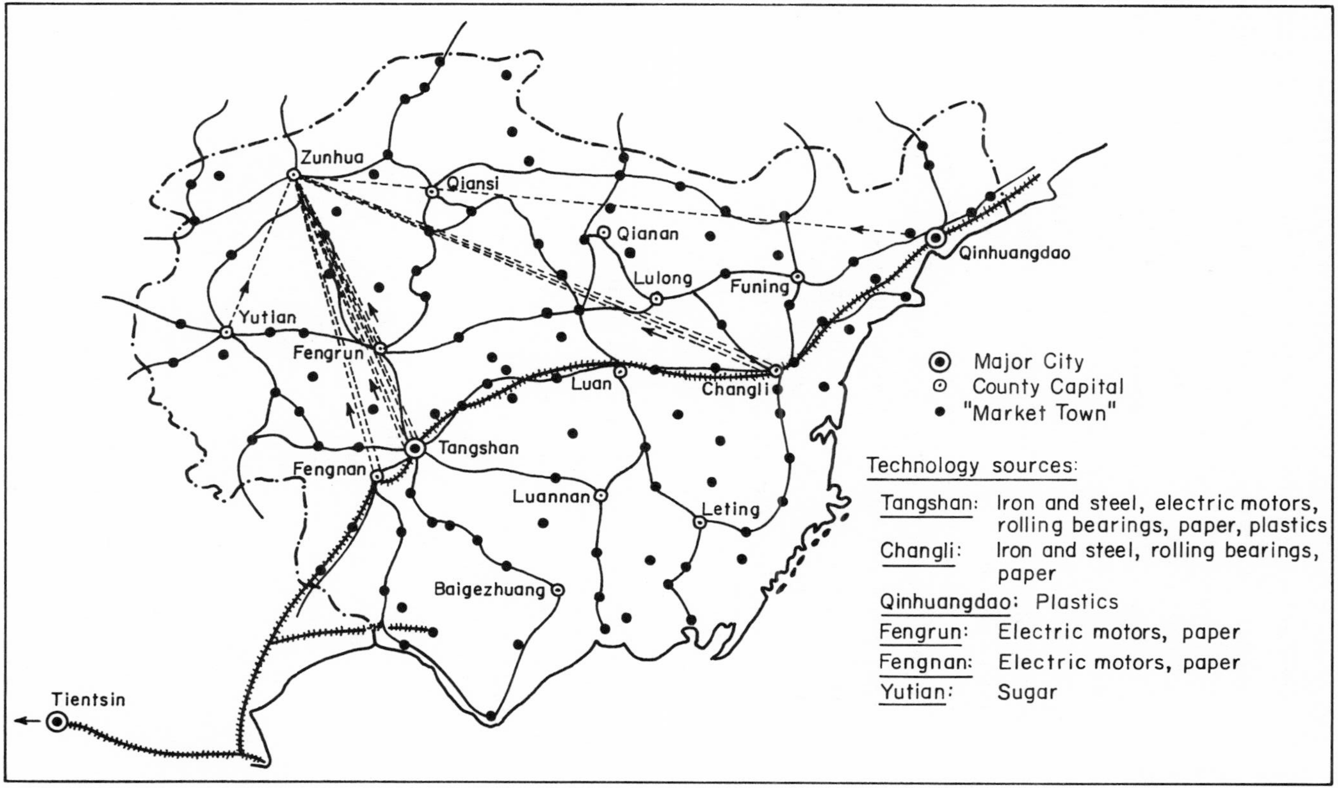
Zunhua
Qiansi
Qianan
Lulong
Funing
Qinhuangdao
Yutian
Fengrun
Luan
Changli
Tangshan
Fengnan
Luannan
Leting
Baigezhuang
Tientsin
Major City
County Capital
"Market Town"
Technology sources:
Tangshan: Iron and steel, electric motors, rolling bearings, paper, plastics
Changli: Iron and steel, rolling bearings, paper
Qinhuangdao: Plastics
Fengrun: Electric motors, paper
Fengnan: Electric motors, paper
Yutian: Sugar

away—and used for the production of chemical fertilizer and pig iron in Zunhua. The importance of Changli as a major source of technology for Zunhua—and most likely for other counties as well— is partly explained by the fact that the county capital is a central place on the railway and was once the capital of the region.

In July 1973 cement was produced in 10 plants located in as many places. Tangshan city has a relatively large modern plant with a rotary kiln. The remaining plants are all small ones and are located in Qinhuangdao city, Funing, Changli, Lulong, Luan, Qianan, Qiansi, Fengrun, Yutian, and Zunhua counties. The distribution of the small cement plants is shown in Figure 24, where the name of each county with a small cement plant has been indicated. It is obvious from the figure that all small plants are located in the northern, mountainous parts of the region, where raw material deposits are located. At the same time, the mountainous areas need more cement for their agricultural irrigation projects than the plains and coastal areas. It should also be noted that approximately 70 percent of the cement from the county-level plants is used for the counties' irrigation projects like dams, canals, wells, and so forth.

The Chinese press in 1972 reported—as earlier mentioned— that Tangshan region had established thirty cement works.[3] During a visit in July 1973, information was given which would indicate that there was only one small cement plant in each of the counties mentioned above. This would then mean that a number of the small cement plants had been closed down. This is, of course, possible. Zunhua county, for example, set up a small cement plant—run by the county construction company—at the beginning of 1971. This plant was closed down two years later when a considerably larger and more modern plant went into production. Similar developments may have taken place in other counties. Another explanation is that the region still has a number of very small commune-level cement plants which produce only intermittently, and which were not explicitly mentioned during the discussions in July 1973.

Tangshan region has eight nitrogen chemical fertilizer plants located in the following counties: Funing, Lulong, Fengrun, Zunhua, Yutian, Luannan, Leting, and Baigezhuang. These plants show a very

Figure 24. Distribution of Cement Plants, Fertilizer Plants, and Paper Mills in Tangshan Region

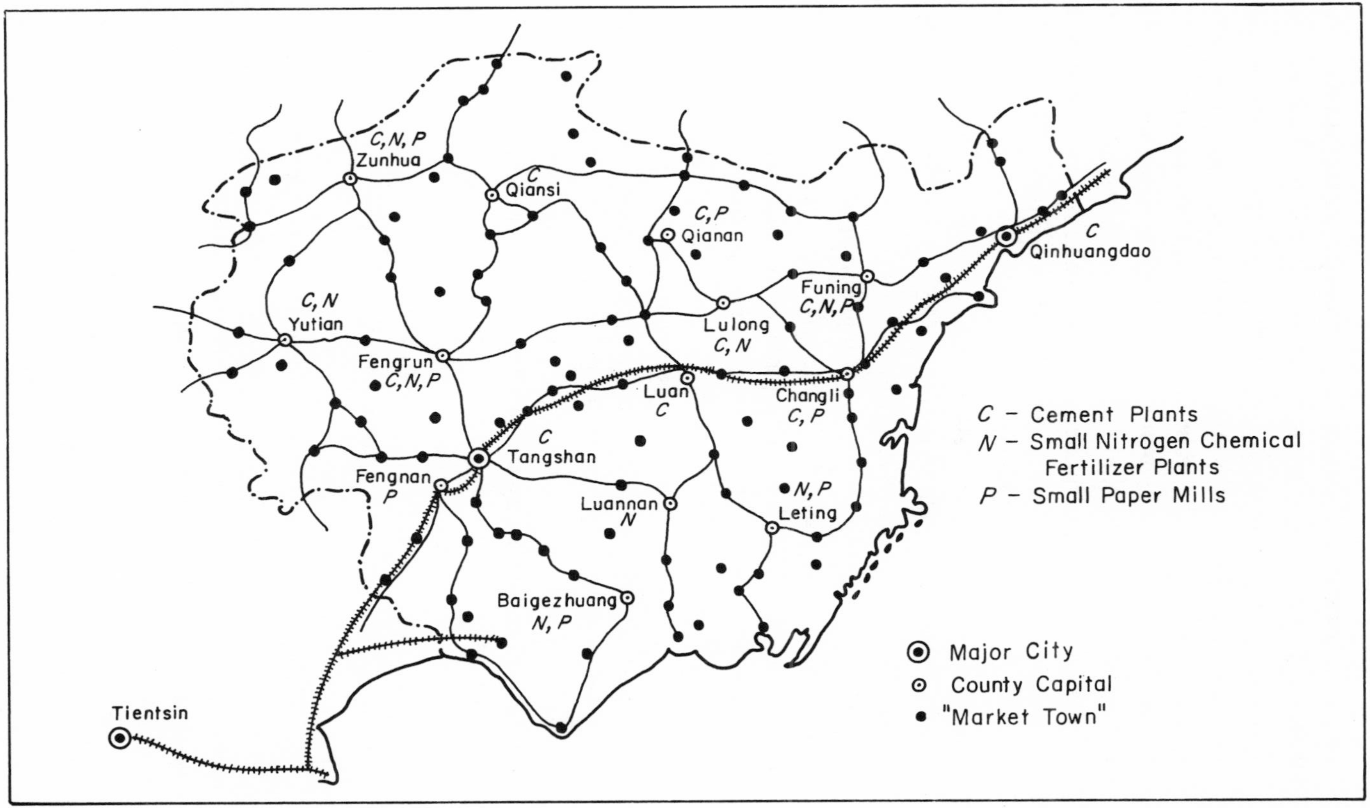

C — Cement Plants
N — Small Nitrogen Chemical
      Fertilizer Plants
P — Small Paper Mills

◉ Major City
◎ County Capital
● "Market Town"

Qinhuangdao
C

Funing
C,N,P

Changli
C,P

Leting
N,P

Qianan
C,P

Lulong
C,N

Luan
C

Luannan
N

Qiansi
C

Baigezhuang
N,P

Tangshan
C

Zunhua
C,N,P

Yutian
C,N

Fengrun
C,N,P

Fengnan
P

Tientsin

different distribution pattern from that of the cement plants. The three central places south of the railway line all have their own plants where the potentiality for increasing agricultural production may have played an important role in deciding to set up local plants. It should also be noted that none of the small fertilizer plants are located on the main railway line. Coal is the main raw material for all the small nitrogen fertilizer plants, and all coal in the region comes from mines in or near Tangshan city. Altogether there are more than twenty-three small coal pits run by counties, city districts, and neighborhoods. The production from these small coal mines was approximately 1 million tons in 1972. All twelve counties have their own coal mines. The production of the one run by Zunhua county was 87,900 tons in 1972.

One indication of the continuing economic and industrial integration of the region is the cooperative network which in 1971 was reported to have been set up between a number of the small chemical fertilizer plants. At least four units, those in Zunhua, Funing, Lulong, and Baigezhuang, have formed a network. The purpose of this is to share the responsibilities for providing certain spare parts often needed in the plants. The plants mentioned have agreed on a division of labor and the small nitrogen chemical fertilizer plant in Zunhua is responsible for the manufacture of certain valves needed by the plants involved in the cooperative network. In return the Zunhua plant gets other spare parts manufactured in the machine workshops of the other plants. It may be noted that the counties involved in this network are not those previously indicated as major technology source for the industrialization efforts in Zunhua.

The region also has some phosphate fertilizer plants—but their number and distribution are not known to the author. However, it may be noted that, in Zunhua, communes and not the county were responsible for the manufacture of phosphate chemical fertilizer. Zunhua has at least three commune-level phosphate fertilizer plants located near the sulphuric acid plants providing one of the two necessary ingredients. Phosphate rock—the other raw material—is being mined in Zunhua but was said to be of poor quality.

Tangshan city has a medium-size iron and steel plant. In addition to this, Tangshan city as well as Qinhuangdao city each has a small iron plant with a 13 cu. m plant. There are four other county-level iron plants—in Funing, Changli, Qianan, and Zunhua. Funing and Qianan only produce pig iron but three of the small plants—Qinhuangdao, Changli, and Zunhua—also produce steel. Steel-rolling is carried out in only one of the small plants, Zunhua. It should be noted that all four steel-producing units are in places located on the main railway line or at the end of the new railway link between Tangshan city and Zunhua completed in 1972. See Figure 25, where the Tangshan-Zunhua link, however, is omitted.

Basic industries like mining and steel have been developed in counties that have the necessary mineral resources. In counties lacking mineral resources—near the sea—a number of single-product chemical industries have been established. The local saltfields form part of the necessary basis, and the industries manufacture caustic soda, detergents, dyestuffs, etc.

In a number of places, including Zunhua, there has been serious discussion of providing the faraway brigades and communes with electricity from very small hydroelectric plants located in small streams. However, the great fluctuations over the year in water flow and other complications would require dam constructions that are too expensive to justify the benefits accruing from small electric plants. Consequently, certain places will have to wait for electricity while most places are connected to the general grid covering the area—at least at commune and brigade levels.

Small paper mills have been set up where suitable raw materials are available. Different types of raw materials can be used, but from discussions in Zunhua it appears that wheat stalks are preferred. A small paper mill of standard design produces two tons per day. The Zunhua paper mill is now being expanded to produce four tons per twenty-four hours. When the Zunhua paper mill was set up, technical expertise was reported to have come from similar small plants in Fengrun, Fengnan, Changli, and Tangshan city, where a considerably larger plant is located. Additional information given in July 1973 indicates that Baigezhuang, Leting, Funing, and Qianan also have

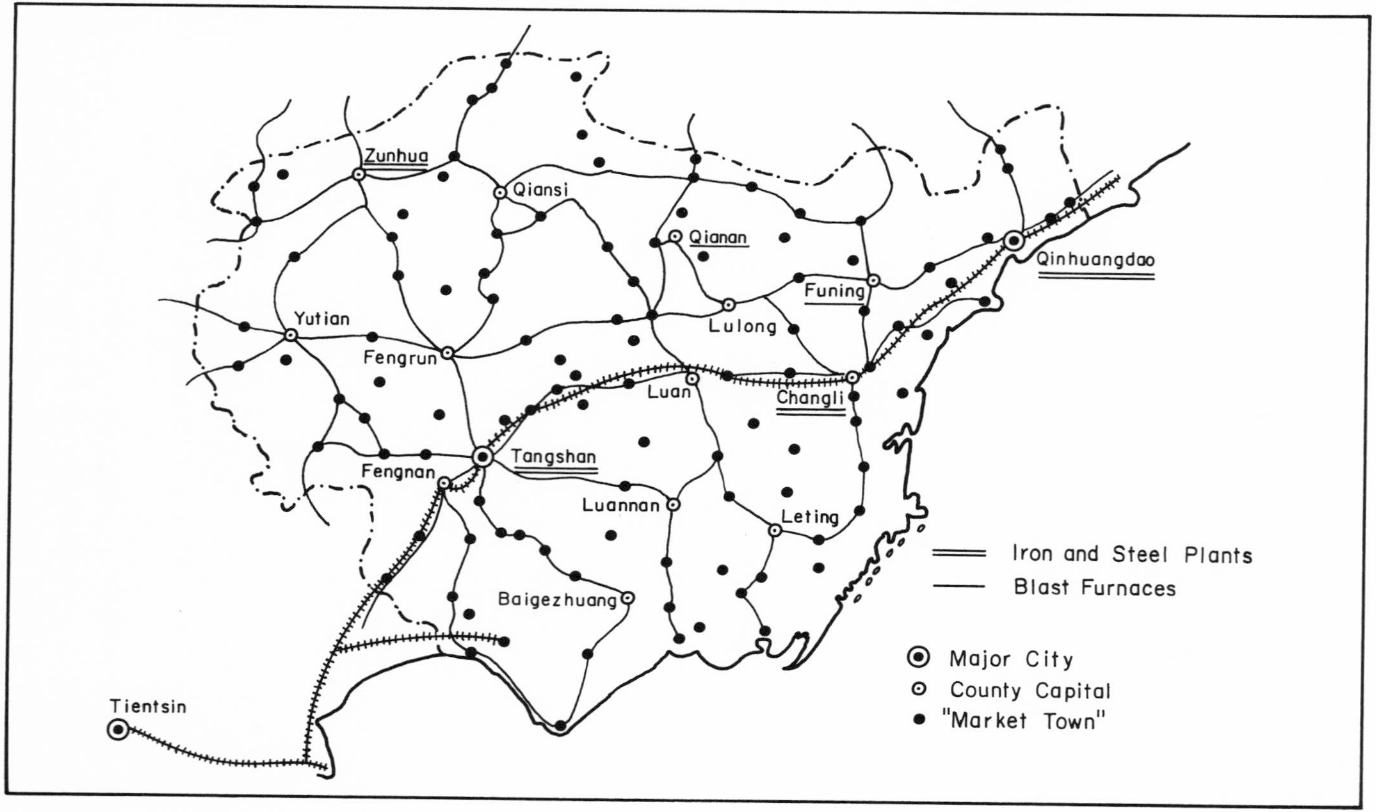

Figure 25. Distribution of Iron and Steel Plants in Tangshan Region

small paper mills. Figure 24 shows that the small paper mills are spread all over the region, which of course shows that the resource base is widely distributed. Furthermore, it should be remembered that scrap paper usually represents a considerable component in the supply of raw materials.

Chapter 6

THE RATIONALE OF RURAL INDUSTRIALIZATION
IN CHINA AND ITS RELEVANCE TO
OTHER DEVELOPING COUNTRIES[1]

It has taken time to develop the necessary institutions and
attitudes towards a development strategy that emphasizes large
numbers of small-scale industries in rural areas. At the same time,
China's rural industrialization programs have undergone sharp
oscillations between acceptance or rejection of major portions of
a development strategy. These oscillations reflect a political struggle
and changing internal and external conditions. The struggle involves
contention over the most fundamental questions of socio-economic
goals, and it affects every aspect of economic policy. No doubt
rural industry will continue to play a role in China's development
strategy for a number of reasons made clear in earlier chapters.
However, rural industry will play a less important role than was
once envisaged during the Great Leap Forward and possibly a
reduced role compared with the early 1970s.

It is obvious that the encouragement of efficient small-scale
industries in rural as well as urban areas has never been presented
as an alternative to the development of medium- and large-scale
enterprises. They have always been seen as a complementary element in the industrialization process. And the requirements of the
large industrial enterprises can never be neglected for long periods
of time because of their importance to overall economic construction and defense. Today—in 1975—there are certain indications
that, in planning her industrial imports and allocating scarce
resources, China has somewhat shifted the emphasis to modern
large-scale, city-based industries.

But the experience of already developed countries suggests
that a balanced industrial structure requires a considerable scale
span of enterprises. The provision of a development base for small-
scale industries in rural areas is then likely to give China significant
economic as well as social advantages for the future.

213

Industrialization in rural areas proper appears to have been more successful when the local character has been stressed. In other words, those activities with high coefficients for backward linkages to agriculture and for forward linkages to final users in the localities have been successful. A distinct difference between rural industrialization in the late 1950s and that since the Cultural Revolution is the latter's apparently higher coefficients for forward and backward linkages in the locality.[2]

It must be remembered, however, that rural industrialization is not pursued as a policy in isolation. It should rather be seen as the outcome of a combination of strategies—for various industrial sectors on one hand and for integrated rural development on the other hand. Industrial sector strategies aimed at expanding the lower end of the spectrum can be nothing more than part of an overall policy to develop rural areas. The sector strategies cannot usually operate in isolation, as they are dependent on demand and on resources that are influenced through rural development.

The development of institutions, technologies, and so forth for the lower end of the industrial spectrum in various sectors has made it possible to locate industries in rural areas—in city-near locations as well as in rural areas proper. The sector strategies are naturally undergoing constant changes due to changing internal and external conditions. Consequently, the lower end of the industrial spectrum is expanding rapidly in some sectors while it is contracting in others—thus influencing the rural industrial system.

Integrated rural development, on the other hand, includes rural industry only as one component of many instruments where improved public health, education, and introduction of agricultural technology all contribute to achieving policy objectives like increased gainful employment, increased productivity, and reduced differentials between urban and rural areas.

The justification of rural industrialization is obviously economic as well as social. Economic growth may, however, in the short run have slowed down because of the need to transfer technical, financial, and planning resources to rural areas in order to start rural modernization and industrialization programs. In the long run, however, rural industrialization is likely to contribute to a more rapid economic growth than would otherwise have been possible. First, a decentralized pattern of urban development is likely to lead to a less capital-intensive expansion of industrial growth, which is better adapted to prevailing factor availabilities and relative factor prices. Second, if a majority of the rural population—through integrated rural development—might be persuaded to remain in villages and expanding county capitals, this is likely to require less investment for expanding large urban centers. Third, rural industrialization provides the opportunity of simultaneously promoting agricultural and non-agricultural elements in the same local areas, and non-agricultural elements are just as dependent on a thriving increase in farm output and income as the latter are dependent on them. Fourth, a rural industrialization which has a strong core of local engineering enterprises is likely to play an important role in any decentralized industrialization policy.

An attempt is first made to summarize the economic reasons into three main categories—to reduce short- and medium-term capital requirements, to incorporate the economy of many locations into long-term planning, and to achieve resource mobilization—before the social aspects are mentioned.

The capital requirements are reduced in a number of ways. First, capital expenditures needed for housing and infrastructure are likely to be considerably lower in rural areas than in urban areas. Second, rural industries will in many cases reduce transportation costs, high transportation costs being partly a reflection of capital scarcity affecting the transportation sector. Third, as almost all equipment and machinery in small plants can generally be produced within the country, the requirements for foreign exchange are reduced. Fourth, capital savings may also be achieved if the economic lifetime of "obsolete" equipment from plants in the modern industrial sector can be extended through use in small- and medium-sized enterprises. Fifth, local small-scale mining and other industrial activity can sometimes be carried out with lower capital per output ratio than in big units. Sixth, the shorter gestation period for a number of the small-scale plants also has an important bearing on capital requirements.

The development of small-scale industries is similarly of importance for *long-term planning*. First, industrial bases can be located and gradually developed where the potential demand is and where the raw materials are. Second, they enable a domestic engineering industry and design capability gradually to develop, which is likely to lead to a higher utilization of plant capacity in the machine-building sector than would otherwise have been possible. Third, skill formation takes place within local industrial systems and can first adapt to future local needs and later on to the future needs of the modern industrial sector. Fourth, the industries become complementary and interrelated and can be used for large-scale subcontracting. And the system character facilitates the multi-purpose utilization of human and physical capital which may reduce the influence of bottlenecks.

Resource mobilization is another important area where the system of small-scale industries plays a role. First, the local character and extensive local control is likely to induce investment, particularly for commune- and brigade-level enterprises, and thus tap local savings arising from increased agricultural productivity which might otherwise be consumed. Second, the existing wage differential between cities and countryside can be utilized—through subcontracting—to reduce costs and thus increase investible profits. Third, the lower average wage level in the rural industrial sector might be an important factor in controlling the rate of increase of the wage level in the modern industrial sector.

On the other hand, there appear to be short-term contradictions in the simultaneous development of rural and urban industries. The urban-based, predominantly large and modern enterprises are affected in two important ways by the rapid development of local industry. First, as local enterprises in rural areas begin to manufacture producer and consumer goods, the urban-based industries which previously supplied such goods lose part of their markets. Since local industry is expanding all over the country, certain industrial sectors are likely to become increasingly affected. This may necessitate changes in the urban-based production profile, which would require a decision on the division of labor between urban and rural industries.

Many large industries are increasingly specializing in larger and more complicated products. Future industrial development in the large industrial cities will certainly emphasize products of high quality and complicated manufacture. Since the rural local industries are becoming more numerous, more sophisticated, and larger in scale, this shift in direction from the large industrial cities is likely to continue for some time. One effect will be to hasten the obsolescence of machinery in urban plants. However, since rural industries badly need equipment, it may be transferred to rural areas and adapted to the different economic conditions and their smaller scale of production.

The growth of rural industry is also affecting urban-based industry in another way. Rural industries are critically short of industrial technology. Part of this need is fulfilled through mutual study and exchange among local industries in rural areas. However, a large number of problems cannot be solved locally and must be resolved with the assistance of engineering and technical personnel from the urban-based enterprises. A considerable amount of the training necessary for personnel in rural industries is also carried out in the large enterprises.

These two problems—the gradual shift of industrial production from urban to rural areas and the lack of personnel for problem-solving and technical training—require a system of planning that reduces the independence of individual enterprises. If the urban-based enterprises were allowed to maximize profits, they would certainly have little interest in providing industrial training and problem-solving know-how to rural industries. In addition, few urban-based enterprises would be willing to give up their markets. As a result, much of the responsibility for individual enterprises must rest with local government planning agencies.

In broad political terms the leadership in China has committed itself to a policy aimed at reducing the differences between industry and agriculture, and between cities and countryside. This has meant, among other things, changing the terms of trade between industry and agriculture, and it has also meant a considerable expansion of services—public health, education, transportation, communications, and so forth—in rural areas. Rural industrialization plays an important role in this development in locating budding industries where the future potential demand is, in providing local agriculture with local industry, and generally in providing local people with some of the necessary tools of modernization. Thus, the majority of the population can at an early stage of development be drawn into the modernization process.

The principles of rural modernization and rural industrialization were spelled out early, but China had to carry out a considerable amount of experimentation in finding the appropriate forms of implementation. There has not always been a consensus on what rural modernization and rural industrialization policies should be, and the Cultural Revolution that started in 1966 is in many ways a new starting point for more active rural policies first initiated in 1958. Although many approaches of rural industrialization today are identical or similar to those of the Great Leap Forward period, there are also distinct differences. This book deals almost exclusively with the present stage of development of rural industries in China. However, the basic difference that must be mentioned is that rural industrialization today does not aim at rapid transfer of manpower from agriculture to industry, which was the case in 1958. Many development economists have in recent years tended to assume that China is achieving a considerable employment generation in the rural industrial sector. There is little evidence to support this notion, and there is nothing to indicate that Chinese planners are primarily aiming in that direction. Far more important is their objective of achieving a complementarity between agriculture and rural industry.

At present rural industrialization programs in China should basically be seen as one important instrument for influencing rural development—in combination with a number of other programs which have the same objective. And the immediate industrial employment increase appears to be rather limited, except in city-near locations. But the indirect effect on manpower utilization may be quite considerable.

Many Western economists have argued that the Chinese emphasis on small and medium industries in rural areas has been motivated by a need to create employment to absorb manpower outside the established industrial centers. This may be so in the long run, but there is little to support the view that this is a short-term objective. Moreover, the view that agricultural mechanization was not needed since China had plenty of manpower has been modified in recent years. The peak requirement for manpower in agriculture has increased considerably as a result of more transplanting, improvement in farming standards, and the expansion of arable land. Consequently the discrepancy between agricultural development and insufficiency of manpower has become increasingly prominent during certain periods of the vegetation cycle.[3]

A gradual development of the capacity for manufacturing farm machinery is now an important ingredient of the Chinese approach to rural industrialization. Great differences in soil, cropping, and climatic conditions are among the main factors explaining the dominance of the small-scale manufacture of farm machinery. Thus it is possible for a locality to decide for itself what machines should first be produced, and how they should be produced, even if types and models are roughly decided by the central authorities.

In view of complicated natural conditions and the present limited capacity for building farm machines, a fairly strict priority system appears to have been adopted. In sum, priority is given to the production which plays an important role in agricultural production, saves more manpower, uses less material, works at greater efficiency, and requires shorter time to build. In areas where multiple cropping takes place, the machines used in sowing and harvesting are the first to be produced, to ensure timely farming and to reduce the requirements for farming.

The provision of inputs to agriculture together with relevant policies appears to be important as it influences cropping practices and cropping intensity and consequently decides the labor absorption potential in agriculture proper. And the labor absorption potential in agriculture proper appears in the short run to be more important than any employment generation in rural industry. Furthermore, the expansion of education, public health, and other services is important for employment generation and it should be noted that their development in essence depends on the economic development of the localities.

Shigeru Ishikawa has pointed out that the competitiveness or complementarity of capital (mechanical inputs) in agriculture in relation to land and labor depends on the categories of capital. Thus, irrigation and other water control facilities are complementary with labor but are competitive with land.[4] The same applies to fertilizer. Agricultural machinery and implements—together with draught animals—are sometimes competitive and sometimes complementary with both land and labor. It cannot yet—by foreign observers—be ascertained whether the introduction of agricultural machinery and implements is competitive or complementary with land and labor. However, when pumps powered by electric motors or diesel engines enable intensified cultivation, the employment impact is definitely going to be positive. Similarly, there is likely to be a positive net effect when the introduction of power tillers enables an increase in the cropping index.[5]

Migration from rural to urban areas is dependent on a number of factors. The most important one may be the differential in employment and income opportunities, which is likely to contribute to the internal brain drain of young and mobile people in many developing countries. The differential in services and culture—including education—is another important factor. The migration of young and talented people is likely to be greatly influenced through employment and career opportunities provided outside agriculture where rural industry at least partly serves this objective.

Every person in rural areas in China is a member of a people's commune, which provides him with basic security. Agricultural mechanization is—in principle—controlled and people hindered from migrating into the cities. However, there can be no doubt that it will be impossible for China to mechanize agriculture as well as keep a majority of an increasing labor force in agriculture, so China has to come to grips with the problem of releasing manpower from agriculture. It certainly appears that different forms of rural industry—small-scale industry in areas dominated by agricultural or stock-farming activities—will play an important role. However, during the first stages of rural industrial development, employment is not primarily created in industrial production, but in repair and maintenance, in production of industrial raw materials, in transportation, and in other services, and in an increasingly diversified agriculture.

China's considerable progress in solving migration and regional problems is dependent on a well-organized party; increasingly competent administration at all levels, and collectively owned enterprises have contributed to the results. The necessary interaction and close cooperation among small local industries on the one hand and between rural industries and urban industries on the other hand would probably have been much more difficult if the enterprises were privately owned.

However, rapid development of rural industries has consequences for the balance between state and collective control, and the issue of ownership in China raises problems for the future. The many local industries which mobilize resources in order to speed up economic and social development have been made economically feasible by a number of factors. The use of appropriate technologies is part of the explanation. Moreover, the quality differential (and sometimes a wage differential) between small and large enterprises is sometimes a crucial explanation for the feasibility of the small enterprises. Chinese planners have apparently created a temporary dual economy, where the rural industries with lower wages and lower productivity are producing goods mainly used within the rural sector, while the urban-based industries with higher wages and higher productivity continue to support the building of a modern industrial base. These differences must for political reasons not continue to exist except in a transitional stage.

Socialist development requires an increase of ownership by all the people while ownership by small collectives decreases. The secular economic trend facilitates this social change: the value of industrial output increases more rapidly than that of agriculture. Since industry is run by larger collectives than agriculture, it appears that the trend is toward socialist transformation in rural areas. Many small industries, however, are collectively owned by brigades or communes, or jointly by the collectives and the state, while the big enterprises are owned entirely by the state. Since the small local enterprises are responsible for an increasing share of total industrial production in certain sectors, this may mean that fairly small collectives will have a considerable influence on the creation and disposal of industrial profits and investments. This may result in certain contradictions in long-term planning even if the higher administrative levels (region, province, and nation) have instruments at their disposal to encourage regional balance in rural industrialization.[6]

It should be noted that rural industry is part of a communications network where an important task is to spread innovations as quickly as possible within a local technology system. New things and ideas often look complicated to an outsider, and therefore people have to be able to ask questions, test things, and try ideas, and to get a feeling for them to fully understand and accept them. A tightly meshed network is then a consequence of the fact that the links of personal communication are heavily restricted by distance for most individuals. Yet, personal communication between pairs of individuals and direct observation are still the basic instruments for the diffusion of innovations.

Further, small-scale industries serve as an important training ground for peasants who are learning manufacturing skills and adapting to an industrial environment, and thus to conditions found in larger enterprises. This training is part of a general process of breaking down the barriers to a transition from a traditional to a modern economy. Consequently, rural industrialization has positive implications for the social development of the country. This is apparently one of the major reasons why the leadership has attempted to make rural industries reach almost every corner of the country, and thus contribute to the local promotion of technical and organizational skills.

A number of foreign observers have seen rural industrialization as an integral part of China's defense strategy. There can be no doubt that a potential capability to produce simple weaponry and explosives is now widely spread through the development of rural industrial systems. However, China's choice of defense strategy influences the viability of rural industry in two very different ways. An emphasis on "traditional" advanced weaponry would tend to reduce the role and the support for rural industry. On the other hand, an emphasis on guerilla-based defenses would give strong support for rural industry. In either case, the country is less vulnerable from an enemy attack if comprehensive industrial systems exist in a large number of places outside major urban centers. Consequently, part of possible higher production costs within the rural industrial systems should then be covered by the defense budget.

The traditional emphasis on a policy of macro-economic growth has in most developing countries proved ineffective in generating balanced socio-economic development. The existence of a dependency structure has usually created a wide gap between the modern and the traditional sector of the economy—particularly in the demand for and use of local resources. That unbalanced growth has tended to increase the disparity between the main urban centers and the rural areas.

Rural industrialization could play an effective role in rectifying this imbalance—as a means for equating local resources to local demands. But reduction of the differential between urban and rural areas requires a multi-faceted development program. Such development would include improved public health, education, introduction of agricultural technology, all of which are different aspects of upgrading the infrastructure in rural areas. And it would usually be necessary to effect these improvements, at least partially, before rural industry can be introduced.

Rural industrialization in China has involved two basically different elements. First, rural industrialization has been part of an industrial dualism strategy in a number of industrial sectors. Second, rural industrialization has also been part of a rural development strategy where repair/manufacture networks, modernized village crafts, reforms in public health, and education have all been components of an integrated approach. The lesson of this latter approach is likely to be of more interest to other developing countries than the industrial dualism in itself, even if it is not possible to separate the two completely.

There can be no doubt that rural industry will continue to play an important role in the modernization process of rural areas in China—even if changing strategies in some industrial sectors in the future might withhold certain pieces of the rural industrial systems.

Many aspects of rural development implemented in China in recent years are also desired in other developing countries. These include improved medical and public health facilities, improved education, and an efficient popular-based extension system in agriculture, all of which appear to reach a very high percentage of the population in rural areas in China. A comparison of achievements in China with rural development plans in other developing countries reveals considerable similarities. What are, then, the constraints hindering other countries—with a dominant majority of people still in rural areas, engaged in agriculture—from implementing such policies?

The immediate constraints are technical as well as political. Among the first is the question of distribution of costs and allocation of resources. China, as a planned economy with publicly (or collectively) owned enterprises, is able to regulate a distribution of costs not possible in most developing countries with their capitalist economies. Consequently, it is possible in China to plan and set lower profit margins for enterprises located in rural areas if this is considered justified because of reduced infrastructure investments in the economy as a whole, or for other reasons. China's widespread rural industrialization and other rural development strategies had to—and must in any other developing country—be based on adapted technology initially involving large numbers of paratechnical personnel. Neither technology nor technicians are immediately on hand and their procurement will require a strong political commitment to develop rural areas.

The political constraint is likely to be the most serious hindrance to a full-scale development of rural areas in most developing countries because of their dependency structure favoring mainly the modern structure. The Chinese Communist Party which today exercises leadership reached control of the country through its power base in rural areas. This political power base is still being maintained even if the economic power may be shifting towards urban areas. Such a political situation is not parallelled in any other country. So, even given the desire—in theory—in most developing countries, rural development plans will not be effectively implemented except as pilot or limited-area projects. The present dependency structure provides too strong an urban bias.

No doubt the technical constraints can be overcome. But the political constraints can scarcely be overcome unless there is a political shift towards rural areas.

Appendix 1

SELECTED STATISTICS FROM ZUNHUA COUNTY, TANGSHAN REGION, HOPEI PROVINCE*

Table A1-1. Zunhua county

Total area	1,640 square kilometers = 164,000 hectares—355 persons/sq km.
Cultivated area	64,000 hectares
Irrigated area	1971—18,700 hectares (22%)
	1973— (35%)
Grain production	3.8 tons per hectare (1971)
Value of grain production	about 50 million yuan (1972)
Total industrial production value	18,000,000 yuan (1970)
Income from side-line occupations	22,700,000 yuan (1972)
Total population	1966—485,000
	1971—553,000
	1973—584,000 (possibly only 570,000)
Number of households	116,000
Labor force	about 200,000 (estimate)
Production teams	2,499 (average of 200 persons per team)
Production brigades	691 (average of 800 persons per brigade)
Communes	43 (average of 12,800 persons per commune)

*All data in the three appendices are either data given by Chinese officials during visits in December 1971 and July 1973 or calculations based on such data.

227

Table A1-2. Some Statistical Information on Zunhua County
Public Health System and Schools System

Total population		553,000 (1971)
Number of households		116,000
Production teams		2,499
Production brigades		691
Communes		43

Public health system (1971)

678 brigade-level health service stations	2,105 medical personnel
41 commune-level clinics	
8 county-level hospitals (located in districts)	376 doctors
2 county-level hospitals	
	+4,138 "barefoot doctors"
	6,619 medical personnel

School system (1971)

Primary school, 5-year	698 units	(>44,000) all students attend
Junior middle schools, 3-year	187 units	26,121 students
Senior middle schools, 2-year	46 units	4,983 students
		>75,000 students

Re-education of students among peasants and
    workers (1971)

Total number received	4,624
Selected for university studies	40
Selected for commercial work	70
Selected for industrial work	821

Table A1-3. The Administrative Structure in Zunhua County

County Revolutionary Committee (1971)
21 cadres
5 PLA representatives
31 mass representatives
11 standing members   Altogether 70 cadres in 1971
    1 chairman (Wang Kuo-fan)
    4 deputy chairmen
Under the Revolutionary Committee
Administrative office
Political department
    organization
    propaganda
    mass organization (has been abolished since the revival of the trade
       unions, the youth league, and other mass organizations)
Production command
    planning group
    production group
    science and technology group
    general
Under the Three Departments (17 bureaus including the bank)
Industry
Commerce
Agriculture and Forestry
Grain
Public Health
Culture and Education (under political department, all others except public
    security are under production command)
Finance
Materials
Transportation (includes highway construction and road maintenance stations)
Civil Affairs
Water and Electricity
Post Office
Telegraph Office
Farming Machinery
Animal Husbandry
Bank
Public Security (under direct leadership of the revolutionary committee)
Under the Industry Bureau (30 cadres in 1973, 20 in 1971)
Administration
Production
Technology
Labor and Wages—about six in each unit plus leader.

Table A1-4. Zunhua County Industrial Activities

39 county-level industrial units—27 light industrial units	5,500 employees (1971)
71 commune-level industrial enterprises	2,500 employees (1971)
Brigade-level industrial activities	5,500 employees (1971)
Three-level agricultural machinery repair and manufacturing network (included above)	
3 county-level central farm machinery units (located in the county capital)	
7 county-level units (located in the county districts)	
43 + 1 commune-level units (1973)	37 units (1971)
620 brigade-level units (1973)	407 units (1971)
In addition, the county also has (not included above)	
"May 7" factories run by county and market town neighborhoods.	
"May 7" factories run by middle schools and some hospitals.	

Table A1-5. The Administrative Structure in Tangshan Region
(tentative outline)

Special District Revolutionary Committee
Under the Revolutionary Committee, 3 groups, with their respective bureaus,
 altogether approximately 400 cadres (1971)
1. Production command group
   a. Finance
   b. Trade
   c. Cadre Education
   d. Public Health
   e. Industry and Transportation
      light industry
      heavy industry
      machine-building industry
   f. Science and Technology
   g. Civil Affairs
   h. Agriculture and Forestry
   i. Aquatic Products
2. Political Group
   a. Organization
   b. Propaganda
   c. Reporting
3. Administrative Group

Under the Science and Technology Bureau, altogether 14 cadres
1. General
2. Agriculture
3. Industry
4. Archives and Data

Appendix 2

EXAMPLES OF COUNTY-LEVEL AND REGION-LEVEL ENTERPRISES

Table A2-1. County-Level Industrial Enterprises
in Zunhua County, Tangshan Region, Hopei

	Employees	
	1971	1973
1. Farm machinery plant 1 (farm machinery)		283
2. Farm machinery plant 2 (tractor repair)	90	147
3. Farm machinery plant 3 (power equipment)	210	225
4. Hardware factory		100
5. Tinsmith		
6. Bicycle repair factory		
7. Rubber tire repair factory		
8. Iron and steel plant	460	
9. Cement plant		307
10. Nitrogen chemical fertilizer plant		
11. Phosphate fertilizer plant (sulphuric acid)		
12. Farm insecticide plant		
13. Pharmaceutical plant		
14. Paper mill		
15. Coal mine		300
16. Brick kiln		
17. Porcelain factory		
18. Glass factory		
19. Cotton mill		
20. Oil pressing plant		
21. Textile mill	275	
22. Knitting mill	326	369
23. Carpet factory		
24. Clothing factory		
25. Tanning factory		
26. Shoe factory		
27. Plastics factory		46
28. Soap factory		
29. Food processing plant	230	
30. Printing shop		
31. Gold purifying plant		
32. Mine(s)		

Total county-level enterprises   39   Total employees   5,500

Total light industrial units   27

Table A2-2. County-Level Industrial Enterprises
in Lin County, Anyang Region, Honan

	Employees	
	1971	1973
1. Farm machinery plant (tractor repair)	208	
2. Farm machinery plant (farm machinery)		130
3. Power machinery plant (power equipment)	267	
4. Hardware factory		
5. Iron plant	207	130
6. Cement plant	250	210
7. Nitrogen chemical fertilizer plant	285	285
8. Phosphate fertilizer plant		115
9. Farm insecticide factory		
10. Coal mine	1,400	
11. Mine		
12. Brick kiln		
13. Porcelain and ceramics factory		
14. "Black light tube" factory (fluorescent lamps)	85	
15. Cotton processing plant 1		
16. Cotton processing plant 2		
17. Oil pressing plant		
18. Textile mill (spinning, weaving, dyeing)		
19. Tanning factory		
20. Shoe factory		
21. Fruit processing factory		
22. Food plant		
23. Printing shop		

Table A2-3. County-Level Industrial Enterprises
in Sulu County, Shihchiachuang Region, Hopei

	Employees 1973
1. Electromechanic factory	
2. Farm machinery plant 2 (tractor repair)	
3. Farm machinery plant 3 (diesel engines)	500
4. Cotton oil factory (ginning machines)	
5. Rubber tire factory	

Table A2-4. Region-Level Industrial Enterprises

Tangshan Region, Hopei

1. Farm machinery plant, Fengrun county

Shihchiachuang Region, Hopei

1. Farm machinery plant, Sulu county, approximately 700 employees
2. Chemical factory, Sulu county, approximately 1,000 employees

Anyang Region, Honan

1. Chemical fertilizer plant, Anyang county, 5,000 tons of synthetic ammonia/ year
2. Cement plant, Anyang county, designed capacity 30,000 tons/year
3. Printing shop

Appendix 3

SELECTED STATISTICS ON SMALL-SCALE CHEMICAL FERTILIZER, CEMENT, AND IRON AND STEEL PLANTS

Table A3-1. Some Statistical Information
on Local Nitrogen Chemical Fertilizer Plants

	Jiading county *Shanghai*	*Lin county* *Honan*	*Zunhua county* *Hopei*
Capacity synthetic ammonia	15,000 tons	3,000 tons	3,000 tons
Capacity solid fertilizer NH_4HCO_3	60,000 tons	12,000 tons	12,000 tons
Investment	¥8,000,000	¥2,800,000	
Investment/ton synthetic ammonia	¥530/ton	¥935/ton	
Investment/ton solid fertilizer	¥133/ton	¥250/ton	
Number of workers	630	285	338
Average wages	¥55	¥45	
Yearly total wages	¥415,000	¥154,000	
Wages per ton synthetic ammonia	¥28/ton	¥51/ton	
Wages per ton solid fertilizer	¥7/ton	¥13/ton	
Cost per ton solid fertilizer	¥90/ton	¥160/ton	¥150/ton
Profits 1971	¥700,000	¥160,000	¥80,000
Investment/workers	¥12,700	¥9,800	

Table A3-2. Some Statistical Information on Local Cement Plants

	Zunhua county, Hopei	Lin county, Honan
Constructed	1970	1958
Closed down		1962
Reconstructed		1965
Employment	97 workers	250 workers
Average wages	¥38/month	¥43/month
Total wages	¥44,000	¥129,000
Daily production	30 tons (December 1971)	60 tons (December 1971)
Production: 1970		17,000 tons
1971	2,400 tons	20,000 tons
1972	9,000 tons (planned)	22,000 tons (planned)
Wages per ton (1971)	¥18.40/ton	¥6.50/ton
Cost	¥68/ton (1971)	¥36/ton (1971)
Price (quality no. 400)	¥75/ton	¥47/ton
Investment		
Fixed capital ⎫	¥270,000	¥330,000
Working capital ⎭		¥100,000

Table A3-3. Some Statistical Information on
Local Iron (and Steel) Plants

	Zunhua county, Hopei	Lin county, Honan
Constructed	1958	1958
Closed down	1960	1962
Reconstructed	1970	1969
Blast furnace	8 cu m—operating	6.5 cu m—operating
Pig iron	8 ton/day	6.5 ton/day
1971 production	2,500 tons	2,000 tons
Ratio between daily production and blast furnace volume	1.0	0.946
Ratio between coke consumption and pig iron production	1.6	2.0
Iron content of ore	38–40%	38–39%
Employment	460	207
Average wages Total wages/year Wages/pig iron	¥40/month	¥40/month ¥99,000 ¥50/ton
Cost of pig iron Price	¥400/ton	¥277/ton ¥110–160/ton
Other facilities	8 coke ovens 20–30 ton/day 0.5 ton electric furnace 2-ton steel converter	Coke ovens
Expansion plans	Steel-rolling mill (1972) 28 cu m blast furnace (planned 1972) Oxygen plant (planned 1972) Ore dressing plant (planned)	13 cu m blast furnace (1972) Steel converter (planned)

NOTES

Preface

1. "The Role of Small Scale and Rural Industry and its Interaction with Agriculture and Large Scale Industry in China," EFI, Stockholm, July 1974 (Mimeo), 168 pp.

Introduction

1. The objectives and organization of the two main sectors of small-scale industry appear to be quite different. The urban small-scale sector has three main objectives. First, to train and utilize manpower that would otherwise not have been drawn into the production sector—like housewives and retired people. Second, to make use of "waste" products from big factories—including everything from sheet metal to chemicals—and also to collect and utilize discarded products. Third, to produce a number of products and components—on a subcontracting basis—for larger companies. There are three major categories of enterprises: factories under industrial bureau leadership, factories run by the street committees, and industrial teams organized by the "neighborhoods." Almost all these enterprises are collectively owned. The teams are small but very numerous in most cities. Shanghai reported in 1972 that the city had 380 neighborhood factories and 4,000 teams employing altogether 210,000 persons. On the basis of such scanty information from Shanghai and other cities, it may be inferred that 3%–5% of the urban population—of approximately 150 million—is engaged in small-scale industrial activities. This would give a total figure of about six million.

2. Localities with less than 5,000 inhabitants are defined as rural in international statistics.

3. The Chinese labor force is estimated to be approximately 350 million, which is about 70% of the population between the ages of 15-64. A couple of provinces have, since the summer of 1973, clearly indicated that—based on local conditions and relevant instructions from higher authorities—the number of workers used by industries at county, commune, and brigade levels should not exceed 5% of the labor force in a county. (Information provided by officials of Lin County Industrial Bureau, Honan province, Summer 1973.)

239

4. China has—with few exceptions—chosen not to publish any aggregate
    figures since 1960. This makes it almost impossible to discuss rural
    industrialization on the basis of available statistics. However, sufficient
    information is available from the Chinese press and from visitors to get
    a fairly comprehensive picture of what is attempted in rural industriali-
    zation and how the present stage of development has been achieved.
    Sometimes the presentation may be supported with figures—which in
    particular applies to the heavy industry component of rural industry—
    but the reader should be warned that the author may sometimes have
    confused policy and implementation with his own interpretation of
    rural industry in China.

Chapter 1

1. The presentation here aims only at providing a rudimentary frame of
    reference for the discussion of rural industrialization. For details, it is
    suggested that the reader consult:
    a. Audrey Donnithorne, *China's Economic System,* London, 1967
    b. Alexander Eckstein, "Economic Growth and Change in China,"
       China Quarterly, No. 54 (1973)
    c. Joint Economic Committee of the Congress of the United States,
       China Reports 1967, 1972, and 1975
    d. Franz Schurmann, *Ideology and Organization in Communist China,*
       Los Angeles, 1968
    e. Barry Richman, *Industrial Society in Communist China,* N.Y.,
       1969.

2. The description here is based on a summary which was published in
    China Reconstructs, Peking, August 1973, pp. 21-23.

3. It is essential to differentiate between the "two-leg" policy of develop-
    ment and the Great Leap Forward approach in 1958-1959. The former
    still applies while the latter, with its heavy emphasis on the lower end
    of the industrial spectrum to achieve industrialization objectives, no
    longer applies.

4. "Let the whole party develop agriculture energetically," by Chao Tzu-
    yang, *People's Daily,* July 23, 1960 (SCMP 2319).

5. "Raise labor productivity constantly," *Shanghai Chieh-fang Jih pao,*
    May 2, 1959 (SCMP 2048).

6. The discussion in this section is partly based on "Rural Industrialization in Mexico—A Case Study," prepared for the U.N. Expert Group Meeting on Rural Industrialization in Bucharest, 24-28 September 1973, Document ESA/SD/AC/.5/9, 27 February 1973.

7. These categories would in the Chinese context correspond to:
    1. County capitals and all smaller (market) towns
    2. Most seats of regional administration, e.g., Anyang in Honan
    3. Some of the seats of regional administration and a few provincial capitals
    4. Peking, Shanghai, Tientsin, and many of the provincial capitals.

8. Information available in 1975 indicates that approximately 11 million middle-school students have gone to rural areas for semi-permanent settlement.

Chapter 2

1. See, for example; Audrey Donnithorne, "China's cellular economy: Some economic trends since the Cultural Revolution," *The China Quarterly*, No. 52 (October–December 1972), 605-619.

2. A detailed discussion of the wage system is found in Charles Howe, *Wage Patterns and Wage Policy in Modern China, 1971-1972*, Cambridge, Cambridge University Press, 1973.

3. "Way to solve population problem in China," *People's Daily*, February 1, 1958.

4. See, for example, *Making Green Revolution—the Politics of Agricultural Development in China*, by Benedict Stavis, Ithaca, Rural Development Committee, Cornell University, 1974.

5. *World Population Prospects as Assessed in 1968 Population Studies*, No. 53. United Nations, New York, 1973.

6. See, for example, Carl Djerassi, "Some Observations on Current Fertility Control in the People's Republic of China," *China Quarterly*, No. 57 (January–March 1974), 40-62.

7. In the rural areas around the big industrial cities the level of industrial

employment is for several reasons relatively high. First, rural manpower is recruited into big enterprises. Second, certain categories of industrial production are transferred from national enterprises to collectively owned enterprises at commune level. Third, agriculture has reached a higher level of mechanization, and manpower can be spared.

8. *Site and Transport Planning for Industrial Enterprises,* compiled by Peking Industrial Construction Planning Bureau, Ministry of Construction and Engineering, Peking, China's Industrial Publishing House, January 1963.

9. Total employment is 700, which is distributed in the ratio 4:3:3 among the three communes. The justification for choosing the present location depends on two factors. First, gas, which is required in large quantities, was available in Chiating county seat, which is only about 1 km. away. Second, the short distance between the county seat and enterprise location facilitates transportation. Almost all the machinery had been taken over from one of the large bulb enterprises in Shanghai. However, the communes plan to install an automated line for the bulb production in the near future. Four different types of lamps are manufactured: railway signal lamps, low voltage lamps, ship lamps, and ordinary bulbs. The problem at present is the high reject rate.

The spatial distribution of enterprises in rural areas in Shanghai is based on the following two principles. First, industry should not be concentrated in only one or two counties. Second, industry should not be located in the near suburbs. Another important consideration is the complexity of the technology involved, and the case of the small tractor exemplifies this. The departments concerned originally planned—in the early 1970s—the transfer of small tractor production from the Shanghai Tractor Plant to several counties in Shanghai rural areas. It was then realized that too many complex parts were involved, and it was decided that the tractor plant should continue to manufacture the walking tractor as well as a 45 hp tractor.

10. *New China News Agency,* as reported in BBC Summary of World Broadcasts, *Weekly Economic Report,* FE/W713 (28 February 1973).

11. BBC FE/W571.

12. BBC FE/W713.

13. "Relationship between agriculture, light industry, and heavy industry," *Peking Review,* No. 34 (1972), 7–9, 20.

Chapter 3

1. China has, since the 1960s, registered a number of outstanding technical and scientific results. Among these are insulin synthesis, advanced research in polymer chemistry, the orbiting of earth satellites, development of nuclear weapons and rockets, a high level of sophistication in the machine tool industry, a technical performance of electronic products that matches what the outside world can do. These achievements suggest a successful technology and science policy. But such fragments give us only very limited information about the strengths and weaknesses of China's technology system.

2. Illuminating information on the commune as a technology system can be found in Ward Morehouse, "The Commune As a 'Technological System': Notes on Hua-Tung Commune," *China Quarterly*, No. 67 (September 1976), 582–596.

3. "China Develops Science and Technology Independently and Self-Reliantly," *Peking Review*, No. 46 (1974), p. 14.

4. The increased wheat/maize intercropping also changes the raw material situation for the local paper plants which use wheat stalk for the manufacture of low- and medium-grade paper.

5. Adapted from "Technology Transfer, Institutional Transfer, and Induced Technical and Institutional Change in Agricultural Development," by Vernon M. Ruttan, a paper prepared for presentation at a seminar on technology transfer in modernizing nations, sponsored by the West Pakistan Institute of Management, Karachi, November 1973.

6. Hupeh provincial service, December 14, 1971, BBC–FE/W653.

7. Transfer of human-embodied technology can be initiated within the enterprise or within the local administration with responsibility for the enterprise in question. Both ways are common.

8. Fukien provincial service, December 30, 1971, BBC–FE/W658.

9. Liaoning provincial service, October 29, 1972, BBC–FE/W701.

10. BBC–FE/W586.

11. BBC–FE/W676.

12. BBC–FE/W668.

13. Liaoning provincial service, December 10, 1972, BBC–FE/W706.

14. BBC–FE/W661.

15. Shansi provincial service, February 4, 1971, BBC–FE/W608.

16. See, for example, "Provincial R and D Activities in Post-Cultural Revolu-
     tion China," a preliminary report on Kwangtung province by Ward
     Morehouse, Director, Center for International Programs and Comparative
     Studies, State Education Department, University of the State of New
     York, July 1973.

17. This figure is likely to be an underestimation as it includes the popular-
     based extension activities only insofar as they involve specific projects
     or formally trained technicians. Consequently, manpower allocated and
     other costs borne by the communes, brigades, and teams do not show up
     in the budget presented above.

18. Shigeru Ishikawa has pointed out that a system of centralized physical
     planning often generates serious micro-economic problems if partial
     indicators of the total enterprise activities—usually physical output of
     most important products, total output in monetary terms, or total
     profits—are used as success indicators for the evaluation of the perfor-
     mance of an enterprise. The result often is that those enterprise activities
     that are not reflected in the success indicators are neglected. The quality
     improvement of existing products and the trial-manufacture of new
     products—all of which are very important activities in developing the
     farm machinery industry—are those to be sacrificed first. ("Chinese
     Method for Technological Development—The Case of Agricultural
     Machinery and the Implement Industry," paper presented at OECD
     symposium on Science, Technology, and Development in a Changing
     World, Paris, April 21-25, 1975.)

19. The use of appropriate technologies in rural industries is dependent on
     a number of factors where transfer of technology mechanisms and simple
     local adaptations often have played an important role. Even if responsi-
     bility has largely been delegated to the localities—counties and com-
     munes—there is at the same time a clear distinction whereby overall

supervision and coordination still rest with the higher administrative levels—regions and provinces. That this must be so is clear from the following measures that appear to be important in fostering the use or development of technologies appropriate for the economic development of rural areas in China:

1. The development of "entirely" new technologies in research and design institutes. This approach is not very common and the only apparent examples are the designs for small chemical fertilizer plants.
2. The use of old designs and processes and second-hand machinery which were developed for factor proportions resembling those in rural areas. "Second-hand" may not primarily mean old and worn-out machinery, but rather equipment which has become obsolete and is uneconomic in the economic factor climate of the cities. Such equipment may still have years of life under economically favorable conditions in the countryside.
3. The adjustment of factor prices to reflect the relative scarcities in rural areas so that local industries generate innovations appropriate to their factor endowment. The modified machine tools are an example of the consequence of this policy. The different pricing of idle equipment and machinery "imported" into a county may have been calculated to achieve a substantial shift toward the use of labor instead of capital both in making and using equipment.

20. "Industrialization and Productivity," *Bulletin No. 17* (1970), UNIDO D/SER A.

21. Information provided by Anyang region industrial bureau (Honan), 1973.

22. The transfer of old machines is facilitated by the fact that wages and social overheads are lower in local industry in the countryside than those in urban-based industry. The average wages in county-run enterprises are likely to be about 35% lower than in urban ministry-controlled enterprises.

23. BBC–FE/W756.

24. The concept of rural small hydroelectric stations still receives considerable attention from planners in China. This is obvious from the fact that regionally and provincially published books on the subject are printed in 60,000–70,000 copies. The Kwangtung Irrigation and Electricity Bureau has compiled *Village small scale hydroelectric power stations,* printed in

63,000 copies (Kwangtung People's Publishing House), and this is only one example among many.

25. "Struggle for nationwide preliminary electrification," by Lan-po Liu, Vice-Minister of Water Conservancy and Electric Power, *People's Daily*, June 21, 1958.

26. *Basic knowledge for the electrification of rural areas*, Northeast Power Bureau, Shenyang, 1971.

27. Information from Fokang county in Kwangtung province as reported in BBC–FE/W586. In a more recent book, instructions are found on how to make turbines out of ferro-cement (*Village Hydroelectric Stations*, 2 vol., compiled by an editorial committee in the Irrigation and Electricity Bureau of the Hunan Provincial Revolutionary Committee, Hunan Publishing House, 1st edition 1974, 12,000 copies).

28. BBC FE/W706, FE/W698.

29. Methane gas (biogas) produced from anaerobic fermentation of organic waste materials has in recent decades become a source of renewable energy in a number of countries. Large-scale plants are in operation in the USSR, USA, Federal Republic of Germany, and a number of other countries. Smaller-scale plants are in operation in India, the Republic of Korea, Pakistan, and other developing countries. The United Nations Development Program has recently decided to organize workshops on biogas technology and utilization in India and China (Project of the Governments of the Economic and Social Commission for Asia and the Pacific [ESCAP] Region, 11 November 1974). For reasons unknown to the author, China was excluded, and the background study focused on Japan, the Republic of Korea, the Philippines, Pakistan, and India. Workshops have been organized in India and the Philippines. The following documents—among others—are available:

"Report of the Workshop on Biogas Technology and Utilization," E/CN./IHT/L.18, 22 August 1975.

"Report of the Preparatory Mission on Biogas Technology and Utilization," IHT/BG(2)/4, 2 October 1975.

These and other documentation on biogas from ESCAP countries appear to be good on technical information but weak on the economic and social issues involved.

30. Those interested in alternative energy sources for rural areas should

consult Norman L. Brown, *Energy for Rural Development: Renewable Resources and Alternative Technologies for Developing Countries,* National Academy of Sciences (Washington), 1976.

31.   BBC–FE/3953.

32.   Leadership improvement can, in fact, deal with a number of different aspects, such as willingness to try new seeds, the popularization of new seeds, accounting systems, and willingness to make investments which will pay off later on, as well as the more strictly political matters generally referred to in press reports.

33.   These issues are thoroughly dealt with in *Making Green Revolution* by Benedict Stavis. (See Chapter 2, n. 4.)

34.   *Current Background,* No. 891, 8 October 1969, p. 56.

35.   *Peking Daily* Editorial, September 6, 1960 (SCMP 2354).

36.   However, the issue of uneven development may not be easily solved in China's present stage of development. Stavis (*Making Green Revolution*) in a concluding chapter deals with the emerging problems of regional inequalities and the existing equalities within the villages. He states that:

> because the (agricultural) production units can retain the bulk of the increments in income from improved productivity, and because wealthier communes invest more, it is clear that the richer production units can become even wealthier. This would suggest a general pattern of increasing inequality in the Chinese countryside. There are no statistical data that would conclusively show this pattern of increasing inequality, but a variety of reports from many communes from visitors to China show that family income is much higher in communes with good natural conditions and near cities than in the other communes.

37.   An avalanche effect is achieved by training first a group of instructors in accelerated training courses. These instructors are then assigned to lower level units to transfer their knowledge within the various networks.

38.   The total number of barefoot doctors exceeds 1 million, and the number of people in the agricultural mass scientific network exceeds 10 million. The opportunity costs for providing the services rendered by these groups

through "Western-trained" personnel are likely to have been many times higher than present realized costs. Furthermore, it would have taken many years to develop such technical forces. However, even if there is a strong commitment to integrate theory and practice in all Chinese training programs, there is no indication that the Chinese leadership sees the use of paratechnical personnel as a long-term solution.

39. This information is based on a broadcast report (Hopei radio, September 27, 1972, BBC–FE/W695) and further confirmed by interviews.

40. An excellent introduction for the automobile industry is found in "Technology Transfer in the Automotive Industry in the People's Republic of China," a report by Jack Baranson, 1973.

41. See, for example, "Local automobile industry expands rapidly," *China Reconstructs,* October 1970, pp. 32–34.

42. BBC–FE/W 601.

43. BBC–FE/W592.

44. The new provincial truck plants are not comprehensive plants but rather assembly plants where major components still come from centralized manufacturing units. Consequently, there is a certain similarity to the decentralized knocked-down car manufacture which is being practised in many parts of the world.

45. BBC–FE/W644.

46. BBC–FE/W603.

47. BBC–FE/W628.

48. BBC–FE/W628.

49. BBC–FE/W597.

50. BBC–FE/W605.

51. BBC–FE/W675.

52. BBC–FE/W578.

53. BBC–FE/W670.

54. BBC–FE/W639.

55. BBC–FE/W642.

56. BBC–FE/W684.

57. BBC–FE/W610.

58. *Hung ch'i* (Red flag), No. 10 (1972), article by Yu Chung-yuan on relations between industry and agriculture, BBC–FE/W4127.

59. BBC–FE/W677.

60. BBC–FE/W684.

Chapter 4

1. The overall development of China's fertilizer industry is described in *China's Fertilizer Economy* by Jung-chao Liu, Edinburgh University Press, 1971.

2. It should be observed, although the theoretical nitrogen content is 17.5%, it may actually be lower for a number of reasons. The Chinese news media actually say that "as this fertilizer decomposes very easily, heavy losses are caused by evaporation in transport, storage, and application ... To solve this problem ... tried to pelletize powder-form ammonium bicarbonate and applied the pellets deep in the soil. By using this method, which the masses call 'pellet deep-soil application,' evaporation of ammonium bicarbonate is curbed and fertilizing effectiveness increased by one third." (Information from the Nanking Soil Institute and reported by NCNA–BBC–FE/W845/A10.)

3. These were apparently not promoted until it became clear that the commune-run nitrogen chemical fertilizer plants represented an unrealistic alternative.

4. Information provided by the Swedish manufacturer of nitrogen fertilizer, SUPRA in Landskrona.

5. It should be pointed out here that we don't know the exchange rates

used by planning agencies in order to decide plan prices for imported machinery, equipment, and complete plants. Furthermore, it has been assumed that the prices mentioned for domestically manufactured plants are plan prices.

Instead of using the official exchange rate one would have liked to use a computed rate of exchange expressing in terms of yuan the national *average* of domestic input required to procure one dollar by means of exports. It may be argued that the marginal input required to improve foreign exchange balance should be used instead of the average input. However, the former may not be known even to Chinese planners. It should be noted that the marginal input required at present to improve the foreign exchange balance will most likely be higher than the present-day average input. Improvement in commodity structure and market distribution of exports and decreased domestic production costs will change this. Consequently, the marginal input which will be required in future to improve the balance of foreign exchange can, therefore, be expected to decrease and approach the present-day average. (These comments are based on the discussion of exchange rates in Janos Kornai, *Mathematical Planning of Structural Decisions*, Amsterdam, North-Holland Publishing Company, 1967.)

6.   Cement production is a rather complicated process. The main process consists of heating certain basic substances at a very high temperature in correct proportions to produce clinkers which when crushed provide portland cement. In actual operation this process requires a system of mechanical devices for breaking stones, carrying them to silos, mixing the various products, heating them in kilns which yield clinkers, which are then ground to cement. Further, arrangements for packaging and transportation have to be made.

Designs of mechanical supports for the various operations such as conveyor systems, silos, nodulizers, and kilns depend on the types of raw materials used, the scales on which the operations are carried out. Technologically there is no special factor restricting the scaling down of the process. However, the process must be economically viable—when all externalities are taken into consideration.

7.   This is, of course, surprising in the light of the history of the vertical kiln which can be summarized in the following words: "The vertical kiln is the oldest method of cement manufacture. However, in its early form, manufacturing difficulties were frequent, the labour force to

operate it was high and the quality it produced could not keep in step with the increasing requirements of modern concrete. In the early twenties the vertical kiln was practically abandoned; only a few plants survived until after world war II but soon these too were replaced by other, more up to date cement manufacturing processes." ("Development Note for the Calcining and Sintering of Cement Clinker and Other Materials in a New Shaft Kiln," prepared for UNIDO by Steven Gottlieb, UNIDP/ITD.223, 13 November 1973.)

8.   The kilns of China's modern small cement plants—usually operated by counties or regions—generally have the following features:
    1. The feed is uniform nodules obtained from a simple disc nodulizer.
    2. The kiln is fed more or less continuously by a team of men working on the top of the kiln.
    3. Clinker formation is confined to the upper portion of the kiln.
    4. Draught is usually induced and heat exchange takes place in the lower portion of the kiln.
    5. Clinker discharge is usually discontinuous.
    6. Fuel economy is good because of:
        a. fuel being interground into the nodules;
        b. efficient heat exchange within the kiln;
        c. porous clinkers, which need less energy for grinding.
    7. Solid fuels with higher ash content are often used.

9.   The managers of small-scale plants in China claim that the quality number of their cement usually exceeds 400. This means 400 kp per cm^2 and is the test value when measuring compressive strength after 28 days. This corresponds to 39.5 MN/m^2. Altogether there are in accordance with state regulations six classes of cement—in terms of compressive strength. These are 200, 250, 300, 400, 500, and 600 kp/cm^2. On the assumption that testing methods are comparable with those specified by the British Standards Institution, the cement produced in small-scale plants compares favorably with portland cement from large-scale plants. However, recent visitors to small-scale cement plants in China have questioned the quality statements and claim that the locally produced cement would fall in the range of 250–325 if tested according to BSI standards. In spite of this controversy, the Chinese use of locally produced cement for most construction purposes in rural areas has not been questioned on quality grounds.

10.   The China Construction Publishing House in 1972 provided a number of booklets under the general heading of "Small Cement Technical

Material." The series consisted of approximately 15 issues dealing with instrumentation, problems of testing, etc. Two of the booklets describe alternative kiln designs which had been tried out in Liaoning and Honan. The basic design for both was ground-level firing chambers that resemble limekilns being used in India. I have not, however, come across any information that indicates that these alternative designs have been widely introduced outside their original locations.

11.   A major reason for these comparatively low production costs may possibly be that plants have been constructed using large amounts of idle or scrap equipment. This has then been provided at opportunity costs which have been much lower than if new equipment would have been available through central plan allocations.

12.   "Small cement plants play big role," *Peking Review,* No. 49 (1972).

13.   Costs for conventional cement plants of this size are still higher. However, recently a designed compact precalciner permits the feeding of completely decarbonized raw mix into a rotary kiln with still acceptable exit gas temperature; this might reduce total investment costs to US $35.0 million. (Information provided by an engineering consultant.)

14.   If the existing shadow-pricing for imported machinery is considered, the cost would be still higher. However, the use of foreign technology would be limited to certain critical components of the plant which might amount to 20–25% of the total costs mentioned above. Other components, construction costs, and peripherals should then be calculated at Chinese domestic prices—which would most likely be considerably lower.

         In the report commissioned by UNIDO in 1973 it is claimed: "Today it is possible to build a vertical kiln cement plant at a fraction of the cost of conventional plant, which permits the economical establishment of cement industry on a small scale." The author, Steven Gottlieb, points out that "during the late 1950s studies were conducted and published about a new modernized vertical kiln which led to a better understanding of the processes involved in it. Based on this work, substantial improvements were made—vertical-kiln plants were built which proved that they can produce uniform and excellent quality cement in a smooth, troublefree operation. Vertical-kiln cement proved to be competitive in every respect, performing well in the most involved concrete structures such as concrete platforms for oil drilling in the sea bed off shore Australia." ("Development Note for the Calcining and

Sintering of Cement Clinker and Other Materials in a New Shaft Kiln,"
prepared for UNIDO by Steven Gottlieb, UNIDO/ITD.223, 13 November 1973.)

15.   It has been argued among certain analysts that total cement production
in 1973 was only around 29.9 million tons (and 31.6 million tons in
1974) which are figures used in *China, A Reassessment of the Economy,*
Joint Economic Committee, US Congress 1975.

In India cement demand has increased by twice the percentage of the
gross domestic product with little change in the relative prices of sub-
stitutes. If one would use such correlation figures for gross domestic
product and cement demand on Chinese time series as given in The
Joint Economic Committee compendium one would get a cement production figure close to the nearly 40 million tons for 1973 given in
Table 38. Without detailed knowledge of changes in prices for substi-
tutes like iron and steel, timber, bricks, tiles, etc., and the various
planning mechanisms it is not justifiable to rely too much on a comparison of this kind.

However, there is an important structural difference that is significant
in discussions of cement demand and production in the two countries.
The small-scale cement plants in China are basically serving localized
rural markets. Consequently, it is safe to assume that construction
activities in rural areas in China contribute a much higher proportion
of total demand for cement than is the case in India. (G. S. Gupta,
"Demand for Cement in India," *The Indian Economic Journal* 22: 3,
January–March 1975.

16.   When I was completing this manuscript for publication my attention
was drawn to the fact that UNIDO had prepared a development note
on this subject. The author, Steven Gottlieb, had written extensively
on the subject in these and other references:
      "The Modern Vertical Kiln," *Rock Products,* June 1966;
      "Revitalized Vertical Kiln Processes Yields More Profit Per
Barrel," *Rock Products,* May 1969;
      "Development Note for the Calcining and Sintering of Cement
Clinker and Other Materials in a New Shaft Kiln," prepared for UNIDO.
UNIDO/ITD.223, November 1973.

17.   It appears that the experimentation in small-scale cement plants in India
can be traced back to the Indo-Chinese war in 1962 when people within

the Indian defense establishment took a number of initiatives for providing localities in outlying areas with cement. The pilot plant at Jorhat in Assam is obviously such an example (Vertical Shaft Kiln for Cement Production–Feasibility Report, Regional Research Laboratory–Jorhat, 1971 [?]).

18. This and earlier information has been taken from "Report of the subgroup on scaling down cement plants," published in Group Reports, Second National Seminar on Appropriate Technology, Hyderabad 17–18 July 1973–Appropriate Technology Cell, Ministry of Industrial Development and Science and Technology, New Delhi.

19. British Standards 12: Part 2: 1971: Specification for Portland Cement (Ordinary and Rapid-hardening).

20. *Science Today* (Bombay), January 1975, reports in a special section on cement that "the shaft kiln technology has not become popular in the country. The first shaft kiln was put up rather hurriedly by the defense scientists in a border area in 1963 with imperfect know-how and transferred to the Tamil Nadu Industrial Development Corporation the same year. The plant failed. The development of shaft-kiln technology later was stalled to a certain extent by the big rotary kiln manufacturers. It is well known that, in the 1960s when shaft kilns were gaining ground elsewhere, the Cement Advisor to the Government of India also happened to represent a large Danish cement machinery manufacturing firm in India."

21. The information in this paragraph was given by the Chinese Agricultural Machinery Association in Peking, 1973.

22. Information provided by the Chinese Agricultural Machinery Association Peking, 1973.

23. BBC–FE/W761.

24. "Chinese method for technological development–Case of Agricultural Machinery and Implement Industry," paper presented at OECD seminar on Science, Technology and Development in a Changing World, Paris, April 21–25, 1975.

25. The role of workers' innovations is discussed in "A Note on the Sources of Technological Innovation in the People's Republic of China," by Genevieve Dean, *The Journal of Development Studies,* 9:1 (October 1972).

26. BBC–FE/W731.

27. There are several reasons for this choice of example. First, the product is sufficiently distinctive so that one can distinguish plants reported to be responsible for the manufacture of this particular product. Second, a certain amount of material was published on local rolling bearing manufacture during the Great Leap Forward which adds to an understanding of the underlying planning policies. Furthermore, I have been able to visit briefly four rolling bearing enterprises which fall into different categories of the Chinese rolling bearing industrial hierarchy.

28. The information on the early development of the local rolling bearing industry is taken from the following items:
   1. "Locally made ball-bearings help peasants," NCNA, June 12, 1958 (SCMP 1794)
   2. "Ball bearings in rural areas," NCNA, August 1, 1958 (SCMP 1833)
   3. "Ball-bearings mass-produced in provinces," *People's Daily*, August 1, 1958 (SCMP 1833)
   4. "Further report on the campaign for introducing ball bearings," *People's Daily*, August 2, 1958 (SCMP 1833)
   5. "Ball bearings exhibition held in Chengchow," *People's Daily*, August 2, 1958 (SCMP 1833)
   6. "More ball bearings for countryside," NCNA, September 2, 1958 (SCMP 1849).

29. From *The Rise of the Chinese People's Communes—and Six Years After,* by Anna Louise Strong, Peking, New World Press, 1964, pp. 41-47.

30. "Farm machinery and tool network in North China Province," NCNA, November 29, 1959 (SCMP 2149).

31. "Some questions posed by the outlook of the Great Leap Forward to economic geography, by Teng Ch'ing-chung, Assistant researcher of the Research Institute of Geography, Chinese Academy of Sciences," *People's Daily,* January 20, 1959 (SCMP 1951).

32. Production of bearings in small enterprises has often started within existing farm machinery repair and manufacturing plants. With the policy of the three-level repair and manufacturing network being implemented and the networks being expanded, two trends are emerging that are changing conditions for the local manufacture of bearings. First, more and more bearings are needed for horse-drawn carts, agricultural machinery, and simple machine tools which are locally manufactured

within the three-level network. Second, the fairly experienced, county-run repair stations have free capacity available when many of their repair responsibilities are transferred downwards to the commune and brigade stations. The county repair and manufacturing stations can then move into the production of industrial commodities, and one of these products has been bearings.

33.   BBC–FE/W705 and BBC–FE/W682.

34.   The following monograph provides an excellent introduction to China's steel sector strategy: M. Gardner Clark, *The Development of China's Steel Industry and Soviet Technical Aid,* Cornell University, 1973.

35.   The role of the small blast furnaces and the technology choice in general have been thoroughly discussed in the following two papers by Shigeru Ishikawa: "Choice of techniques in Mainland China," *The Developing Economies* (Tokyo 1962), No. 2; "A Note on the Choice of Technology in China," *The Journal of Development Studies* (London), 9:1.

36.   Straw holds the dominant role in providing the raw material for the present annual production of 4 million tons of paper—accounting for 60% of the total, followed by 30% for wood, and 10% for waste paper and rags. (*Japan Pulp and Paper,* 12:2, July 1974.)

Chapter 5

1.   See, for example, "Running industry in the 'pauper spirit'," *China Reconstructs,* November 1971, and "On the road of mechanization," *Peking Review,* No. 51, 1971.

2.   "Industrialization in a Hopei region," NCNA, June 7, 1972, BBC–FE/W677.

3.   Hopei provincial service, July 22, 1972, BBC–FE/W685.

Chapter 6

1.   Many will find that this monograph lacks an analytical model to deal with rural industrialization. However, it appears to me that the justifications of small-scale industries in rural areas are so multi-faceted and so varying from sector to sector that they elude the grasp of a single analytical model. Furthermore, one must differentiate between

various sector strategies on one hand and the integrated rural development approach on the other.

2. It seems that the greatest merit of small enterprises as experienced in China lies not in the superiority of their capital/labor or capital/output ratios but in the overall savings in resources they make possible.

Watanabe argues that "small enterprises seem to contribute most to the economic development of countries with surplus labor and shortage of capital (which applies to China at her present stage of development) under the following conditions:
1. where they can be set up without heavy overhead capital expenditure on buildings, land, and infrastructure;
2. where the diseconomies of small enterprises are compensated for by the use of idle capital, labor, and raw materials;
3. where division of labor between enterprises in different size groups, e.g., in the form of subcontracting, enhances the overall efficiency of the industry."

Susumu Watanabe, "Reflections on Current Policies for Promoting Small Enterprises and Subcontracting," *International Labour Review,* 110:5 (November 1974), 405–422.

3. Agricultural mechanization appears under present conditions first to be carried out where a great amount of labor is being used. The central emphasis of mechanization is planned for those projects which demand large amounts of labor, high intensity of labor, or urgent attention during the farming season.

Such operations as ploughing, hoeing, etc., could be mechanized early, but mechanization must be based on a number of considerations. First, it must conform to the country's tradition of intensive farming. Second, it must be suited to the varied natural conditions. Third, the universal existence of the communes must be taken into consideration; this among other things requires that farm machinery should be usable for many purposes, and if possible all the year round. In this way communes, which are both social and economic organizations, may prove more efficient than would otherwise have been the case. Fourth, farm machinery should be produced in medium and small factories as well as in big ones.

4. "Technological change in agricultural production and its impact on agrarian structure—A study of the so-called green revolution," by Shigeru Ishikawa, *Keizai Kenkyū,* 22:2 (April 1971).

5. Private communications from Shigeru Ishikawa.

6. Resource mobilization in rural areas, which may initially have been very important, will eventually become less important. As transportation networks are developed and the level of industrial technology raised, many of the small enterprises may become obsolete. They must then be closed down, expanded, or transformed to other relevant production. These problems will require constant attention and foresight by the planning agencies at different levels to make the partially decentralized economy work.

SELECT BIBLIOGRAPHY

This is not an extensive bibliography, but it serves to introduce the reader to some of the more important works dealing with rural industrialization and related subjects. A more complete list of references to primary sources can be found in works by Carl Riskin and other China scholars, including two volumes in Danish by Kjeld Larsen.

Behari, Bepin. *Rural Industrialization in India.* Delhi, 1976.
Bhalla, Ajit S., ed. *Technology and Employment in Industry.* Geneva, 1975.
Biehl, Max. "Die dezentralisierte Kleinindustrie Chinas im grossen Sprung und heute," *Internationales Asien Forum,* Heft 2 (April 1970), 202–14.
Brown, Norman L. *Energy for Rural Development: Renewable resources and alternative technologies for developing countries.* National Academy of Sciences (USA), 1976.

Carin, Robert. *Power Industry in Communist China.* Union Research Institute, Hong Kong, 1969.
China: A Reassessment of the Economy. Joint Economic Committee, Congress of the United States, Washington, 1975.

Don, Yehuda, ed. *The Role of Group Action in the Industrialization of Rural Areas.* New York, 1971.

An Economic Profile of Mainland China. Joint Economic Committee, Congress of the United States, Washington, 1967.
Edwards, Edgar O., ed. *Employment in Developing Nations.* New York, 1974.

Gurley, John G. "Rural Development in China, 1949–1972, and the Lessons to be Learned from It," *World Development,* 7–8 (1975), 455–471.

259

Haissman, R. Rural Industrialization in Mexico—A Case Study. Prepared for the UN Expert Group Meeting on Rural Industrialization, Bucharest, 1973, ESA/SD/AC.5/9. (Mexico's rural industrialization programs have also been analyzed in various internal documents of the World Bank and the Inter-American Development Bank.)

Halperin, Haim. *Agrindus: Integration of Agriculture and Industries.* London, 1964.

Ishikawa, Shigeru. "Choice of Techniques in Mainland China," *The Developing Economies,* September–December 1962, pp. 24–56.

Johnston, Bruce F. and Peter Kilby. *Agriculture and Structural Transformation.* Oxford, 1975.

Lang, Wong Y. "Establishment of Industrial Estates in Rural Setting" in *Industrial Estates in Asia and the Far East.* United Nations, New York, 1962.

Larsen, Kjeld Allan. *Den kinesiske lokalindustri på xian-niveau under og efter kulturrevolutionene* (Chinese local industry at xian-level during and after the Cultural Revolution). 2 vols. Copenhagen, 1975.

Liu, Jung-chao. *China's Fertilizer Economy.* Chicago, 1970.

Mathai, P. M. "Rural Industrialization in India, A Case Study." Prepared for the UN Expert Group Meeting on Rural Industrialization, Bucharest, September 24–28, 1973.

"Notes on Small Industry and Handicraft Development in Mainland China 1952–1958." Research Program on Small Industry Development, International Industrial Development Center/ Stanford Research Institute. Miscellaneous Paper No. 2, December 1958.

People's Republic of China: An Economic Assessment. Joint Economic Committee, Congress of the United States, Washington, 1972.

Report on Evaluation of Rural Industries Projects. Planning Commission, New Delhi, 1968.

Report of the Evaluation Study Group on Rural Industries Projects Programme. Rural Industries Planning Committee (Department of Industrial Development), New Delhi, 1968.

Richman, Barry M. *Industrial Society in Communist China.* New York, 1969.

Riskin, Carl. "Local Industry and the choice of techniques in the planning of industrial development in Mainland China," in *Planning for Advanced Skills and Technologies,* Industrial Planning and Programming Series No. 3 (UNIDO). New York, United Nations, 1969.

——— "Small Industry and the Chinese Model of Development," *The China Quarterly,* No. 46 (1971), 245–73.

——— "Rural Industry: Self-Reliant Systems or 'Independent Kingdoms'?" Department of Economics and East Asian Institute, Columbia University, draft 1972.

"Rural Industrialization." Report of the UN Expert Group Meeting on Rural Industrialization in Bucharest, 1973, New York, 1974 ST/ESA/4.

"Rural industrialization in developing countries." Neilson Alexander and United Nations Secretariat. Prepared for the Expert Group Meeting on Rural Industrialization, Bucharest, September 24–28, 1973.

Schran, P. "Handicrafts in Communist China," *The China Quarterly,* No. 17 (January–March 1964), 151–73.

Schurmann, Franz. *Ideology and Organization in Communist China.* Berkeley, Los Angeles, London, 1970.

Sigurdson, Jon. "Rural Industry—A Traveller's View," *The China Quarterly,* No. 18 (April–June 1972), 315–32.

——— "Rural Industry and the Internal Transfer of Technology in China" in Stuart R. Schram, ed., *Authority Participation and Cultural Change in China.* Cambridge, England, 1973.

600 Million Build Industry. Foreign Language Press, Peking, 1958.

Wheelwright, E. L. and Bruce McFarlane. *The Chinese Road to*

262

Socialism; Economics of the Cultural Revolution. New York, London, 1970.

The Writing Group of the Peking Municipal Revolutionary Committee. "China's Road of Socialist Industrialization," *Peking Review,* No. 43 (1969), 7–13.

The Writing Group of the State Capital Construction Commission. "Simultaneously Develop Big and Small and Medium Enterprises," *Peking Review,* No. 48 (1970), 14–17.

Wu, Yuan-li. *Spatial Economy of Communist China: Railway Transportation and Industrial Location in Communist China.* New York, 1967.

Yu, C. L. "Local Industry and Its Impact on Agricultural Development in China," *The Asia Quarterly,* No. 4 (1971), 32–42.

INDEX

Note: Page numbers in italics indicate references to illustrations and tables.

Acids, sulphuric, *63*, 67, 200, 204, 208

Accumulation Funds. *See* Capital

Administrative levels, 1, 3-5, 20-21, 42, 182; reforms in, 28-29; political structure and planning in, 35, *36*, *39*, 40, 115-117, 127-131; and control, 69, *70*-73, 75-77, 122, 129, 138, 168-169, *174*-175, 195-*196*, 221-222, 244-245n19; of science and technology, 70-71, 81, 85, *86*, 87, 96-97, 201. *See also* Brigades, Committees; Communes; Counties; Provincial level; Regional level; State-level control

Administrative talent, 7, 29, 75-76, 81, 96-97. *See also* Leadership; Management and organization

Agricultural machinery, 16, *54*, 168, 173, *174*, 175, 179, 188, 220; and mechanization, 4, 11, 18, 21, 23, 43, 48-*49*, 55-57, 61, 203, 219-220, 242n9, 257n3. *See also* Farm machinery

Agricultural Mechanization Institute (Fukien), 173-*174*

Agricultural production value, 4, 53, 98, 221, 244n18

Agricultural productivity and yields, 61, 73, 215; need for increased, 18, 20-21, 23, 25, 41, 48-*49*, 55, 71, 77, 115, 138, 147, 198. *See also* Cropping; Crops; Grain production; Land; Seeds

Agricultural research: extension and popular-based networks, *24*, *70*-71, *78*, 80-84, 96, 120-*121*, 224, 244n17; experimental centers and farms, 80-81, *84*, 85, *86*, 97, 173-*174;* local institutes, 80, 82-*84*, 85, *86*, 87, 97, 245n22; reclamation areas, *84*, *86*, 195-*196*, *205*, 206, *207*, 208, *210*. *See also* Farm machinery; Mass scientific network; Seeds

Agricultural side-line occupations, 23, 29, 33-34, 51, *70*, 98, 197-199. *See also* Food processing

Agricultural technology, 10-11, 23-*24*, 33, 55-57, *70*, *78*, 80-*86*, 87-89, 96-98, 119-*121*, 214, 223. *See also* Technical training and technicians

Agriculture, 1, 4-5, 11, 13, 38, 55, 116, 221; development policy in, 1-2, 7-11, 28; and manpower, 2, 4, 10-12, 18, 20-21, 23, 48-*49*, 58, 60-61, 71-73, 87, 105, 110, 156, 179, 188, 218-221, 241-242n7, 257n3; and industry, 2, 8-9, 11, 13, 15-21, *24*-25, 33, 58-60, 69, *70*-73, 76-77, 115-116, 130, 198-202, 208, 214, 218, 220

Agrochemicals, 23-*24*, *70*, 115

Agro-industries, 17, 33-*34*, *59*-60. *See also* Food processing; Fertilizers

Allocation of industry and equipment, 67-68, 93, 129-130, 168-169, 186, 192, 242n9

276

Public health. *See* Health units, public
Public welfare funds, *66*
Purchasing power, 17, 20-22, 33-*34*, 60, *79*, 100, 115
Pyramid structures: in population, 44, *47, 56;* in the industrial system, 77, 89, 94; in infrastructure services, 120-*121;* in rolling bearing industry, 183-*184*

Qianan county, *196*-197, *205*, 206, *207*, 209-*210*
Qiansi county, *196*-197, *205*, 206, *207*, 210
Quality control. *See* Product quality; Standards and standardization
Qinhuangdao city, *196*-197, 203-*205*, 206, *207*, 209-*210*

Rationing cards, 28
Raw materials, 1-2, 8, 22, 127-128, 131, 133, 139, 190, 199, 203, 206, 221; accessibility and transport of, 12, 62, 64, 134, 161, 216; agricultural to local industry, 18, 20-23, 33, 51, 115, 130; scarcity of, 113, 192, 209; in fertilizer industry, 134, 137-*141, 143,* 147-148, 208; in cement industry, 161, 164; in iron and steel industry, *189*-190; in paper industry, 190, *191,* 192, *193,* 209, 211, 243n4, 256n36. *See also* Natural resources
Reclamation and research areas, *84, 86,* 195-196, *205,* 206, *207,* 208-*210*
Red Flag, 131
Red Star Chinese-Korean Friendship Commune, 53-*54*
Reforestation, 55
Regional capitals, 197. *See*

also Tangshan city
"Regional industries," 14-*15*
Regional level, *111;* control and planning, 5, *36*-*37, 39,* 75-76, *78*-*79, 155,* 175, 244-245n19; industry, 8, 65, *66, 67,* 68, 121-*123,* 124-126, 129-131, 135, *138,* 164, 168, 195-*196, 205, 207, 210;* science and technology, *78*-*79,* 89-90, 96-97; institutes, 83, *84*-86. *See also* Center and central authority
Regions: number and size of, 5, *36, 39,* 162, 175; as administrative units, 5, *36,* 241n7; autonomous, and special districts, *36, 39*
Repair units and workshops, 3, 19-20, 94-*95,* 105, 181-182, 255-256n32. *See also* Farm machinery, repair and manufacturing network
R and D, national, *79,* 82-83
Research institutes: central, 77, 103, 133, 172-*174;* local, 80, 82-*84,* 85, *86,* 87, 97, 244-245n19. *See also* Industrial research and innovation
Residents' groups, *39*
Resource mobilization, 1-2, 22-23, 25, 27, 33, 58, 133, *151,* 168-169, 211, 213, 215-216, 221, 224, 258n6
Resource-specific industries. *See* Forward linkage industries
Retirees, 27, 44-*45,* 48-*49,* 239n1
Revenue sharing and transfer of resources, 65, 68
Revolutionary committees. *See* Committees, revolutionary
Road building. *See* Construction industry and materials; Transportation

HARVARD EAST ASIAN MONOGRAPHS